Sidi Bou Sa'id, Tunisia

Structure and Form of a Mediterranean Village

Sidi Bou Sa'id, Tunisia

Structure and Form of a Mediterranean Village

Edited by

Besim S. Hakim

This book is the work of ten senior architecture students while residing in the village of Sidi Bou Sa'id, Tunisia for nine weeks during the Fall term of 1975. The study trip was conceived and organized by Professor Besim S. Hakim, who also accompanied the students.

School of Architecture, Technical University of Nova Scotia, Canada.
Amalgamated in 1997 with Dalhousie University, Halifax, Nova Scotia, Canada.

The book was first published in August 1978 in a limited edition in landscape format.
It was subsequently made available upon demand by the Books On Demand program of University Microfilm International, which is currently a part of ProQuest Company. UMI's Books On Demand program was terminated in March 2008.
The editorial assistant for the first 1978 edition of this book was J. Alexander Wilson, and the graphic design assistant was Arthur B. Carter.

This is the 2009 edition, in portrait format, with a new preface by the editor. All illustrations and photographs were scanned from the 1978 edition at high resolution for inclusion in this edition.

ISBN-10: 0-9683184-1-X
ISBN-13: 978-0-9683184-1-6

Library of Congress Control Number: 84204583

Book and cover design by Olaf Nelson, Chinook Design, Inc. www.chinooktype.com

To order additional copies visit: www.booksurge.com or www.amazon.com

DEDICATION

This book is dedicated to the residents of the village of Sidi Bou Sa'id—past, present, and future—and to the ten participating senior architecture students of Term 7, Fall 1975, whose hard work while residing in the village made this book possible:

Harriet E. Burdett-Moulton

Carmen G. Caulfield

Brian A. Gillis

George H. Guimond

Miklos P. Jablanczy

Maria K. Jones

Jainarine Lalla

Paul M. Ledaire

James K. Ogden

James H. Wright

CONTENTS

PREFACE TO THE 2009 EDITION

This preface was written in January 2009, thirty-one years after the first publication of this book in 1978. I have decided to re-publish it now due to its importance as an example of a built environment that came into being due to a generative system that is based on a sustainable framework of decision-making characterized by a bottom-up approach and guided by overarching generative proscriptive codes. The emergent result is a dynamic complex built environment that is not the brainchild of a master planner or architect. The exact configurations and form of the built environment is not known during the process of its formation and has a characteristic of unpredictability. This is one of the main features in natural systems that are associated with the phenomenon of emergence. What is known is that the result would fit well and in full balance within its immediate surroundings and will be a contribution that would maintain the integrity and quality of the village as a whole. The process is a result of small acts that in aggregate produces built form that is compatible with its immediate neighbors and that contributes to the high quality of the village's character. I have researched and published in recent years numerous studies that explain how such an underlying generative system works.[1]

In August 1915 a decree was officially enacted for the village titled: "The protection of Arabic buildings in Sidi Bou Sa'id" (see Appendix B). This was one of the earliest such laws for preservation in the Mediterranean region. The decree's intention was to preserve the character of the village's built form by requiring that modifications must be approved by the local governing authority to ensure that changes and/or additions do not negatively impact the character of the village. Ornament and color must be similar to the existing customary practice. The decree includes penalties for infractions that include, if necessary, demolition of non-conforming acts. This top-down code did help to preserve the character of the village but its success was also due to the village residents' sympathy and agreement with the decree's general intent. However, it should be kept in mind that the decree and its codes is a static system that relies on top-down policing for enforcement. It is not a generative code as was the case in traditional practice that shaped the village in the first place. [2]

---

[1] Hakim, B., *Arabic-Islamic Cities: Building and Planning Principles,* 1986. Paperback Edition, 2008. Available from Amazon.com. ——, "The Urf and its role in diversifying the architecture of traditional Islamic cities", *Journal of Architectural and Planning Research,* vol.11, no. 2, 1994, pp.108–127. ——, "Rule systems: Islamic", *Encyclopedia of Vernacular Architecture of the World,* vol.1, 1997, pp.566–568. ——, "Reviving the rule system: An approach for revitalizing traditional towns in Maghreb", *Cities,* vol.18, no. 2, 2001, pp.87–92. —— and Z. Ahmed, "Rules for the built environment in 19th century Northern Nigeria", *Journal of Architectural and Planning Research,* vol.23, no.1, 2006, pp. 1–26, and an abbreviated version titled "The Sub-Saharan City, Rules and Built Form" in *The City in the Islamic World,* vol. 1 (of 2 volumes), edited by Salma K. Jayyusi, et al, Brill, Leiden, 2008, pp. 663–676, and supporting figures in vol. 2. ——, "Generative processes for revitalizing historic towns or heritage districts", *Urban Design International,* vol.12, no. 2–3, 2007, pp.87–99. ——, "Mediterranean urban and building codes: origins, content, impact, and lessons", *Urban Design International,* vol.13, no. 1, 2008, pp.21–40. ——, "Law and the City" in *The City in the Islamic World,* vol. 1 (of 2 volumes), edited by Salma K. Jayyusi, et al, Brill, Leiden, 2008, pp. 71–92, and supporting figures in vol. 2.

[2] Ibid.

The village was selected for award in the first cycle of The Aga Khan Award for Architecture in 1980. The category for its award was for: Search for Preservation of Traditional Heritage. Here is a statement from the award:

> *For the efforts, over a long period of time, by a community toward the conservation of their village. Based on true understanding of the architectural values of the village, legislation has been enacted controlling maintenance, expansion and vehicular circulation, and the sense of place has been kept. The character of the buildings, the relationship between activities and architectural forms, and between the built fabric and the surrounding nature have all been respected. Within the context of North Africa, and in the face of mass tourism, the concept of conservation has been strengthened. Sidi Bou Sa'id has retained not only the picturesque quality of a village, but its very essence.*[3]

As for the conclusion of this study (see pages 143–52) and its link to the patterns in Christopher Alexander's *A Pattern Language,* 1977—at the time of writing the conclusion the only substantive publication that was relevant and available was Alexander's book, published only a few months before I wrote the conclusion. I wanted to communicate, in an accessible manner, the high quality of the village's built environment by linking its physical elements and configurations at all levels of its built form to the patterns that Alexander put forward in his book. The rational for doing so is explained in the first pages of the conclusion.

It should be kept in mind that the generative process that shaped the village's built environment is the essential lesson that should be understood, adapted and applied in our contemporary urban development activities. Nevertheless this study addresses primarily the physical structure and form of the village and therefore communicating its inherent high quality in a way that is understandable and that is to be appreciated by the reader is an important objective in itself. Explaining and communicating the village's qualities by reference to Alexander's book for this purpose, back in 1978, was determined to be an effective method. The more so today since its publication in 1977 *A Pattern Language* continues to be a perennial best seller. In a review of the book in the *Harvard Design Magazine* it is mentioned that the book "could very well be the most read architectural treatise of all time".[4] Almost every architect practicing today has come across it at one point or another in their career. A later book by Alexander: *A New Theory of Urban Design,* 1987 explains a generative process, that is in its essential features, similar to the one that shaped the village of Sidi Bou Sa'id.[5]

For the above reasons, re-issuing this book at this time in early 2009 is important and should be a valuable reference. The village is an excellent example of how a sustainable generative process can produce such a high quality built environment.

Besim S. Hakim
January 2009, Albuquerque, New Mexico

---

[3] From the booklet titled: "The Aga Khan Award for Architecture—Awards, 1980," presented by His Highness The Aga Khan at Lahore, Pakistan, 1980, p. 20.

[4] Review by William Saunders in Harvard Design Magazine, no. 16, Winter/Spring 2002, pp. 74–78. See Alexander's response to Saunders at this link: http://www.natureoforder.com/library/reply-to-saunders.htm (accessed January 2009).

[5] Alexander, et al. *A New Theory of Urban Design,* Oxford University Press, New York, 1987. See my review of this book in *Journal of Architectural Education,* vol. 44, no. 2, pp. 120–123.

INTRODUCTION

Traditionally in the West, an acceptable travel program for a mature student of architecture was constituted by a "Grand Tour" of Europe. This provided the student with a deeper understanding of major architectural monuments and of the social, cultural and historical milieu from which they arose. The concept of the "Grand Tour" persists to this day but has been enlarged by numerous schools of architecture in Europe and North America to include the works of modern architects.

With the knowledge that the values encompassed by architectural education have been gradually shifting from an appreciation of isolated historical monuments to architecture in the wider context of urban agglomerations and the habitat of man, I intentionally designed a travel-study program to fulfil the following criteria:

1. The place to be studied should constitute an environment which has grown incrementally over a period of more than one generation.
2. The place to be studied should be currently inhabited. This would allow the study of the ways in which people interact with the built environment.
3. The place to be studied should, if possible, represent a building tradition of as wide a geographic and cultural area as possible.
4. The history of the place to be studied should closely resemble the long history of the city particularly within the selected cultural/geographic context, in terms of its physical structure/ form and inherent building process.
5. The place to be studied should only have sustained minimal changes to its physical structure and form due to the technological impact of the 20th century (e.g., automobile traffic, steel or reinforced concrete construction etc.).

It was by following these five criteria that I was eventually able to choose the village of Sidi Bou Sa'id in Tunisia as the site of the 1975 student foreign travel-study program for the Nova Scotia Technical College School of Architecture.

Historical factors seem to vindicate the appropriateness of a study site in the Arab-Islamic world. History tells us that the first urban cultures and the roots of Western civilizations go back over 4600 years to the Sumerian civilization in southern Mesopotamia. It seems that the physical pattern of the first Sumerian cities eventually became the predominant norm for the cities of most subsequent civilizations within the region of the Eastern Mediterranean, the Middle East and North Africa. This pattern is based on the courtyard building and the access system of through streets and cul-de-sacs as the primary organizational components. History also indicates that trade, war and written communications allowed for the continuous dissemination of information, skills and especially the ideals/values of the monotheistic religions throughout that region and beyond.

At the beginning of the Christian era, the two prominent powers in the Middle East were the Romans and the Persians. Both acted to modify a basically similar urban model: within the Roman controlled territories we find the influence of the earlier Hellenistic civilization, whereas in the eastern region we find the Sassanian influence. With the sudden emergence and rapid spread of the Islamic faith in the seventh century, these Sassanian and Hellenistic derivatives were carried, with some modifications, throughout the Middle East and North Africa, an area which included and extended from Spain in the west to Afghanistan in the east.

By the time the Arabic-Islamic culture was fully entrenched after a period of 200–300 years, it had developed a complete set of religiously based social and economic norms which included building guidelines. The use and development of these guidelines continued unabated until the beginning of the 20th century. Hence, it can be seen that there was a continuous historical link from the Sumerian civilization of approximately 2700 B.C. via various civilizations culminating with the Arabic-Islamic civilization which extended this linkage to the early years of the 20th century; a period of 4600 years.

The preceding historical sketch partly justifies my choice of an Arab-Islamic environment for the travel-study program in 1975. Tunisia, itself, was chosen due to its accessibility from Europe and, especially, the excellent condition of its traditional towns and architecture.

The study group was fortunate to find suitable accommodation in the village of Sidi Bou Sa'id, just 16 kilometers from Tunis, the capital city of Tunisia. In addition to satisfying the previously mentioned selection criteria, Sidi Bou Sa'id provided us with the following unique factors for study:

1. It was originally developed as a summer resort for Tunisia's wealthy upper class. Therefore it utilized the best building technologies, construction and decorating skills available at the time. Many of these technologies and skills can only be found elsewhere in the historic "Medina" of Tunis and in other few locations.

2. Due to its religious and historical military significance, foreigners were not encouraged to visit the village until recently. This had the effect of reducing outside influences.

3. A preservation decree passed in 1915 has helped the village to retain its traditional physical form and architectural qualities.

4. Its small size made it manageable in terms of a nine week study by a group of ten students.

The approach taken by the group was to examine the total physical environment of the village from general considerations at the total "village scale" to details of the individual "village components". Information on the village was compiled by groups of students working in two's or three's, with the exception of the study of "Materials and Construction" which was accomplished by one person. The first three chapters of this report represent the work of twelve students; the latter four chapters the work of eight students.

This final report is the edited and revised version of the initial findings of the study group. The sequence of chapters was designed to create a logical flow of information so as to enhance the reader's appreciation and understanding of the whole work. The conclusion was written by myself. It is meant to highlight the relevance of the study by linking it to the findings of recent appropriate research.

Besim S. Hakim
September 1977, Halifax, Nova Scotia, Canada

**NORTH AFRICA, THE MEDITERRANEAN
AND THE LOCATION OF SIDI BOU SA'ID**

Chapter 1

GEOGRAPHY AND CLIMATE

TUNISIA[1]

Tunisia is the northernmost country of Africa and the smallest country of the Maghreb (Libya, Tunisia, Algeria and Morocco). It is bordered on the west by Algeria and the Atlas Mountains and faces east with a mostly low Mediterranean coast scalloped by the three large gulfs of Tunis, Hammamet and Gabes. The short north coast rises to the Cap Blanc promontory near Bizerta and the Saharan frontier post of Borj el-Hattaba lies 800 kilometers due south at the point of a long desert prong.

The landscape changes continuously from the well-watered north to the arid south. Along the north coast runs the panhandle of the rugged mountains of Khroumiria with their twin lakes of Bizerta and Ichkeul, and thick stands of pines and cork-oaks. Southwards, the lush pastures and wheat fields of the meandering Medjerda Valley divide this region from the undulating farmlands of the central Tell. To the east the Tell peters out into the flat wheat country which stretches from Bizerta to Tunis. To the south, the Tell is bordered by the Dorsal Mountain Range, the "Backbone" of Tunisia.

From the Mediterranean north, Tunisia then sinks unevenly towards the Sahara, In the center of the country is the steppe region, rich only in Roman ruins. This is bounded to the south by the Gafsa Mountains, stretching from Metlaoui to Maknassy, which make one last stand before succumbing to the vast, arid stretches of the Great Eastern Erg of the Sahara.

POSITION OF SIDI BOU SA'ID

Sidi Bou Sa'id is a village in the northern suburbs of Tunis, at the top of the promontory of Cape Carthage at an altitude of 129 meters, beside a lighthouse whose coordinates are 36°52' North, 10°2' East. The direction to Mecca is 22°56'46" South of East.

---

[1] Source: *Tunisia, A Holiday Guide,* by Michael Tomkinson, London, 1974.

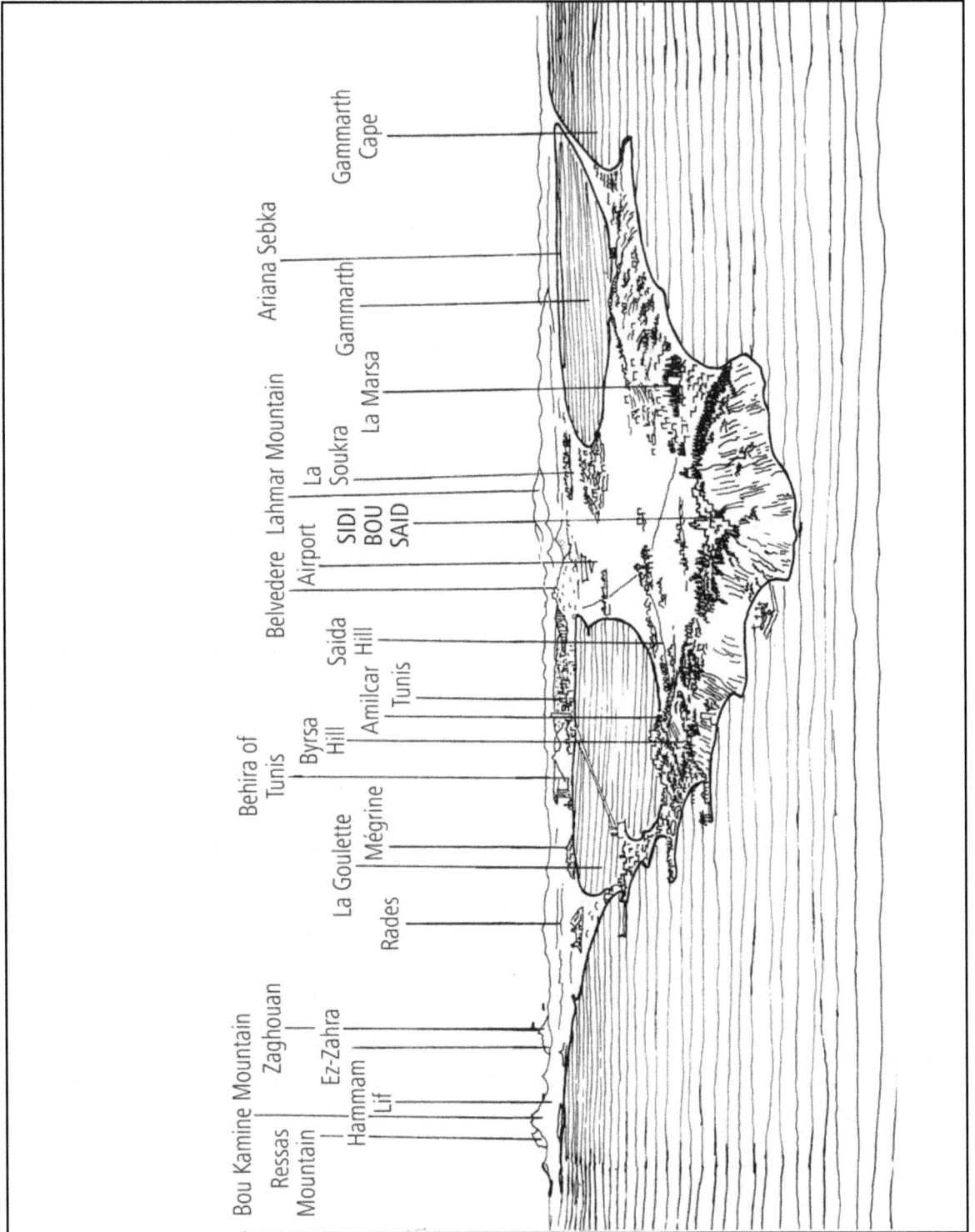

Bou Kamine Mountain
Ressas Mountain
Zaghouan
Ez-Zahra
Hammam Lif

Behira of Tunis
La Goulette
Mégrine
Rades
Byrsa Hill
Saida Hill
Amilcar Hill
Tunis

Belvedere Lahmar Mountain
Airport
La Soukra
SIDI BOU SAID
La Marsa

Ariana Sebka
Gammarth
Gammarth Cape

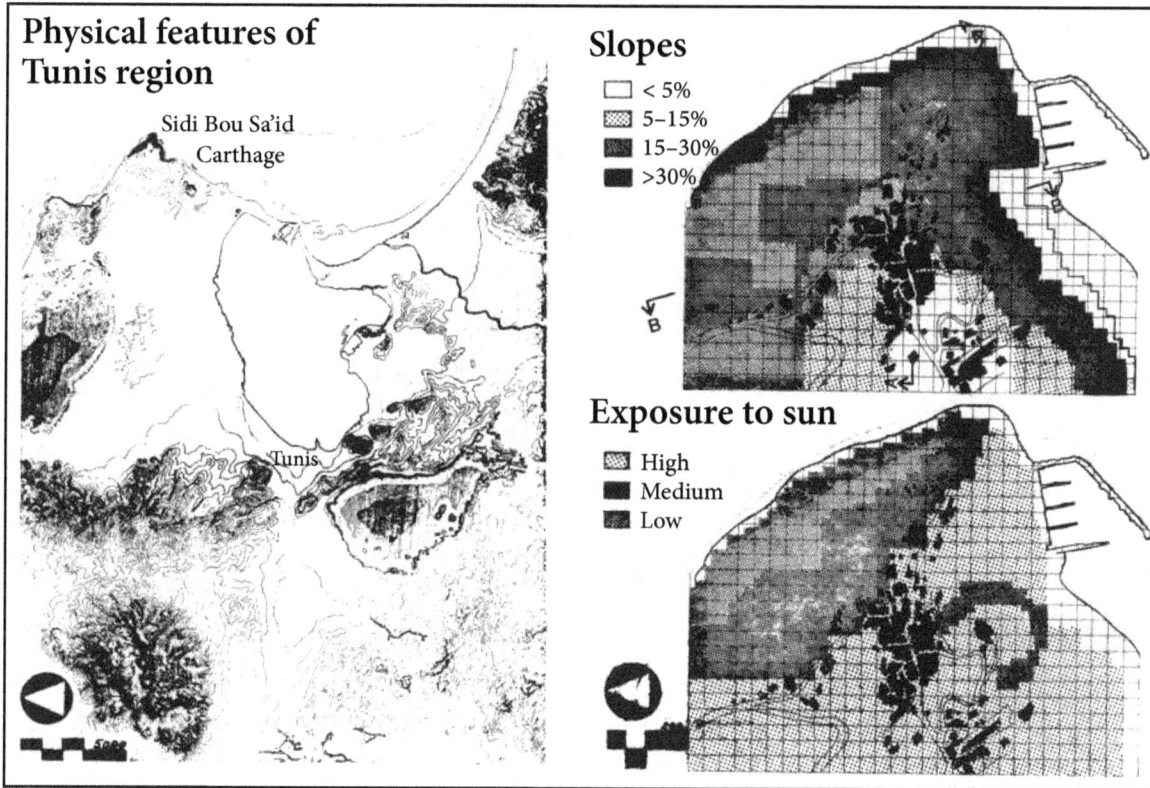

Physical features of Tunis region

Sidi Bou Sa'id
Carthage

Tunis

Slopes
☐ < 5%
▨ 5–15%
▦ 15–30%
■ >30%

Exposure to sun
▨ High
■ Medium
▩ Low

Since its emergence in prehistory, the promontory of Cape Carthage has been under the influence of the erosive forces of the wind, rain and sea which have certainly modified its initial aspect. No doubt its profile was more forbidding than it is today, the pluvial and eolian erosions having laid bare its foundations of clay and limestone, while marine erosions have cut its cliffs, causing landslides into the sea.

This promontory is inaccessible to the east and south, on the sea-coast where the cliffs drop steeply. On the side of firm land to the north and west, with some protective works, it can be considered to be a very strong military position. It is an excellent observatory for the surveillance of the entrance to the Gulf of Tunis and the greater part of the Carthaginian Peninsula, a fact which was well understood by the Carthaginians, Byzantines, Arabs, Hafsids, Spaniards and Turks who each in their turn utilized it for military purposes (see History, Chapter 2).

CLIMATE[2]

RAINFALL:
- 450 mm annually (based on a 30 year period)
- rainy season from September to March
- negligible amount of rain from May to August

---

[2] All information except rainfall calculated on a 5 year data base.

Sections

Section A–A

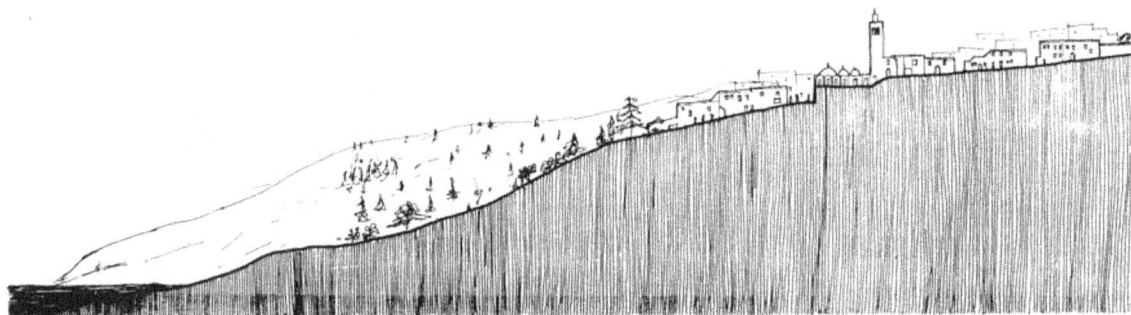

Section B–B

WINDS:
  Winter (October to March):
  • West to Northwest
  • moderate to strong winds (40–80 km/hr.)
  Summer (April to September):
  • Northeast, sea breeze in afternoon
  • moderate winds (20–40 km/hr.)

SEA CURRENTS
Sea currents generally flow in the same direction as the wind.

AVERAGE AIR TEMPERATURES (°C)[3]
  January   11
  April   15.8
  July   26
  October   20.4
  December   12.2
Absolute minimum temperature: 0°C
Absolute maximum temperature: 45°C

AVERAGE TEMPERATURES OF SEA WATER (°C)
  January   12
  April   15
  July   23
  October   21
  December   11

AVERAGE NUMBER OF HOURS OF SUNSHINE PER DAY
  January   5
  April   7
  July   12
  October   7
  December   5

[3] Source: *Practical Guide of Tunisia,* Office National du Tourisme et du Thermalisme, Tunis, 1975.

SOLAR DATA CHART FOR SIDI BOU SA'ID, 36°52' N LATITUDE,
ON THE WINTER SOLSTICE, EQUINOX AND SUMMER SOLSTICE

	Winter Solstice (Dec. 22)	Equinox March 21 (Sept. 23)	Summer Solstice (June 22)
Sunrise	in ESE at 7:00	in E at 6:00	in ENE at 4:45
Sunset	in WSW at 17:00	in W at 18:00	in WNW at 19:15
Max. sun angle (noon)	28°	52°	75°
Mean hours of direct sunshine	5 hr./day	8 hr./day	12 hr./day

WATER RESOURCES[4]

To the west, below the lighthouse there is a well of drinkable water called Ain-Touila meaning "deep spring". Not far from there is another well, called Ain Messaoud, and, on the beach, there are two springs which are actually overflowing: Ain Zalazziya and Ain Belioune. Finally there are wells of potable water in the vicinity of the railway station. These wells may have been sufficient in ancient times but by the mid-1800's, when Sidi Bou Sa'id had become a village, cisterns and earthenware jars had to be resorted to for the assurance of an ample flow of the precious liquid. (See Chapter 5 for a description of the construction of wells and cisterns.) The water supply in these containers was supplemented by specialized donkey-men who transported the water from wells found along the road to La Marsa. The donkey-man was able to make his delivery without entering the house by pouring the water into a clay pipe which led to a reservoir on the inside of the dwelling.

It is interesting to note that it was the custom among public-spirited house owners in the Tunis region to provide a separate water jug inside their home with a copper tube leading to the street. From this "masassa" (as it is called in Arabic) a thirsty traveller could quench his thirst.

The water supply of Sidi Bou Sa'id found its true solution with the branching of the water conduit which feeds the northern suburbs of Tunis. This conduit was reinforced (ca. 1954) by the construction of two immense reservoirs on the hill of Amilcar.

---

[4]Source: "Sidi Bou Said: Le Site et son Histoire," article by Arthur Pellegrin in *Bulletin Economique et Social de la Tunisie,* Tunis, December 1955.

POPULATION[5]

1956 (Census 1.2.56)	3,438 (3,108 Tunisians)
1966 (Census 3.5.66)	3,345
1971 (approximation)	4,000
1976 (projection)	5,000

In 1971, the population of Sidi Bou Sa'id made up less than *5%* of the population of the northern suburbs of Tunis (4,000/82,000) and about 0.4% of the population of Greater Tunis (4,000/862,000).

POPULATION BY AGE GROUP AND SEX

Male	0–4yr.	5–9	10–14	15–19	20–59	60 & over	Total
1966	270	250	200	160	720	110	1,710
1971	300	300	200	200	900	100	2,000
1976	400	400	300	200	1000	200	2,500

Female	0–4	5–9	10–19	20 & over	Total
1966	250	230	370	790	1,600
1971	300	300	500	900	2,000
1976	400	300	600	1,200	2,500

ACTIVE MALE POPULATION

	Population Total	Population Active Males	Available	Employed
1966	3,310	990	800	700
1971	4000	1,200	1,000	800
1976	5,000	1,400	1,100	1,000

The number of foreigners residing in Sidi Bou Sa'id in 1972 was approximately 450.

EMPLOYMENT

With the exception of limited artisan craft, there is no industrial activity in the village. It is therefore in the secondary and service sectors that the majority of employment takes place. The number of jobs in Sidi Bou Sa'id was enumerated in 1971 as follows:

1.	Commerce & Artisan Crafts (in the 52 stores enumerated)	70
2.	Tourism (Restaurants, Hotels and Tours)	15
3.	Administration:	
	Municipal	48
	Primary Schools	22
	Dispensary, PTT, Police	11
	Children's Activity Center	9
	TOTAL	175

---

[5]The information for this section and all succeeding sections of this chapter is from *Plan D'Amenagement Commune de Sidi Bou Said,* Tunis: Ministere Economie Nationale, January 8, 1973.

In comparing the number of employees in the community (less than 200) with the total employable population (approximately 800) we can see a large imbalance which results in many persons commuting to work outside the town limits.

INFRASTRUCTURE

1.MAJOR ROADS

There are three main roads leading from the round-about in the lower part of the village. These are:

- the MC.33, leading to Carthage, La Goulette and Tunis
- the MC.33/GP-9, leading to La Marsa and Tunis
- the Comiche, leading to La Marsa

Leading from these three major routes is a network of secondary roads serving the town. In the older town there are two parking areas:

- Dar Las ram (4,800 m²)
- Sidi Chabane (800 m²)

The town is also served by pedestrian routes.

For a more complete discussion of the streets of Sidi Bou Sa'id see Chapter 3.

2.PUBLIC TRANSIT

An electric commuter train operating between La Marsa and Tunis at a frequency of every 20 minutes in both directions is the most highly utilized transportation link serving the village. After

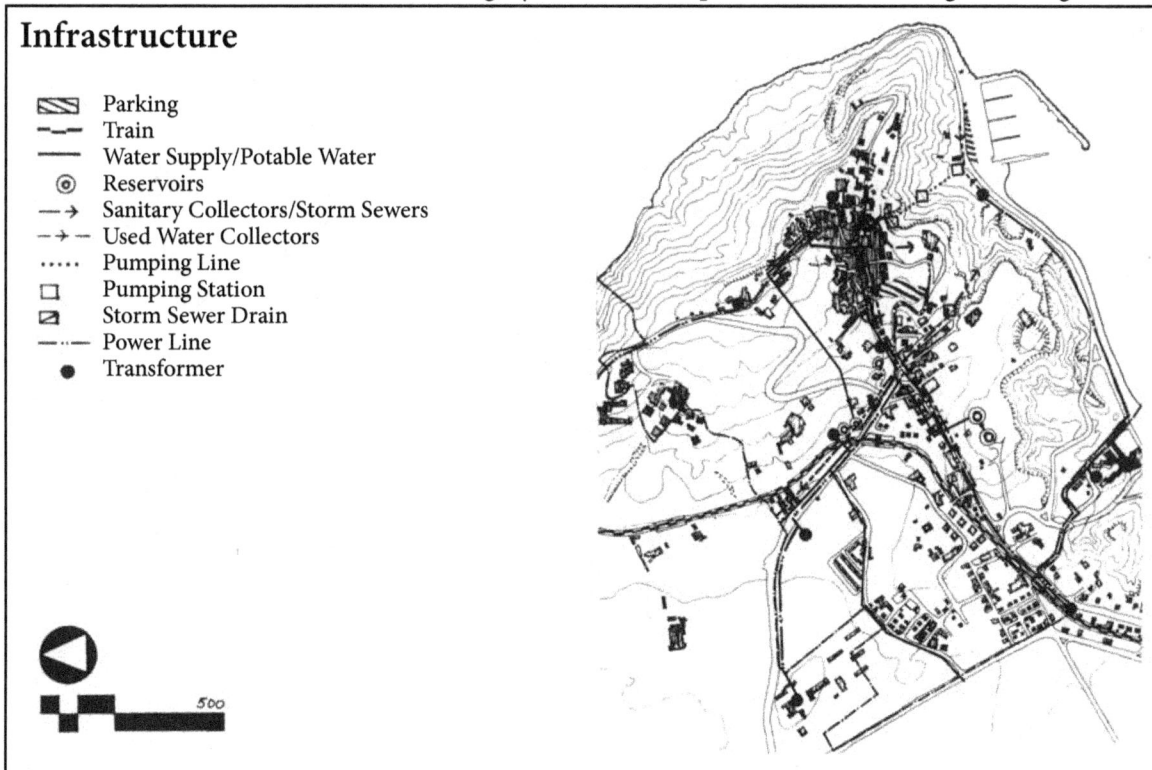

Infrastructure

- Parking
- Train
- Water Supply/Potable Water
- ⊙ Reservoirs
- Sanitary Collectors/Storm Sewers
- Used Water Collectors
- ..... Pumping Line
- Pumping Station
- Storm Sewer Drain
- Power Line
- Transformer

500

21:30 the route is served by transit buses operating every 30 minutes. In addition the village is served by taxis.

3.MARINA
A modern marina constructed in 1968 is equipped with 400 berths to accommodate small boats and pleasure craft. The basin has a depth of 2 m.

SERVICES

1. WATER
A pipeline carries drinking water from Ras to two reservoirs in Amilcar, it is then redistributed through four other reservoirs located in the village.

2. SEWERAGE
A network of sewers serves the entire village. With the aid of three pumping stations, sewage from the marina zone is deposited in the main lines of the town, all of which are directed to La Marsa.

3. ELECTRICITY
The village is served by 110V electricity, arriving by overhead lines and underground cables (along Avenue Habib Thameur). There is no public telephone serving the town except during the hours when the post office is open.

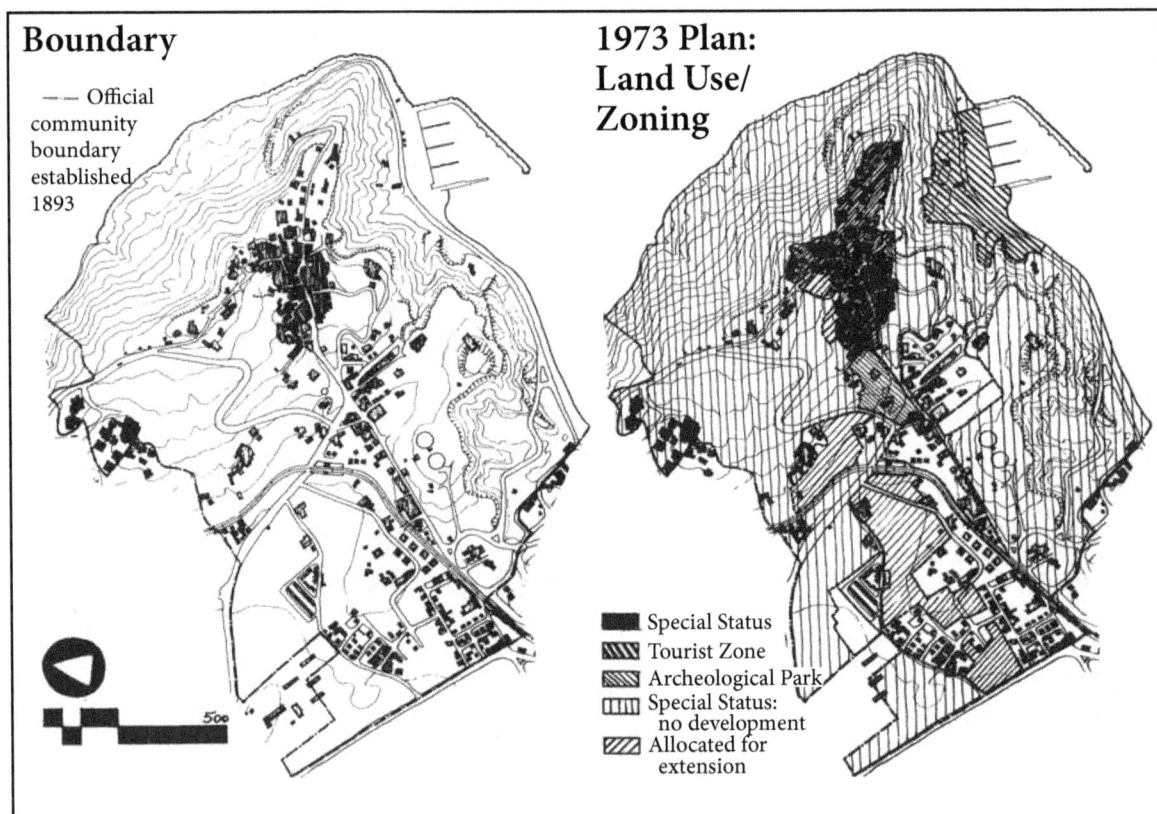

Boundary

--- Official community boundary established 1893

500

1973 Plan: Land Use/ Zoning

■ Special Status
▨ Tourist Zone
▩ Archeological Park
▥ Special Status: no development
▨ Allocated for extension

GEOLOGICAL CONDITIONS

There are certain factors of topography and geology which impose serious constraints on the utilization of certain areas of land within the community. There have not been sufficient technical studies carried out to determine specific causes of soil failure , but based on preliminary information and observations the community can be categorized according to the following areas:

1. STABLE TERRAIN
This area in the central region of the community is considered to pose no hazards to the construction of buildings or other uses.

2. MODERATE EROSION AND SLIDES
This area along the south east slopes of the community is marked by moderate erosion and slides, but the soil seems to have arrived at a natural stability. Until further technical studies are carried out to further understand the conditions, no modifications of the existing status should take place, such as of the new grading or excavations, the extra weight of new buildings or embankments or new drainage, which might endanger the present stability.

3. LANDSLIDES AND ENDANGERED BUILDINGS ALONG THE NORTH SLOPE
For more than twenty-five years, there have been observed movements and slides of the embankments. These slides have sometimes taken place without human intervention, and as well have damaged or destroyed dwellings. It is strongly advised that no further building or alteration is to be attempted in this zone until an overall and detailed study is undertaken.

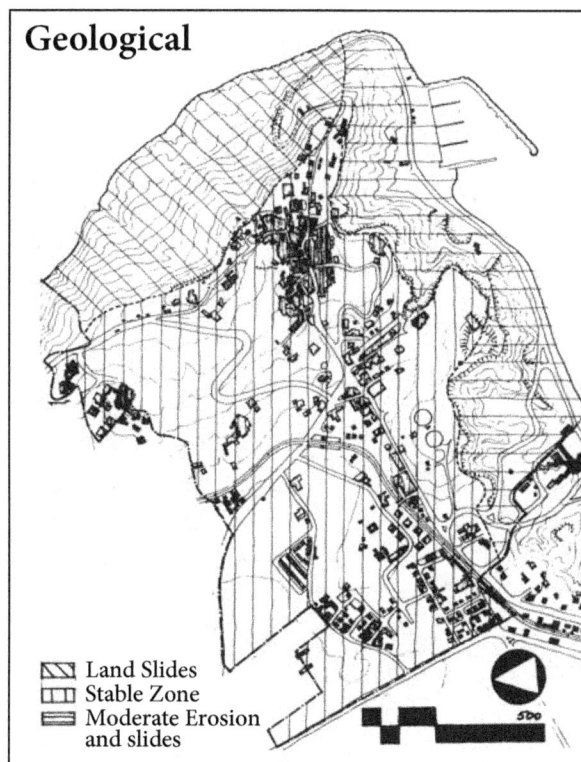

This and the previous three maps were based on information from *Plan D'Amenagement: Commune De Sidi Bou Said,* Tunis, January 1973.

Geological

Land Slides
Stable Zone
Moderate Erosion and slides

THE "KHARJA" IN SIDI BOU SA'ID

CHAPTER 2

HISTORY

PUNIC ERA

Archaeological evidence attests to the presence of people on the site of Sidi Bou Sa'id as early as the 5th Century B.C. It was at this time that Carthage had reached its height as a prosperous trading nation with territory corresponding approximately to present day Tunisia and influence stretching throughout the Mediterranean. Its capital city, Carthage, extended over a large area including the promontory of Cape Carthage where a navigational fire-tower and possibly part of the wealthy suburb of Megara were built.

ROMAN PROVINCE

A series of conflicts between Rome and Carthage over sea power and colonies in Sicily and Italy culminated in the Punic Wars which ended with the defeat and total destruction of the city of Carthage and the surrounding countryside in 146 B.C. It was not until after Roman resettlements in Tunisia after 44 B.C. that Carthage again rose to be a prosperous city—this time as the capital of a province called Africa Proconsularis.

ARAB CONQUEST

The Islamic conquest reached Tunis in 647 but the resistance of the native Berbers of Constantine and of the Byzantines delayed the complete submission of the country until 703. Under the new rulers, Tunisia and part of Constantine took the name of Ifriqiya and the capital was moved from Carthage to Kairouan.

THE AGHLABIDS

In 800, Ifriqiya acquired a large degree of self-government under the ruling house of the Aghlabids. The following hundred years marked a period of great cultural activity in the fields of scholarship, religion and the arts. The two great mosques of Tunis and Kairouan were built during this period.

In order to protect the prosperous mercantile stronghold of Tunis against a sea attack the Aghlabids built a whole series of fortifications along the length of the African shore. Depending on the particular instance, these fortifications were called qcars or ribats and were manned by a force of monk-soldiers. As part of this line of fortifications a ribat and lighthouse tower ("menar") was built on the promontory of Cape Carthage—the present day site of Sidi Bou Sa'id. From the installation of the lighthouse the site gained its early Arabic name of "Jbel al-Menar" (Mount of the Tower), which was the name used for the site and subsequently the village until it was given its official name of Sidi Bou Sa'id in 1893.

THE FATIMIDS

An internal struggle between various North African princes and potentates led to the subjection of Ifriqiya by the Fatimid dynasty in the early 10th century. But in 972 the Fatimids, who had conquered Egypt, established themselves at Cairo leaving Tunisia in charge of their faithful Berber allies, the Zirids. When the Zirids eventually revolted against the Fatimids, the Fatimids retaliated by unleashing the disastrous invasion of Tunisia by the Hilal, Sulaim and Maqil Arab tribes in 1050; subsequently called the Hilalian Invasion. The rampant destruction of waterworks, olive groves, vineyards and urban settlements, much of which had endured since Roman times, reduced the land to arid steppe, a devastation from which it has never fully recovered.

THE ALMOHADS AND THE HAFSIDS

Order was restored to Tunisia in 1159 by the Almohad caliph Abd-al-Mumin from Morocco who united the entire Maghreb (Libya, Tunisia, Algeria, Morocco and Andalusia) under his authority. With the breakup of the Almohad Empire in 1236, Tunisia came under the rule of the Hafsid dynasty. The late 13th and early 14th century was, except for the invasion in 1270 by the crusade of King Louis IX of France, an exceptionally peaceful era for Ifriqiya and Tunis grew in prosperity and influence to become the most important trading post of the Maghreb.

During the Hafsid era, the Ribat of Sidi Bou Sa'id was in times of peace transformed from an essentially military institution into a refuge for religious adepts. There was no urban agglomeration at Sidi Bou Sa'id at this time although there was a cemetery around the Ribat which contained scattered mausoleums and simple shelters used as hotels for visitors. Further down the hill was a secular area consisting of modest rural houses. An important achievement of the Hafsid period was the consolidation of the existing Ribat at Sidi Bou Sa'id into a more extensive defensive work.

SUFISM

Originating in the Middle East, Sufism is a moral and religious doctrine, rigorous both in its principles and in its application. It was brought to North Africa by educated Maghrebians who had gone to Damascus, Baghdad or Cairo to complete the initial instruction which they had received at Kairouan, Fez or Cordoba.

Sufism developed first in Morocco, probably with the help of the Almohad movement which was itself a very vigorous form of Islam. It then spread rapidly into Algeria and Ifriqiya. The success of Sufism can be explained by the fact that it provided its followers with heightened religious experiences. It brought together man and his Creator and allowed his union with the Divinity;

the "elected" or possessors of the Baraka were even able to intercede between God and the prayers of simple believers. Thus began the cult of saints or "maraboutism" which was to play such an extraordinary role in the history of the Maghreb.

One of the great Sufic teachers, Abou Sa'id, chose Jbel-el-Menar as his retreat and it was on the slopes of its hill overlooking the sea that he taught, meditated and prayed. He died there in 1231— his burial place near the lighthouse having since become a place of hermitage for his followers from the various religious brotherhoods which acknowledged Abou Sa'id as one of their greatest spiritual leaders. The annual feast of the "Kharja" still takes place as a ceremony of reunion and homage to the great saint.[1] It is from Abou Sa'id, patron saint of the village, that Sidi Bou Sa'id gets its present name.

SPANISH PROTECTORATE

As the power of the Hafsids declined in the 15th century, the country fell once again into anarchy. Towards the end of the century, Spain and Turkey emerged as the two rival powers fighting for domination of the Mediterranean. With the establishment of a protectorate in Tunis in 1535, the Ribat of Sidi Bou Sa'id was occupied by a large garrison which remained until the Turkish conquest in 1574. It is possible that the Spaniards destroyed much of the Ribat before leaving it to the Turks, as little evidence of their presence remains,.

TURKISH CONQUEST

The conquest of Tunisia by the Turks was completed in 1574, a control which the Turks were not to completely relinquish until the establishment of the French protectorate in 1881. Under Turkish rule, Tunisia was again part of the Islamic world, which, for all of its Muslim subjects, was a commonwealth of equals and powerful protection against the encroachment of Christian forces. Tunisia gained an increasingly large measure of self-government under the dynasty established by Mourad Bey who ruled for most of the 17th century.

During the 17th century the Turkish "Rais" (fleet captains) adopted Abou Sa'id as their patron saint, giving him the title of "Rais el-Abhar" (Master of the Seas).

Before each expedition, the Turkish seamen held ceremonies around his tomb to ensure themselves of a fortunate voyage; and upon returning to Tunisia held another ceremony in which the most prized acquisitions were offered to the "Shaikh of the Zawiya" (Keeper of the Mausoleum) either in kind or in coin.

---

[1]The Kharja: Held each year for many hundreds of years in the middle of August, the Kharja (literally meaning "going out"), originated as much as a military review as a religious procession. Today, the Kharja of Sidi Bou Sa'id is the apotheosis and winding up of all the other Kharjas and is no longer a military display but rather a joyous parade of adherents to Sufism including representatives of the various "Sufi" brotherhoods, who for the most part have occupied ancient ribats called by their names.
The procession begins at dusk at the west entrance to the village and when it finally arrives at the marabout of Sidi Bou Sa'id the great interior courtyard (Sahn) is dark. There, men, women and children wait for hours for the commencement of "Issaouia", a series of driving chants and rhythms obtained with percussion instruments which slowly ascend in volume to bring initiates towards "takmira", a state of ecstasy .

The town of Sidi Bou Sa'id began to take its present form in the early 17th century when the increasing frequency of pilgrimages to the tomb of the saint allowed a few hawkers to build permanent stalls at the site of the Present "souk" (marketplace). Other permanent residents of the town were the families of the readers of the Qur'an, the conductor of prayers, and the "moueddeb" (teacher) who clustered around the mausoleum; and a number of the fleet captains who settled in large residences a short distance from the mausoleum.

HUSAYNIDS

In 1705 Bey Husain ben 'Ali Turki moved the seat of government to Bardo and in 1710 established the Husaynid Dynasty. By this time the Turks had become completely assimilated and the new dynasty was a Tunisian one which was to reign until the formation of the Tunisian Republic in 1956.

During the reign of Bey Husain ben 'Ali Turki (1705–1740) the "zawiya" (mausoleum of the Saint) and the Mosque of Abou Sa'id were restored and, during the reign of Ali Bey (1759–1782) the interior of the zawiya was renovated and a minaret was added to the mosque. Later, under Harnmoud Pasha (1782–1814), a great flight of stairs was erected to serve as an entrance to the mosque. The closing of these stairs in the late 19th century to make way for a cafe caused the main entrance to be shifted to a former women's entrance. Although the minaret was reconstructed in 1906, the mausoleum is almost identical to how it appeared in the 18th century.

In the 19th century the village became more and more a place of retreat for the rich and highly placed officials of the beylical court in Tunis. New construction crowded around the mosque and souk, to assure the protection of the saint. While the princes preferred elaborate and extensive blocks of construction, which included accommodation for house servants and visitors, many smaller summer residences were built by members of the wealthy upper class of Tunis. Thus Sidi Bou Sa'id became a kind of resort town for the well to do, with a large proportion of its population staying during the summer months. Until the end of the 19th century only the great Tunisian families could build their summer homes here, as the hill was considered sacred and therefore forbidden to foreigners (see Appendix A).

EUROPEAN INFLUENCES

European influence had been felt in Tunisia since the establishment of European trading quarters in Tunis in the late 17th century. But it was not until France had gained control of neighboring Algeria in the late 1820's that Tunisia began to withdraw from the influence of Turkey and attempt to modernize itself along Western lines. Unfortunately the well-intentioned but costly reforms of the Husaynid rulers including the abolition of slavery, and the creation of a Tunisian army and navy eventually led to the country's bankruptcy in 1869. Tunisia fell into the grip of foreign control as a commission of creditor powers—Britain, France and Italy—undertook to receive all revenues and distribute them among the creditors.

France's position of influence in neighboring Algeria was a large factor in Tunisia becoming a French protectorate in 1881. Complete French control of defense and internal administration

Growth Pattern

■ Agglomeration after 1831
▨ Growth after 1928
▨ Growth after 1947

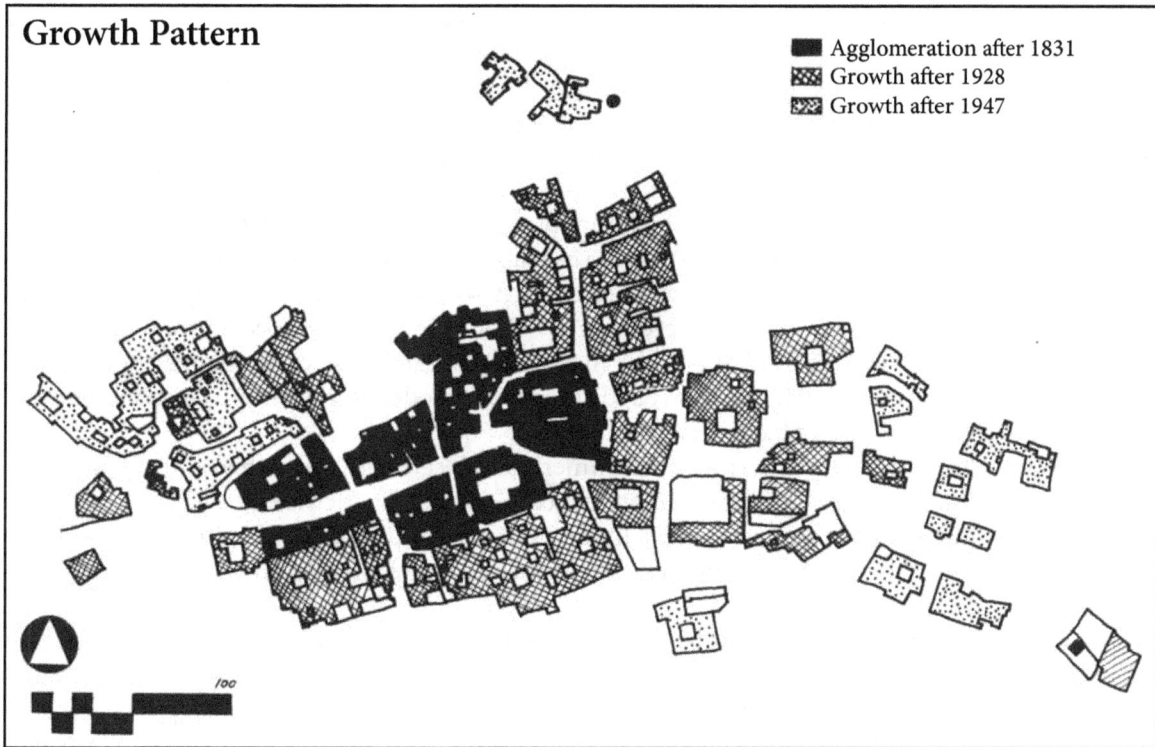

rapidly took place and the groundwork for modernization was laid.[2] Well organized efforts in all fields led to a considerable improvement in the living standard in the next 50 years.

TWENTIETH CENTURY

The French protectorate tended to establish a joint Franco-Tunisian sovereignty in which the Bey became a mere figurehead for the legitimation of French control. Coupled with the hardships of the economic recession of the 1930s this gave impetus to a rise in Tunisian nationalism which had as its central figure Habib Bourguiba, leader of the Neo-Destour party. His influence increased after the heavy destruction of the Second World War and when Tunisia gained its independence in 1956, Bourguiba became president as well as chief of the executive. With considerable amounts of foreign aid, Bourguiba's policies have enabled the country to make steady progress over the last twenty years.

SIDI BOU SA'ID IN THE TWENTIETH CENTURY

The construction of the railway from Tunis to Sidi Bou Sa'id and La Marsa in the late 19th century brought this area within easy reach of a new class of rich town dwellers. The possibility that they had less sophisticated taste or less respect for tradition than their predecessors was of particular

---

[2] The country was provided with a modern infrastructure of railways, ports, hospitals and schools. The olive orchards were replanted on modern lines and a prosperous phosphate mining industry was established.

concern to Baron d'Erlanger, a retired British banker and a resident of Sidi Bou Sa'id, who was very appreciative of the built form and architectural character of the village. Through his influence a decree was passed in 1915 which was designed to preserve the village's beauty and provide guidelines for growth and change (see Appendix B). To prevent unsympathetic alterations to existing buildings or the erection of new buildings the Baron also bought houses and lands as they came on the market. To set an example he had an old house converted into a large villa. Today this is a superb example of traditional Arabic-Islamic architecture built with increasingly rare techniques.

A talented painter, Baron d'Erlanger strove to capture the beauty of the site on canvas, a beauty which he felt was threatened by insensitive modernism. Also a renowned musicologist, he did much to promote a traditional Andalusian music known as "Malouf". As the style became popular, special festivals were held at Sidi Bou Sa'id, especially in the 1960's. The Baron's remarkable encyclopedia of Arabic music[3] is now housed in Sidi Bou Sa'id along with a collection of musical instruments and a library of manuscripts and published works.

Sidi Bou Sa'id remained primarily as a summer residence for the wealthy of Tunis until the Second World War. Since then and particularly since 1960, a dramatic rise in tourism and a large increase in the numbers of foreign residents living here year round have caused major changes in the life of the town.[4] Probably the most noticeable change is the sheer number of visitors to this small village.

A few meters down the road from the main square is a parking lot which used to be a pleasant park until a few years ago; tour buses daily disgorge hundreds of Germans, French, British and other tourists. They stroll up and down the main street, buying souvenirs from shops (which once sold vegetables and housed tradesmen), crowd into cafes or venture into the narrow side streets which once served as places for locals to socialize or for children to play. A hotel and restaurant now exist in what was once a private residence. Locals now do most of their shopping at a supermarket in the lower part of the town.

The local resident's attitude to foreign visitors is an ambivalent one. Many depend on them for their livelihood, yet their social mores and life styles have tended to be eroded by constant exposure to the more worldly habits of Europeans and North Americans. The tangible, physical environment is protected from these alien forces, yet the social and economic basis of the community which engendered that environment is constantly undermined. Property values become inflated—a poor houseowner makes more money by renting out half his home than he can by working at a trade.

Nevertheless, many of the native Tunisians maintain a distinctive life style here; calls to prayer are heard from the mosque every day and traditional music can often be heard near the Cafe des Nattes. The cafes remain the exclusive domain of Tunisian men and foreigners, and most Tunisian women still wear white veils when they go out in public.

---

[3]Entry in British Museum Catalogue of Printed Books to 1955: ERLANGER (Rodolphe D') Baron; *La Musique Arabe,* vols. I–V, (Paris: Guethner), 1936–1940.

[4]Sidi Bou Sa'id's prominence as a tourist attraction began with the government's aggressive promotion of tourism. The industry is a prime earner of foreign exchange in Tunisia.

AERIAL PHOTO OF SIDI BOU SA'ID, 1970, SCALE: 1/3000

CHAPTER 3

SPATIAL STRUCTURE AND BUILT FORM

INTRODUCTION

In general traditional Arabic-Islamic towns are walled and divided into a number of distinct sections or quarters . One quarter usually contains government garrisons, hospitals, palaces and fortresses, the major mosques associated with the particular Islamic school of law or "madhhab" of their ruling elite, and various Muslim school and universities. An important section invariably located close to the government quarter contains the souk or covered marketplace. The souk is a labyrinth of alleyways divided into sectors according to the merchandise sold. Small mosques and mausoleums are usually scattered through it. Residential quarters are traditionally reserved for Muslims who divided themselves into neighborhoods by virtue of their particular "madhhab" and/or original tribal affiliations. Non-Muslims lived within their own quarters inside and/or outside the city with their own schools, religious institutions, etc.

The form of a typical Arabic-Islamic town is the result of a continuous intermeshing of a basic building type—the courtyard house—in response to needs for security, privacy and protection from the climate.

Because of its size and the fact that it is so close to Tunis, Sidi Bou Sa'id did not develop some of the typical characteristics of a large Arabic-Islamic town. The Mosque with its dominant minaret is the focal point as well as the religious, cultural and social center of the town. The souk developed in front of the Mosque as the town grew down the hill. The area containing the police station, pharmacy, municipal offices and most of the schools is located just below the souk. The same sense of highly concentrated urbanity as found in a large Arabic-Islamic town is achieved in Sidi Bou Sa'id by the close association of like buildings developed towards the focus of the minaret. The town moulds itself to the hilly terrain yet is still articulated by the sharp white blocks of its forms.

As in a typical Arabic-Islamic town the exterior spaces in Sidi Bou Sa'id are, for the greater part, evolved from their internal space needs resulting in the fact that the apertures of the houses seem to have no logical arrangement from the exterior. Because these spaces evolved from the needs of interior planning, animal circulation, terrain and drainage they tend to be "negative" spaces, although the need for communality sometimes provokes a "positively" planned space like a square or outdoor cafe.[1]

An outsider coming to Sidi Bou Sa'id is only exposed to the exterior spaces or very public interior spaces due to the impenetrability of the introverted architecture. Wandering through the streets of the village he would be swept into the open where he could view the sea and then suddenly be enclosed in the narrow cul-de-sacs with their cobblestones and, except for their blue doors and window frames, featureless whitewashed facades. The minaret, which appears deceptively close from any point in town, provides orientation. Small neighbourhood squares allow a pause for breath and re-orientation before he is once again engulfed in the narrow streets. There are no hard, right-angled corners but rather softened edges which encourage the flow of his movement around them.

It is hoped that the following quantitative and qualitative analysis of Sidi Bou Sa'id will allow its lessons to be more fully understood and utilized.

MAJOR STRUCTURING DEVICES

PRIMARY STREETS

The Rue Dr. H. Thameur, the most important street in the town, and the one used each year for the Kharja, terminates in the main square which is dominated by the Cafe des Nattes, the former entrance to the Mosque. Another important street, the Rue El Hedi Zarrouk, begins at the small square at the present entrance on the south side of the Mosque, and continues towards the end of the headland. These two streets form a spine off of which all residential streets branch. The semi-private cul-de-sacs in turn lead off the residential streets.

The third major street, Rue Sidi Bou Fares, the coast road from La Marsa, terminates in the small square at the base of the minaret. This square is connected to the square of the Cafe des Nattes by a street along the north edge of the Mosque, and to the Rue El Hedi Zarrouk by a small street (Rue Dar et Toumi) with a set of stairs on the south side of the Mosque.

Because Sidi Bou Sa'id was fully developed before the advent of the automobile, its streets and spaces did not need to be shaped for fast vehicular movement and car parking. However, to prevent automobiles from entering and destroying the intimacy of the main square, steps were placed at the lower end of it and posts were placed in the middle of the two upper tributary streets. Thus cars could come close to the square but not enter it

To allow for some vehicular movement about the town, it was found to be necessary to upgrade two hitherto insignificant roads joining the main spine some distance from the square. Fortunately this was accomplished without forcing a great change in the urban structure and character of Sidi Bou Sa'id.

---

[1] Ashihara in his book, *Exterior Design in Architecture* defines negative space as: 1) Space whose vector diffuses outwards from the center, and 2) Natural space, spontaneous, unplanned. He defines positive space as: 1) Space whose vector focuses inward, 2) Space which indicates the existence of intentions or of planning with regard to the space, and 3) Where boundaries are determined and then order is built inward toward the center.

PEDESTRIAN SCALE

People relate to the built environment in terms of perception and in the way in which it allows them to move around. Because people do not want to walk more than 800 m in performing routine tasks and because normal walking speed is about 4000 m/hr. then a general rule can be stated which says that, within a pedestrian enclave, no two points should be more than about 12 minutes apart. The fact that the location of the major elements of Sidi Bou Sa'id respect this rule is shown by the accompanying diagram.

As opposed to being mere conduits for car and truck traffic, the streets of Sidi Bou Sa'id reflect a major concern for the perceptual needs and movement of pedestrians.[2] Although the three major vehicular routes are relatively straight, there is no straight section longer than 140 m; a sufficiently short distance to discern the body movement of pedestrians. Secondary streets are much shorter; the maximum length without interruption being about 40 m—the upper limit of the size of an "intimate" enclosed urban space. These secondary streets are characterized by changing levels, varying street widths and changing vistas. They may be properly regarded as public spaces for they form not only a means of pedestrian movement but, by mere dimensions, intimate enclosed spaces in which children can play and neighbors can relax and converse. The shorter (less than 15 m) cul-de-sacs are quite private allowing for closer relationships among neighbors.

SYMBOLIC SCALE

It is interesting to note how major ecclesiastical symbols and devices have influenced the design of such a religiously important town as Sidi Bou Sa'id. For instance, because the muezzin calls the faithful to prayer five times a day from the minaret the desire to hear his call has been a factor in deciding where a devout Muslim should build his house. This was proved to be true by experiments that discovered that it was possible to clearly hear the voice of the muezzin up to a distance of 250 m from the minaret. As shown by the accompanying diagrams, nearly all of the old town fits within this radius. Also, the minaret, because of its height always seems deceptively close, is quite strategically placed at the end of major street vistas giving orientation. It also acts as a reminder of the importance of the Muslim faith in Sidi Bou Sa'id. Nowhere does one see the full height of the minaret, which would be oppressively tall, but rather only the top half. The minaret immediately indicates the center of town from almost any public place in the village and, if it is not in view in one place, it usually can be spotted if one moves his vantage point a few meters.

---

[2] In his book *Urban Design: The Architecture of Towns and Cities,* Paul Spreiregen stated that human social interaction is determined by vision and distance. His research determined the following relationships:
1 m – 3 m, conversational distance.
up to 13 m, possible to distinguish facial expressions.
up to 25 m, possible to recognize a friend's face.
up to 40 m, possible to discern body movement.
up to 1260 m, possible to recognize a human figure.

Vehicular Circulation

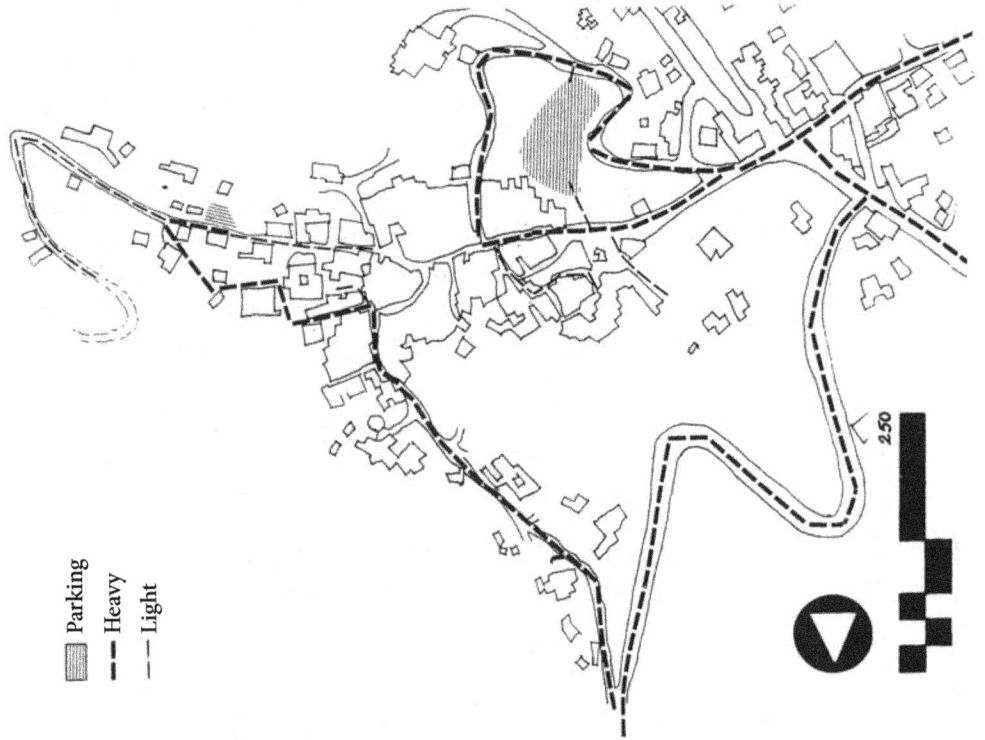

▨ Parking
– – Heavy
‒ ‒ Light

250

Pedestrian Circulation

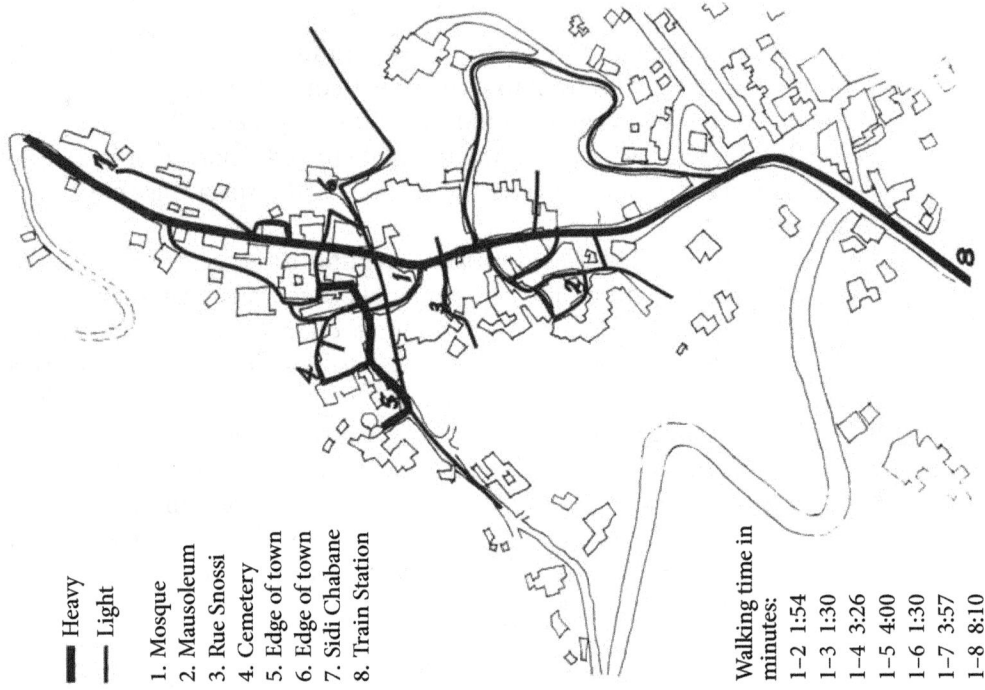

■ Heavy
— Light

1. Mosque
2. Mausoleum
3. Rue Snossi
4. Cemetery
5. Edge of town
6. Edge of town
7. Sidi Chabane
8. Train Station

Walking time in minutes:
1–2 1:54
1–3 1:30
1–4 3:26
1–5 4:00
1–6 1:30
1–7 3:57
1–8 8:10

Call to Prayer Distance

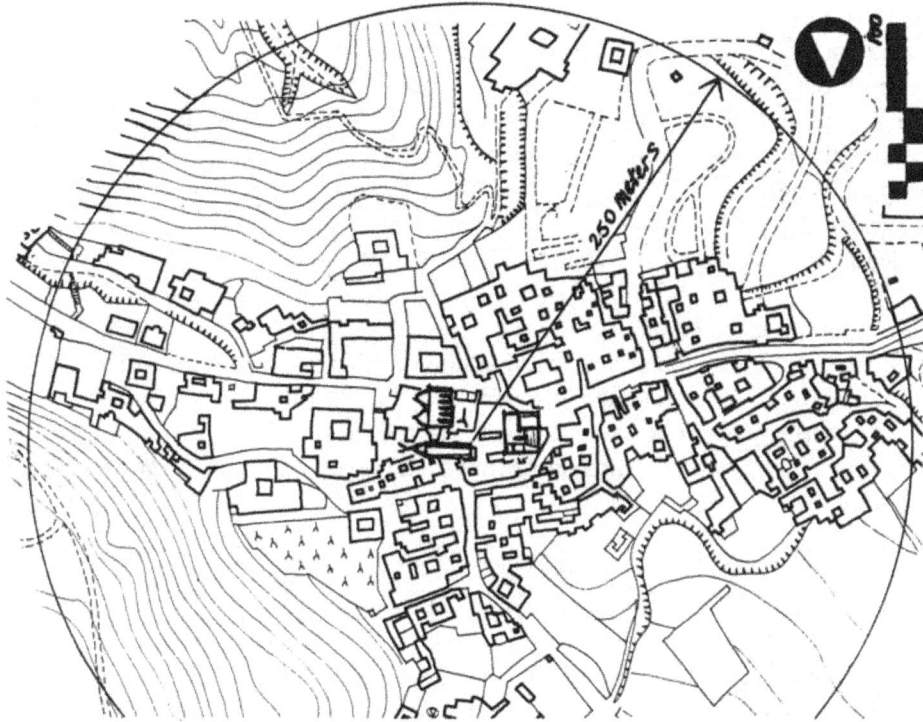

Length of Streets

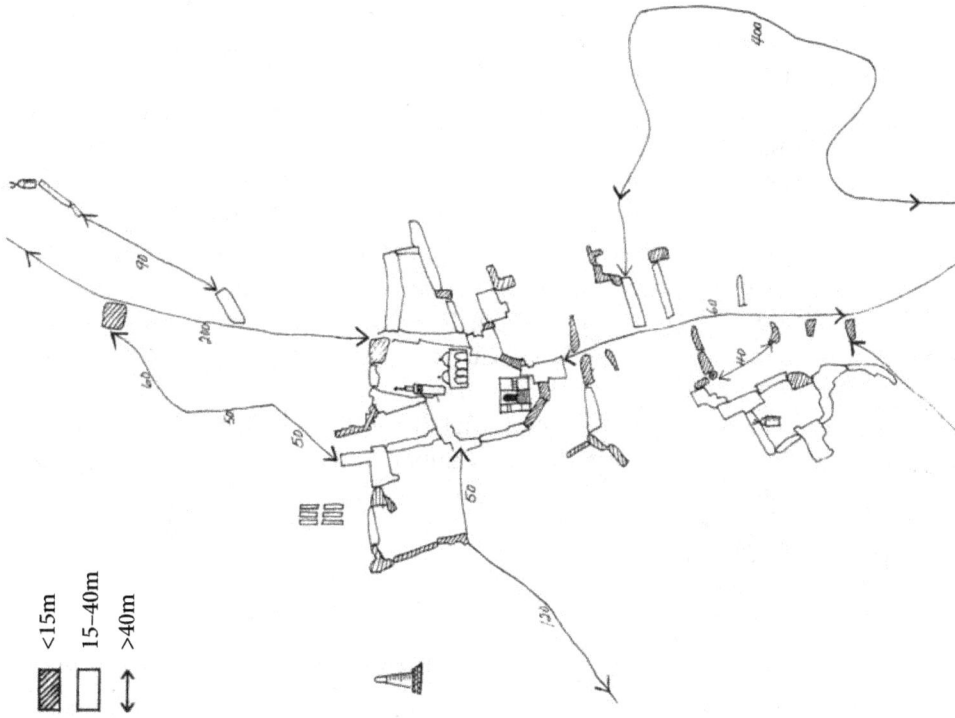

<15m
15-40m
>40m

STREET TYPOLOGIES

The basic urban structure and most of the general details of Sidi Bou Sa'id have been discussed in previous sections of this book through a set of maps showing its size, patterns of movement, density and landmarks, etc. In this section, the streets of the village have been divided into five categories in order to further clarify the nature of the urban pattern. These categories are:

    A—The roundabout street
    B—The connecting street
    C—The dead end street or cul-de-sac
    D—The square
    E—Major circulation streets

    Each of the streets in the village have been tabled in their respective categories and described in detail. It is interesting to note that the cul-de-sac is by far the most prevalent street type unlike the case in North America where connecting streets are the most numerous. Although each type may appear similar on a map, in three dimensions they all have their own unique form, size, atmosphere and specific function.

TYPE A: THE ROUNDABOUT STREET

DESCRIPTION: A street which originates and ends at the same street.
VARIATIONS:

1. This street comes off the principal street in the village and returns to it: it is always noisy as it has three branches onto the main street. It also has a now disused public node: the wells of Ain Touila.
2. This street becomes more private and less noisy as it makes a wide arc away from the main thoroughfare. As the street progresses it climbs higher and higher away from the town affording a fine view of Tunis. Suddenly the street drops back into the village but at a much lower point than where it originated.
3. A very private street which begins and ends on the main thoroughfare. It is only used by the people who live along it for, unlike A2 (above), it is not connected to paths which lead out into the adjacent countryside. It has a small private square far removed from the center of town.
4. This is an extremely private street whose entrance—a set of steps which faces away from the main public thoroughfare—is nearly invisible. It has a few inconspicuous small doors to private residences but seems to be used very little. Although close to the main thoroughfare it is almost completely isolated from public activity by tall buildings.
5. Because this street contains the cafe/restaurant of the biggest hotel in Sidi Bou Sa'id, half of this street is very private and the other half is very public. It seems as if people rarely use this street as a through street.

TYPE B: THE CONNECTING STREET

DESCRIPTION: A street which connects squares or other streets.
VARIATIONS:

1. Connects one of the main vehicular entry points to the pedestrian center of town. It is a pedestrian street often used by people to go to the cemetery, the Mosque or the school. It

contains more modest homes than other areas of Sidi Bou Sa'id which could account for its heavy traffic at various times of the day. Children tend to use parts of this street as play areas. The top of the street enters a busy square full of people, a few cars, etc.

2. This street is often used by people to go to the Mosque, cemetery, etc. Due to a set of steep steps it does not allow rapid or free pedestrian movement. The hotel adds to the traffic and makes this street less public (as in A5).
3. This is a very seldom used street possibly due to its two sets of stairs. Its privacy and orange trees make this an exceptionally beautiful street.
4. This street connects the main square of the Cafe des Nattes with a secondary square. It is short, very public and essentially just an extension of the two squares.
5. This street is the main route to the cemetery and therefore has symbolic significance and atmosphere. People who do not belong on this street are often stared at as they go by.

TYPE C: THE DEAD END STREET OR CUL-DE-SAC

DESCRIPTION: A dead end street or cul-de-sac.

VARIATIONS:

1. This street divides and ends in two private squares. The privacy of one is maintained because it cannot directly be seen on entering the street. The other one has a "sabat" (a room built over it) giving it a very enclosed and intimate feeling.
2. A very short, noisy street very visible from the main street of Sidi Bou Sa'id. The houses leading onto it are obviously well to do. An elaborate door at one end gives the street a strong focal point and makes it seem shorter.
3. Less noisy than C2 but still fairly public. Seems to be a modest street although there is a house at the end with a fine plasterwork ceiling.
4. This private street is covered with arches, giving it the illusion of being a series of private courtyards. Small openings from one section of the street to another protect its privacy. A very elaborate studded door at one end again provides a strong focal point.
5. Similar to C1, but instead of ending in two private squares, one fork leads to a garden and the other one leads to a courtyard. This seems to be a modest neighbourhood.
6. This street originally led to a large, rich man's house—Dar Lasram—with a private courtyard for horses. Its gates are still visible but now stand open and unused. This is the only street in the village where there is an exterior staircase leading to a second storey entrance.
7. This is a narrow winding street with a surprisingly open vista at the top overlooking the cemetery, the lighthouse and the sea.
8. This is a very well kept exclusive street. At the top is the lighthouse and along one side is a large estate. This street contains a stepped sidewalk but no space for cars.

TYPE D: THE SQUARE

DESCRIPTION: A square

VARIATIONS:

1. This is a series of private, unexpected spaces linked by arched openings.

2. This is the square in front of the Cafe des Nattes and is the main focal point of the town. It is fully discussed in Chapter 6.
3. This square is often used by children during their school break.
4. This square has a high traffic volume as it is the main vehicular entry point to the top part of town.

TYPE E: MAJOR CIRCULATION STREETS

DESCRIPTION: A major circulation street.

VARIATIONS:

1. 1 and 1(a) These are two large vehicular streets into town with very few houses except for those close to the main street.
2. This is the main street of Sidi Bou Sa'id and is discussed in detail in Chapter 6.
3. This is a fairly straightforward road with houses on both sides. It is wide enough to allow for cars.
4. This street originally encircled the entire town until it was covered by a landslide.
5. This street used to form part of the major vehicular route provided by E4.
6. This street is a continuation of E3 but is narrower and more intimate.

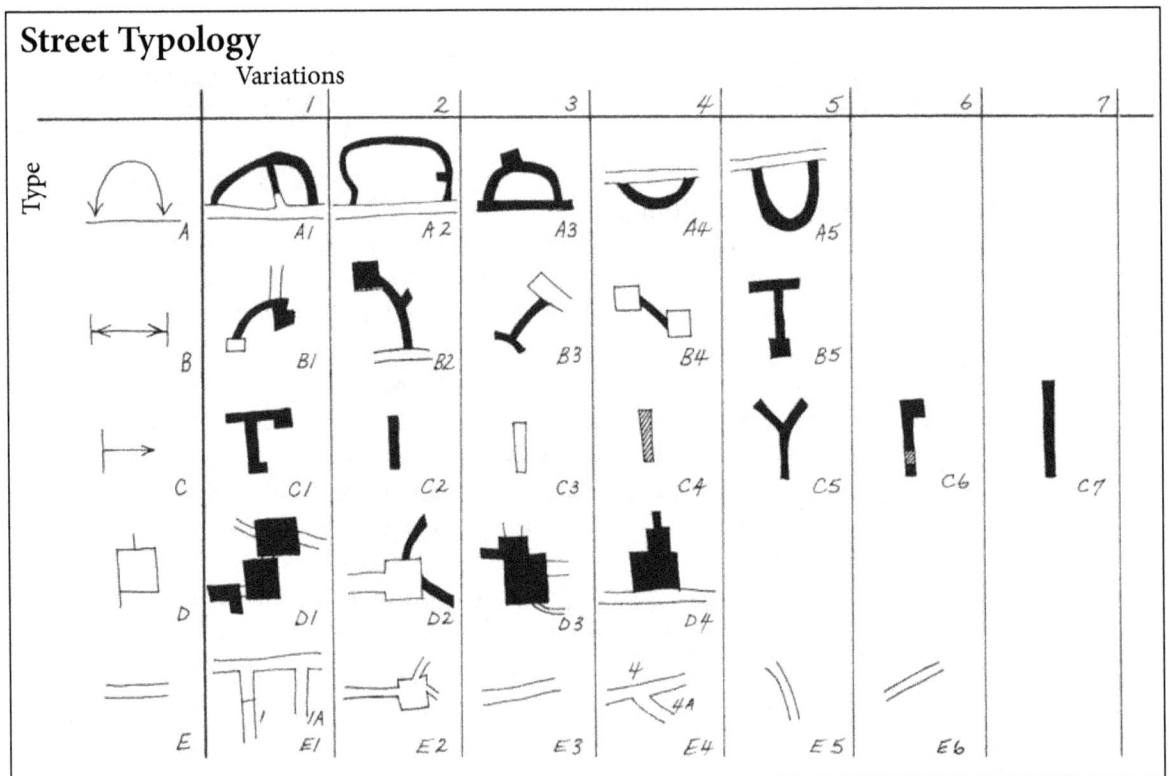

Street Typology

Streets Studied

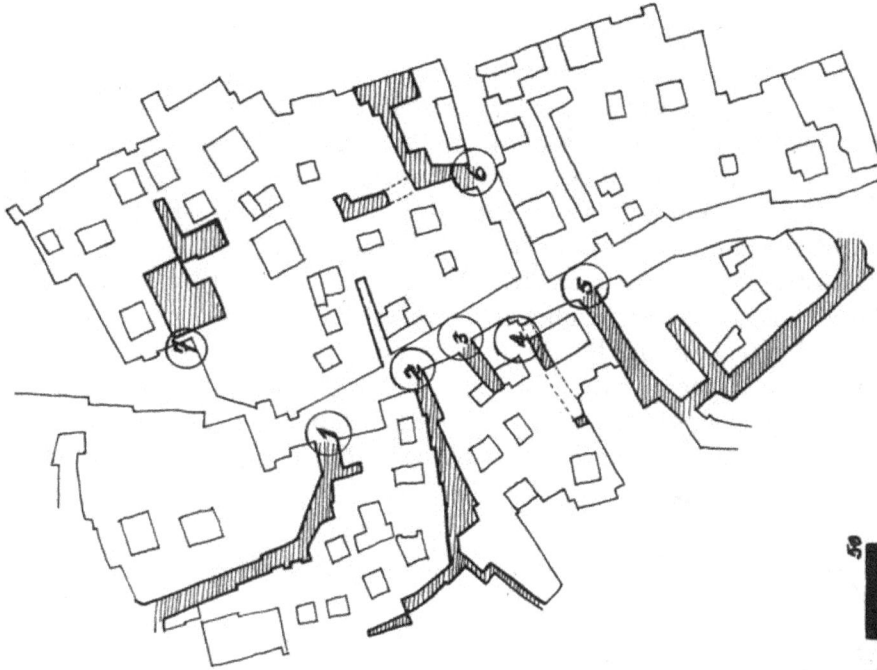

**Street Variations:
Locations**

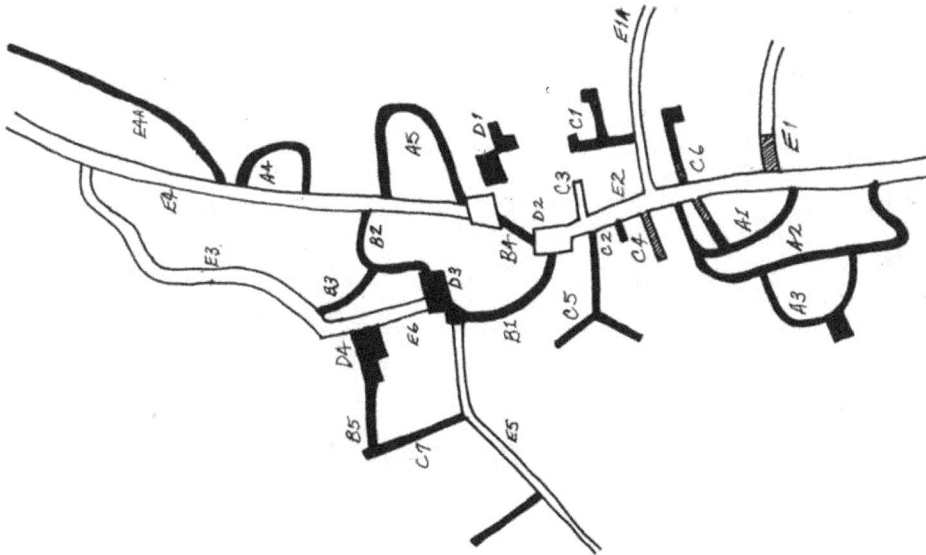

1. RUE BOU FARES

At various times of the day this street is one of the most heavily trafficked pedestrian routes in Sidi Bou Sa'id being used in the mornings (7:45), at noon (12:30 and 2:00) and in the evenings (6:00) by the girls who attend the school near the cemetery. It also used to be the main connecting street between the lower part of Sidi Bou Sa'id (the Souk, Mosque and government quarter) and the upper part of Sidi Bou Sa'id (the lighthouse, cemetery and school).

It is a good example of one of the ramped staired streets which are so prevalent here. The accompanying elevation shows how the builder's individuality prevails even though the basic design idiom and construction materials are kept the same. It can also be seen that the windows rarely have an external order of their own but rather reflect the internal order of the rooms. Every door on the street is different yet each has some elements (color, patterns, etc.) which tie it to the others. There are two typical window styles: the older plain type and the more ornate type of Andalusian influence. Building heights vary, articulating the street and giving it a sense of movement. As the street approaches the Souk, the buildings lower dramatically to open the vista into the more public space.

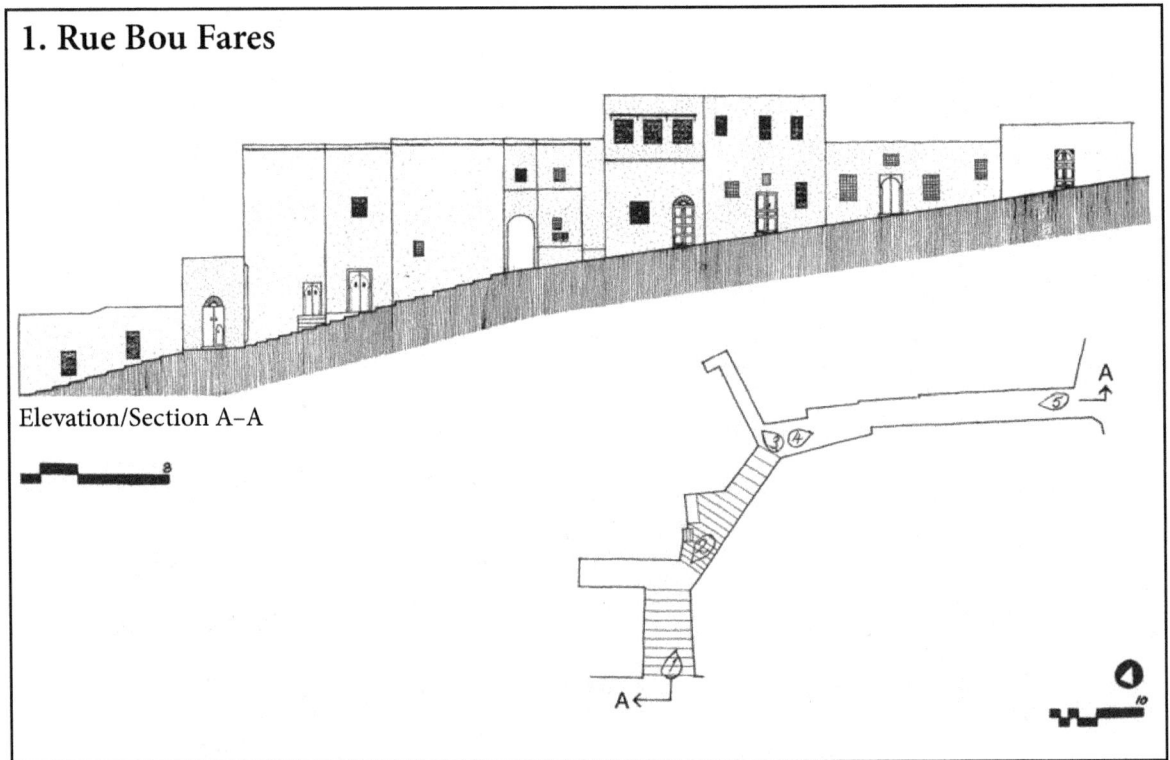

1. Rue Bou Fares

Elevation/Section A–A

Rue Bou Fares

1

2

3

4

5

2. RUE SNOSSI

This street is a good example of two of Cullen's qualitative attributes, hierarchy and serial vision. The best way to illustrate this is to use his method of analysis, a series of photographs.

Hierarchically this street progressively moves from the extremely public to the very private, that is, from the souk area to the private courtyard. During this progression it also passes from a very noisy area to more quiet regions as it moves from the center of the town to the countryside surrounding it, (where the most prominent noises are the birds). There is also a sudden transition in paving—flat asphalt in the souk area and ramped stepped cobblestones on Rue Snossi—forming a clear line of demarcation.

Photo 1: Transition from noisy souk to quieter street. The stairs are fairly close together giving a sense of rapid movement. The focus seems to be on the door to the left but is suddenly shifted to the arch which is the real entrance to the street. This has the effect of suddenly changing one's line of travel.

Photos 2 & 4: On passing through the arch, the street unexpectedly widens into a static square with two small openings. The exit to the right, under a walkway connecting two buildings, is almost hidden since it is very narrow and dark.

Photo 5: The street bifurcates at this point, the left branch being a very narrow alley which makes an S-shaped curve almost immediately so that very little of it is visible. It finally fades out in the countryside. The corners of the building are cut out so that men riding donkeys can get through more easily—a fine example of the awareness of public responsibility by private owners. The space is so tunnel-like and tight that only one person can pass through it at a time.

Photos 6 & 7: The right branch, a cul-de-sac, is wider than the left branch. The attraction here is not the street itself but rather an elaborate door (described as "pinpointing" by Gordon Cullen). The cobblestones have much more texture than the walls, creating a distinct separation between houses and street. An unusual alley leading into a private courtyard/garden joins on to the end of the street.

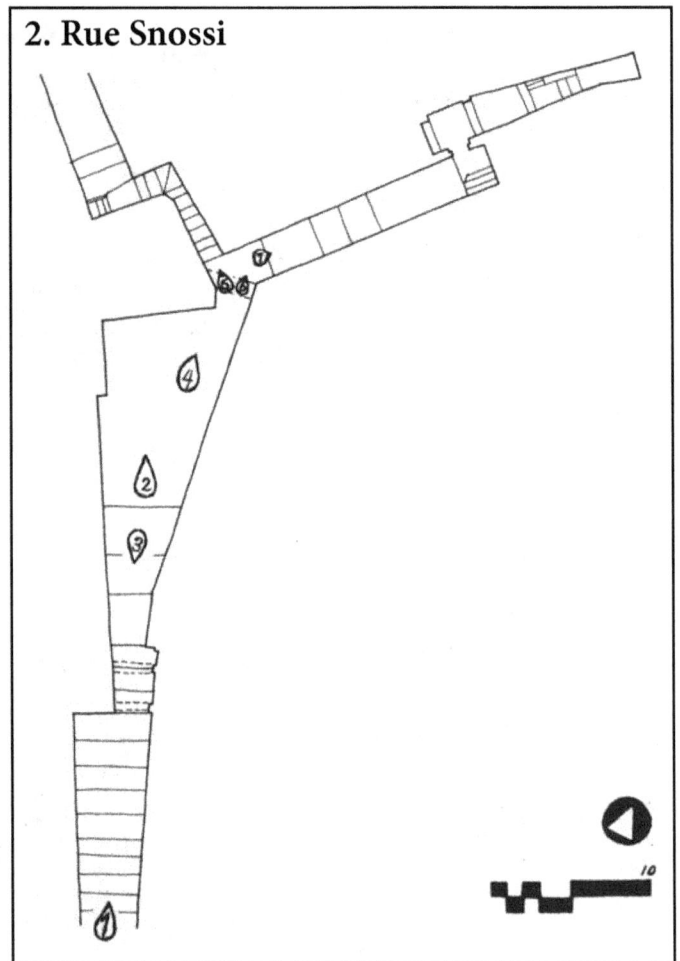

2. Rue Snossi

Rue Snossi

1

2

3

4

5

6

7

3. IMPASSE BEN M'RAB

This cul-de-sac is only 14.7 meters long and, as may be seen from the drawing, can easily be represented in one small perspective. According to Spreiregen (see footnote 2, this chapter) this length is easily within the maximum distance for recognizing a friend's face; making the Impasse Ben M'Rab quite an intimate space. On first entering the street the whole is visible with the 60° degree horizontal and the 27° degree vertical (above eye level) field of human vision. The street slopes upward so that the top is at the eye level of someone standing at the bottom. However, the ratio of the distance to the building (D) to the height of the building (H) changes as one progresses up the street.[3] As one approaches the buildings the details become visible, the most imposing one being the door at the top. Towards the end of the street, as the buildings come closer and closer, a low wall on the right allows visual penetration beyond the white facade into a garden.

This type of street acts functionally to penetrate into a group of attached buildings. Its four separate entrances each lead to individual houses.

It is also interesting to note that the narrowing of this street towards its far end gives it a false sense of perspective.

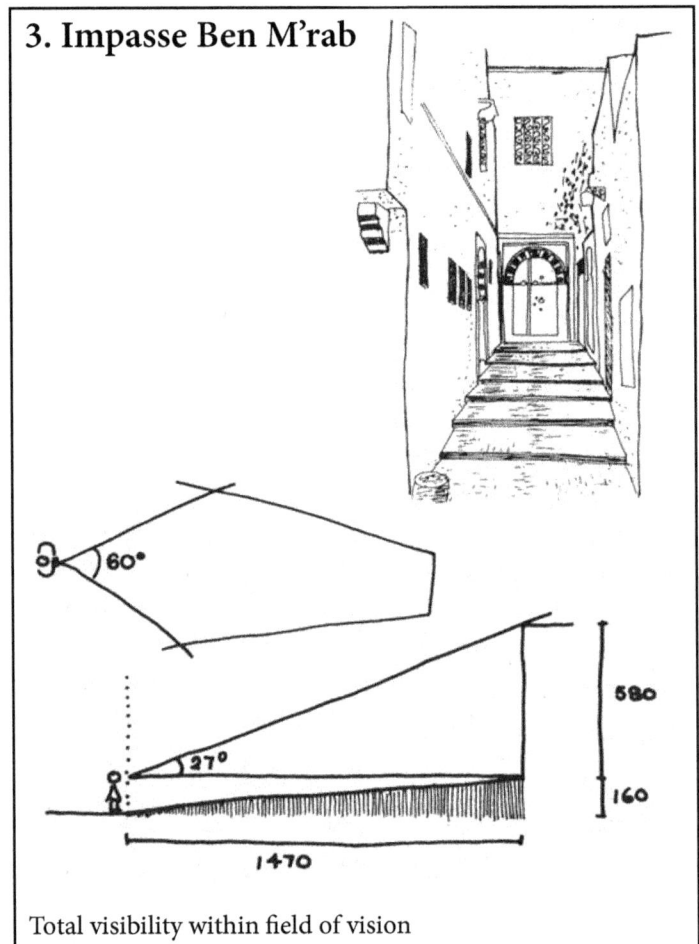

3. Impasse Ben M'rab

Total visibility within field of vision

[3] Ashihara, Y. *Exterior Design in Architecture.*

Impasse Ben M'rab

1. View of impasse from Rue Dr. H. Thameur

2. View of built-in seat "Dukkana" adjacent to mouth of impasse

3. Top of impasse showing courtyard vegetation behind wall

4. THE DRIBA

A driba in Arabic-Islamic town planning is a cul-de-sac with a heavy gate designed for added security from intruders. The gate can only be opened by a key or a guard. Because it no longer has its gate, the "Driba" is not a true driba but, nevertheless, is still one of the most delightful streets in Sidi Bou Sa'id. It is a definitely planned series of spaces divided by portals whose shapes have been formed by the buildings around them. It is a positive space whose "outdoor rooms" are gradually revealed giving it a very private atmosphere.

The first section of the Driba is entered via a small portal. Its pleasant benches ("dukkana") with tile-work on both sides and a flat roof with a lantern above make this a good place to sit out of the sun and noise and watch the people going up and down the busy main street.

After passing through another portal there is a section covered with grapevines on the right and with a walled garden on the left. Next to this is a series of vaulted areas with doors to private houses. Finally, at the end of the Driba, there is a large square opening in the ceiling ("rokba") highlighting the ornate door which was once the entrance to a rich man's house.

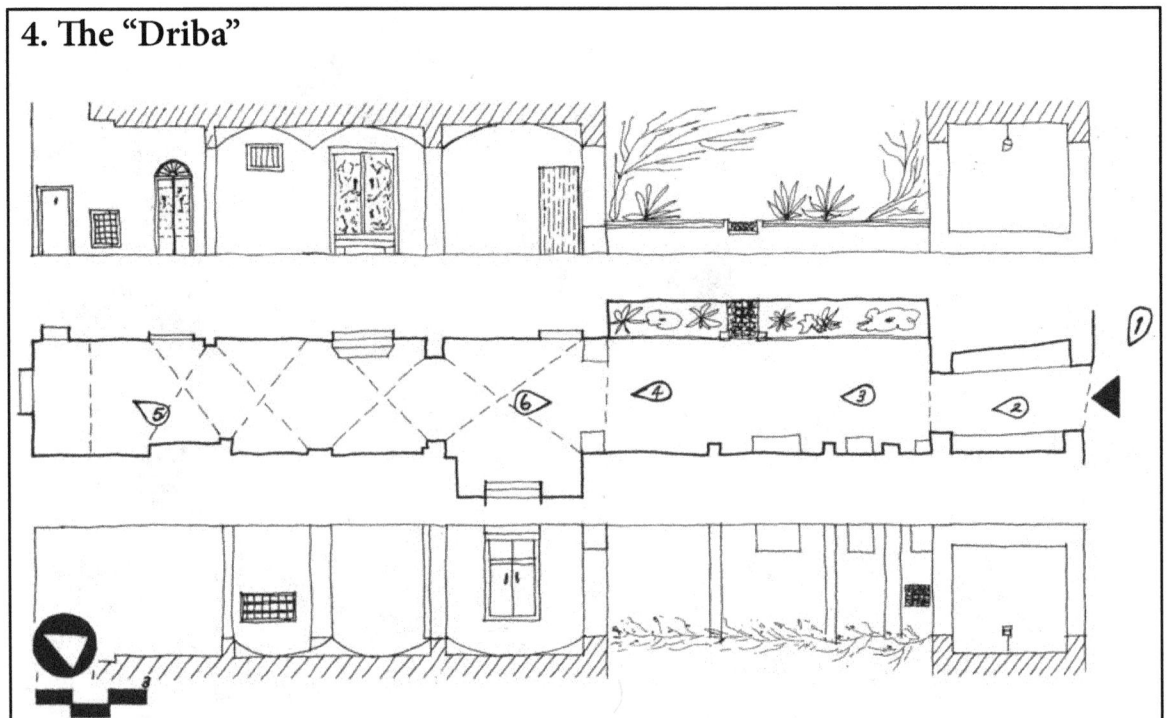

4. The "Driba"

The "Driba"

5. RUE AIN TOUILA

This street is most interesting because of its social, cultural and religious significance; one part of it, Rue Sidi el Ghemrini leads to an important mausoleum while another part of it leads to the now disused wells called the Ain Touila. After the Mosque, Sidi el Ghemrini is the most important religious center in the village. The wells, on the other hand, used to be a social center for the women who came to get water and do the laundry for their families. The frame built above the wells on which the women could hang wet clothing is still there although, with the advent of modern plumbing, the wells are now closed. There is a magnificent view of distant Tunis from these wells. On descending the steps from the Rue Ain Touila one is suddenly plunged into a noisy, heavily trafficked section of the Rue Dr. H. Thameur.

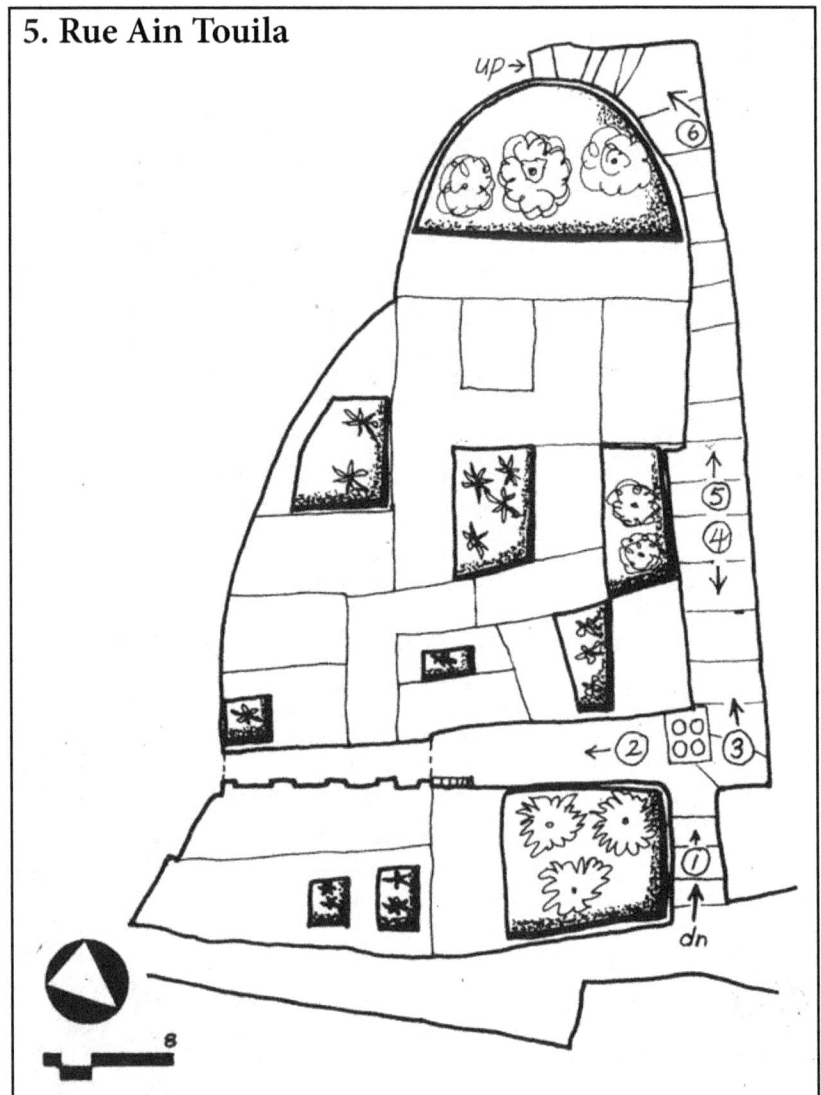

5. Rue Ain Touila

Rue Ain Touila

6. IMPASSE EL KHALSI

Because construction techniques do not allow high buildings to be built and the streets are already too narrow for expansion in that direction, it is very difficult to enlarge an individual house in the urban agglomeration of an Arabic-Islamic town. As a result the architecture has resorted to the concept of air rights to cope with the lack of space by adding rooms out over the street called "sabat". The hatched portion of the plan of Impasse el Khalsi signifies a sabat which was built between two facing buildings long after the block was completed.

This street is also somewhat typical of the residential cul-de-sacs because one arm of it ends at the gate of a small garden to a well-to-do house and the other arm ends at the small door of a modest one-storey house.

The Impasse el Khalsi is more like an elongated square than a street because there is no feeling of movement through space as the whole view is revealed at the outset rather than exposed gradually. However, the enclosing buildings do give a feeling of intimacy and privacy. Where the street forms a small square the feeling is intensified by a lowering of the facades of the building.

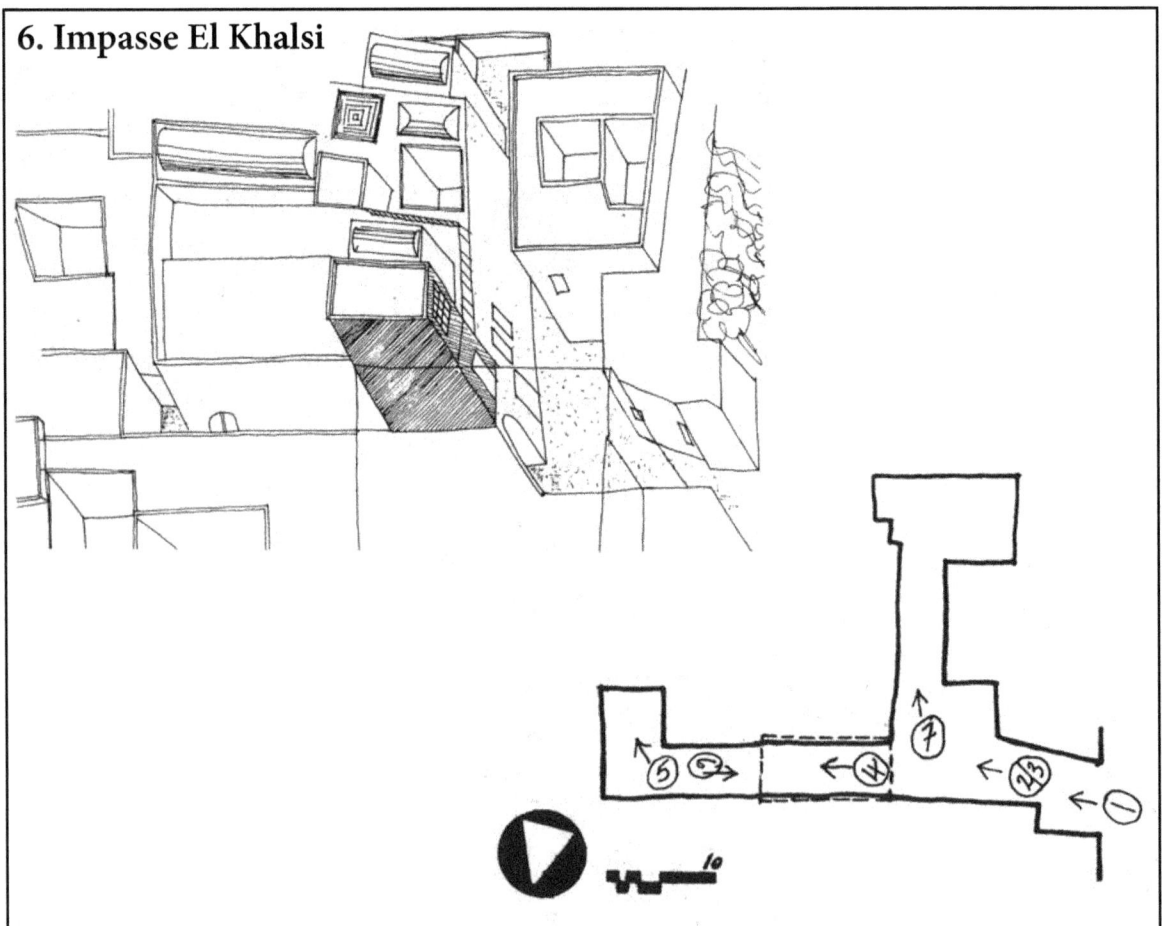

6. Impasse El Khalsi

Impasse El Khalsi

7. IMPASSE THAMEUR

Historically the first courtyard of the Impasse Thameur was a plaza outside the stables of Dar Thameur, one of the largest and oldest houses in Sidi Bou Sa'id. It is entered through a portal which leads off the main street of the town. Today it is used as an outdoor playground, a parking lot and occasionally as a place to play football games. The activities which take place here plus the fact that it is visible from an adjacent rooftop cafe makes this courtyard a semi-public space.

The second plaza, which is smaller than the first, has a more intimate semi-private atmosphere. No cars can enter here due to all the changes in level. One narrow arm of this court slopes down in ramped steps so that the feeling of closure and intimacy is increased. There are only two doors which lead off this alley.

Using the distance to height ratios of Ashihara it may be seen that the ratio of the length of the plaza to the height of the principal building is slightly larger than one. According to Ashihara this means that a definite sense of enclosure and a "plaza" effect is achieved.

It is interesting to examine the noise levels as one steps from the main street into Impasse Thameur. On entering through the main portal into the court there is a sudden drop in noise level yet, at dusk, the call from the Mosque is loud and clear while the music from the neighboring cafe can scarcely be heard.

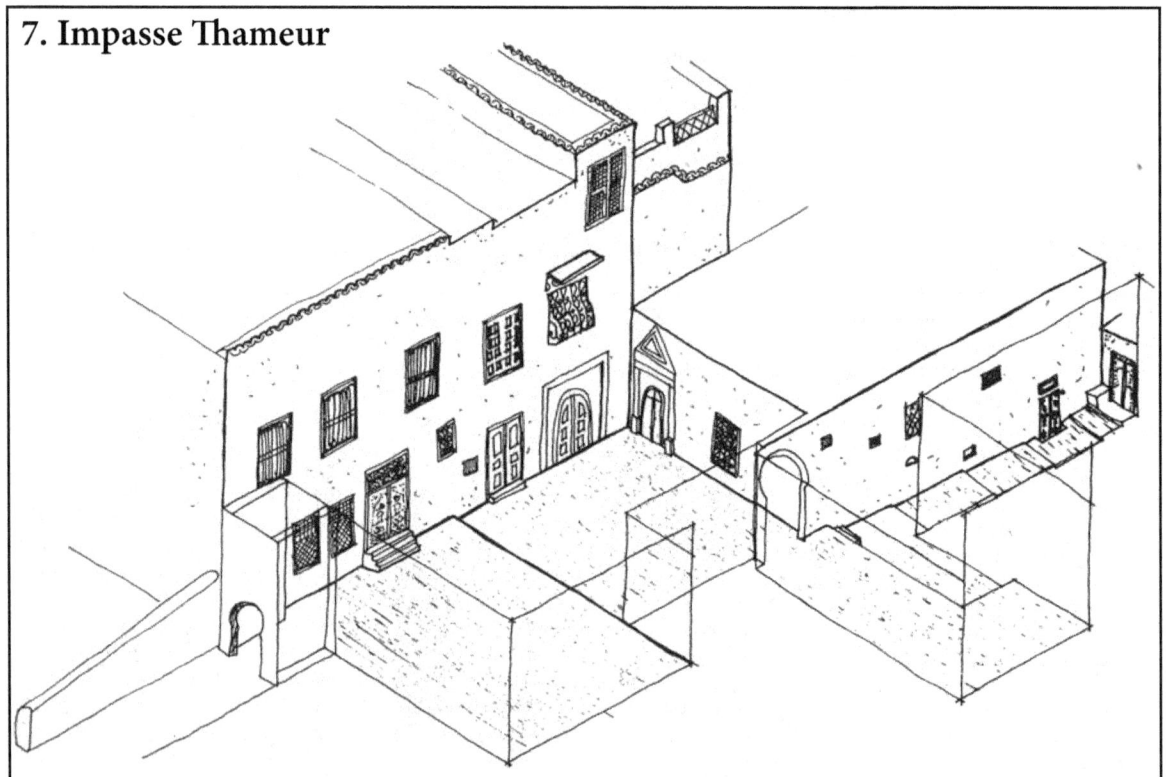

7. Impasse Thameur

Impasse Thameur

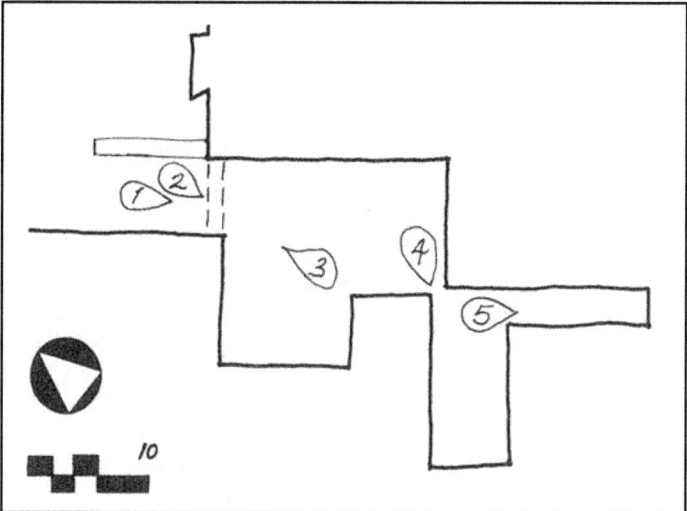

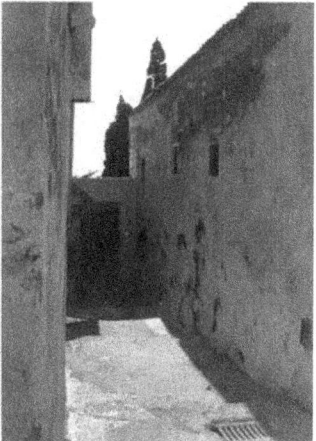

1

2

3

4

5

ENTRANCE TYPOLOGY (PRE 1831)

The map below shows types of entrances into groups of adjoined buildings. The most common entrance type (total number = 58) leads into a "skifa" or entrance hall. A skifa can lead to a courtyard, to a set of stairs going up or down or just to another room. The second most common entrance is to a set of stairs leading to the top half of a house. These stairs (total number = 30) may vary greatly—some are tiled, some are plain—although most have a door at the top. Very few doors (total number = 10) enter straight into a house because traditionally women were to be visually protected from the public. Even now, only foreigners (mostly French) inhabit the houses whose front doors open onto a living room rather than a skifa. Many of the doors on the main street of Sidi Bou Sa'id (total number = 25) open directly onto shops. These usually double as a shop-front in which to display wares. In the study area there were a total of 13 openings to a garden or courtyard and 4 openings leading to garages.

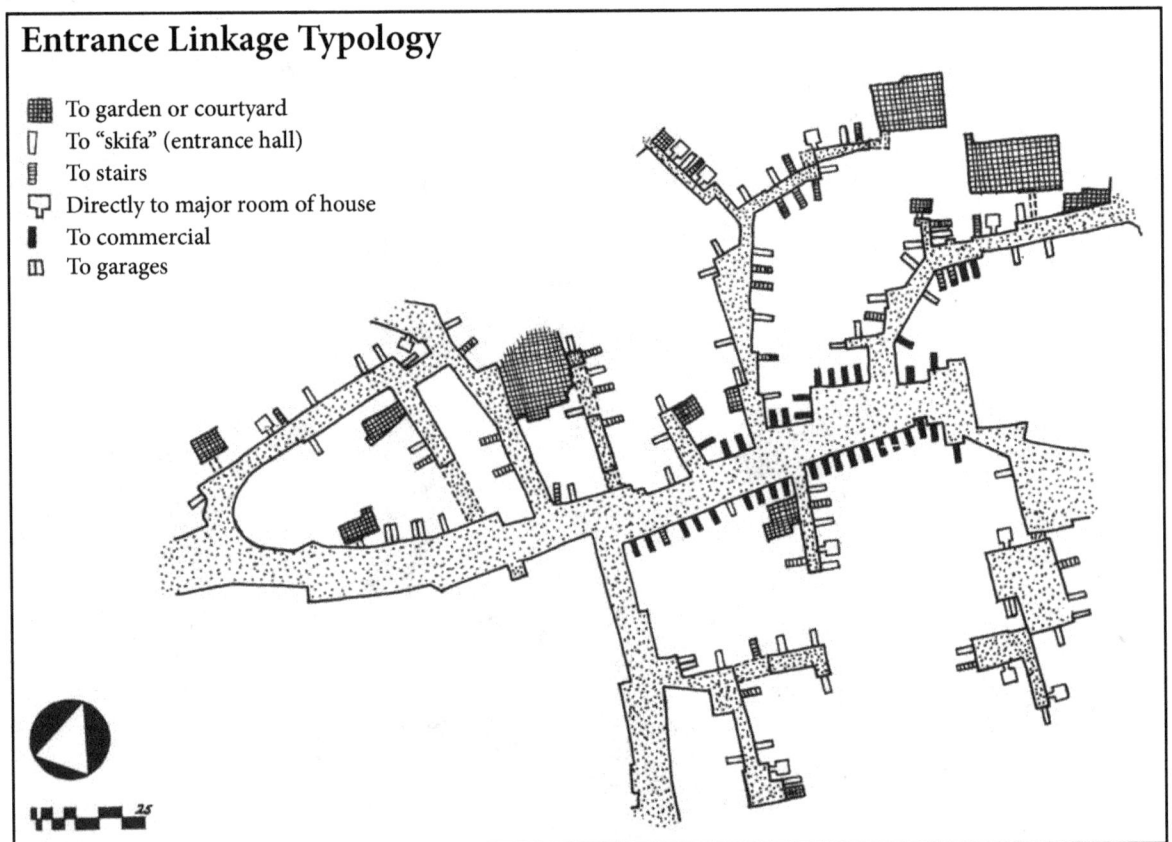

Entrance Linkage Typology

- To garden or courtyard
- To "skifa" (entrance hall)
- To stairs
- Directly to major room of house
- To commercial
- To garages

STAIRS

Basically there are three kinds of stairs found in Sidi Bou Sa'id. These are:
1. ramp stairs
2. public stairs
3. private stairs

RAMP STAIRS:

Almost all streets that have a change in elevation use ramped stairs as these permit the passage of trade animals such as donkeys and camels.

PUBLIC STAIRS:

These stairs are part of the public circulation system and are used only where the grade differential is too great for ramp stairs.

PRIVATE STAIRS:

Those stairs lead directly into private entrance ways. The first step from the street is usually about 50 cm (a cubit) from street level. The other steps are usually about 25 cm high (a handbreadth or 'shiber').

It is interesting to note that the deployment of a staircase in a particular location will determine where functions other than walking (such as street games, use of wheeled vehicles, etc.) will take place.

PUBLIC SEATS

Private individuals often provide seats in left over exterior spaces which encourage people to use the street as a living space rather than a place of continual movement. These seats occur on the main street, large residential streets, small alleys and squares.

Stair Types

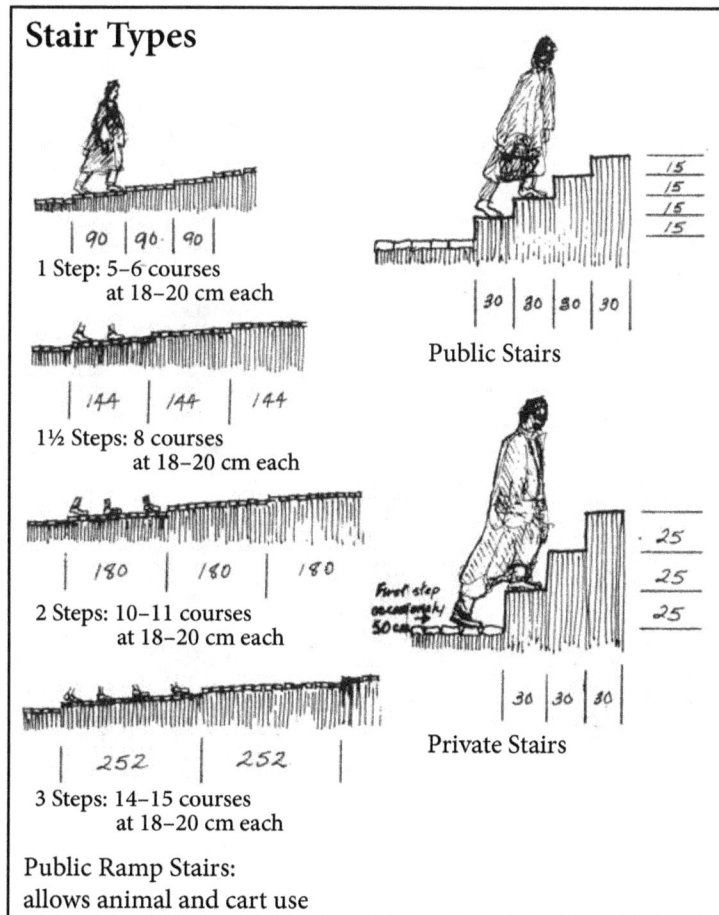

| 90 | 90 | 90 |
1 Step: 5-6 courses
   at 18-20 cm each

| 144 | 144 | 144 |
1½ Steps: 8 courses
   at 18-20 cm each

| 180 | 180 | 180 |
2 Steps: 10-11 courses
   at 18-20 cm each

| 252 | 252 |
3 Steps: 14-15 courses
   at 18-20 cm each

Public Ramp Stairs:
allows animal and cart use

Public Stairs

Private Stairs

Stairs

1, 2, 3, 4: Public Ramp Stairs
5, 6: Public Stairs
7: Private Stairs

1

2

3

4

5

6

7

WALL TYPES AND PURPOSES

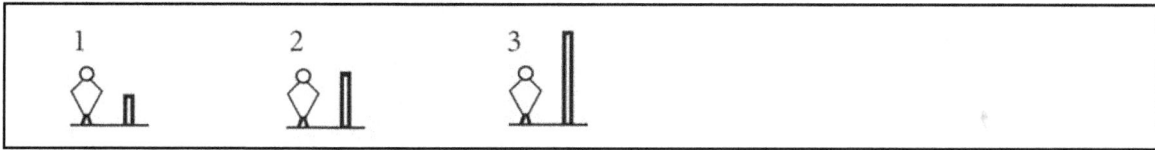

1. Short wall allowing visual penetration. Somewhat of a physical barrier. Often used to keep people from injury.
2. Property boundary for a semi-private place. This can be seen over if only one tries. A definite physical barrier.
3. Property boundary for a very private space. No view. A definite physical barrier.

VEGETATION

Vegetation is used in the following ways:
1. Vegetation in the main street decreases its width and provides a sense of intimacy. In the square of the Cafe des Nattes vegetation is used to create a symbolic separation between the major stream of foot traffic and the people seated around coffee tables.
2. Vegetation from private gardens is often visible as it spills over fences or through gates. Trees are often visible over the white walls.
3. The cactus is often used for security around a building or to mark the boundaries of a private piece of land.

INTERESTING ACCESS RELATIONSHIP

Although the entrance to this house on the Rue El Hedi Zarrouk is very indirect it is very clearly marked by two tall trees.

CORNER TREATMENT

Corners are seldom sharp right-angled corners and are usually off-set; when an intersection is reached there is usually a space before the next street is entered. Corners are also cut out often to

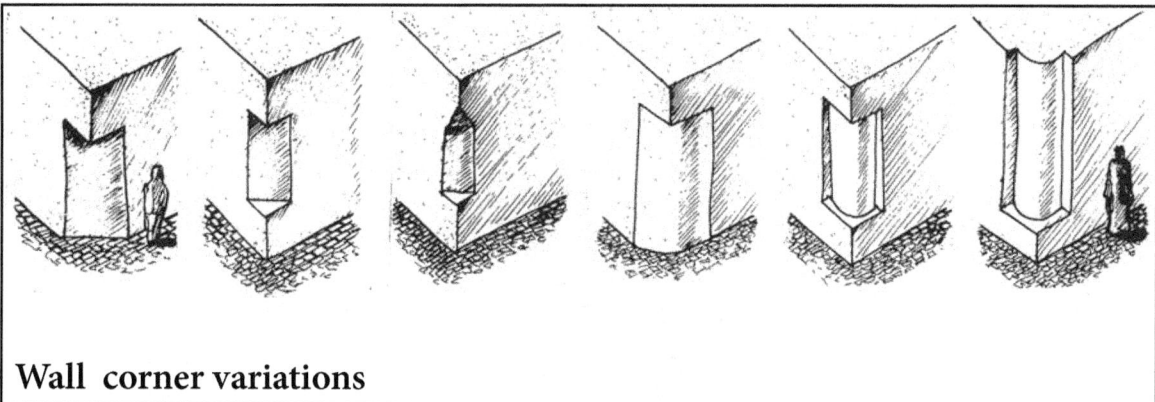

Wall corner variations

**Public Seats
and Wall Corners**

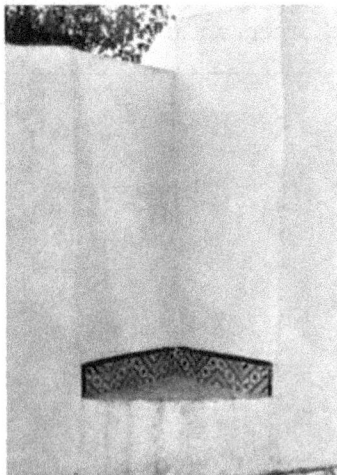

Wall types and use of vegetation

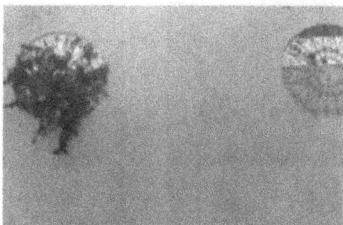

allow donkeys with loads to pass easily. Interior corners will often have planters or seats in them. Private individuals seem to have great public awareness by providing these amenities.

FRAMING THE VIEW

The device of framing brings the distant scene forward into the ambience of our own environment. Joining the whole into a significant pattern makes the view more finite. The feeling of being lost in an infinite perspective is reduced.

VIEWS OF THE MINARET

The minaret, because of its height, always seems deceptively close. It is quite strategically placed at the end of major street vistas giving orientation. Nowhere do you see the full height of the minaret which would be oppressively tall, but rather only the top half is visible. As shown by the photos below it immediately indicates the center of town from almost any public place in Sidi Bou Sa'id, and if it is not in view in one place, it usually can be seen if one moves on a few meters.

VISTAS

Because of its strategic position Sidi Bou Sa'id has many fine vistas, not only the striking ones of the sea, Tunis and La Marsa, but also vistas within the town itself of rooftops and articulated white

Framing the View

Views of the Minaret

blocks of buildings. These vistas are especially significant because of their religious, cultural and processional significance. The minaret, the entrance of the cafe maintains a special significance apart from the beauty of the panoramas.

NIGHT IN SIDI BOU SA'ID

Except during Ramadan, Sidi Bou Sa'id as a town closes very early because most inhabitants work from 8:00–12:00 and 2:00–6:00. Any streetlights in the village, of which there are very few, are placed on street corners. The town therefore looks very different by night than by day.

Vistas and Night Views

Upper left: Vista from balcony of Cafe des Nattes. Upper right: Vista from covered prayer area in mosque. Lower right: Vista toward Rue Korsi es-Sollah at dusk.

A USEFUL DESIGN TOOL USED IN THE ANALYSIS
D/H CONCEPT AND USE

In order to quantify spaces it has been determined by observation that certain ratios of distance (D) to height (H) are the most amenable. The following are some of the observations which may be used to design or analyze space:[4]

Sᴄᴀʟᴇ ᴀɴᴅ Sᴘᴀᴄᴇ Usᴇ

Rooms (based on Japanese mat size, approximately 3 feet x 6 feet):
1. 9' x 9' room—intimate for two people.
2. 90' x 90'—every person can distinguish face of every other person.
3. 30' x 60'—largest space (interior) in which people can interact informally.
4. 192' x 480'—largest exterior space in which people can still retain some sense of intimacy.

Pʟᴀᴢᴀs

1. D/H = 1: minimum size equal to height of principal building, when D/H < 1, however, the exterior space is too small and building interaction too strong.
2. If D/H is between or equal to 1 and 2 a sense of proportion is achieved.
3. Maximum size of plaza must not exceed twice the height of the principal building unless form, purpose or design of building will support greater dimension. Enclosing factors that create sense of plaza begin to diminish if plaza exceeds twice the height of the principal building.

Bᴜɪʟᴅɪɴɢs

1. D/H < 1: distance too small, in extreme feel claustrophobic.
2. D/H = 1: balance between building height and space between building.
3. D/H > 4 interaction between buildings hard to perceive unless we provide structural connections.

Wᴀʟʟs

1. D/H <1: vertical opening has quality of exit or entrance, tempting to go through and see what is on the other side.
2. D/H = 1: balance is maintained
3. D/H > 1: spacious, loses quality of a vertical opening, enclosing force of wall diminishes.

Eɴᴄʟᴏsᴜʀᴇ

1. When facade height (D/H = 1) we feel enclosed higher than upper limit of our view.
2. D/H = 2 coincides with upper limit of view partly feel enclosed, partly distracted.
3. D/H = 3 minimum enclosure, perceive prominent objects beyond space as much as space itself.
4. D/H = 4 space loses its containing quality, loss of enclosure.

---

[4] Source: Ashihara, Y.; *Exterior Design in Architecture.*

D/H Concept: A Useful Design Tool

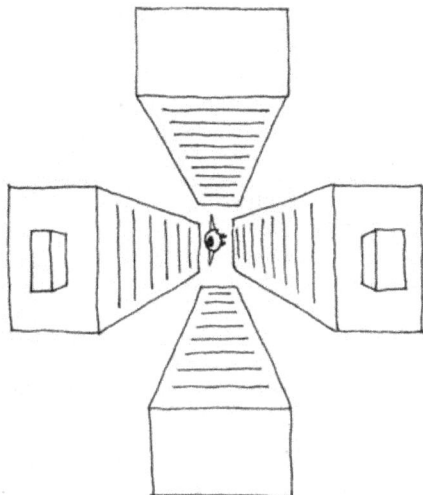

claustrophobic
D/H < 1

balance
D/H = 1

D/H Concept and Buildings

D/H Concept and Walls

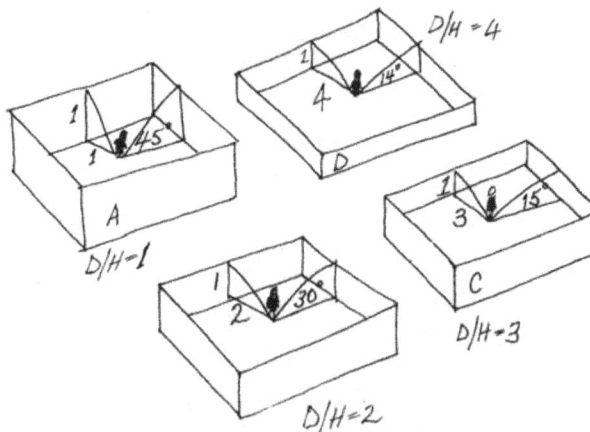

D/H Concept and enclosure

Scale and Space Use

9' X 9' ROOM

30' X 60' ROOM

90' X 90' exterior space

SIDI BOU SA'ID: STATISTICAL DATA

Location coordinates: 36°52' North, 10°21' East
Elevation above sea level: 129 meters beside the lighthouse
Orientation to Mecca: 22°56' 46" South of East.

DESCRIPTION		AREA (m²)		PERCENTAGE
TOTAL LAND AREA WITHIN BOUNDARY		110600		100%
I	GROSS BUILT UP AREA (INCLUDING COURTYARDS)	49332		44.6%
II	CIRCULATION & PARKING AREAS	24014		21.7%
III	OPEN SPACES (GARDENS, CEMETERY, FUTURE USABLE LAND)	37254		33.7%

	AREA		PERCENTAGE	
I—GROSS BUILT-UP AREA (INCLUDING COURTYARDS)	49332			100%
1. Residential (with courts)	44107			89.4%
2. Commercial	3585		100%	7.3%
a–Shops	825		23%	
b–Hotels	2360		65.8%	
c–Cafes	400		11.2%	
3. Institutional	1640		100%	3.3%
a–Mosques	1000		61%	
b–Schools	600		36.6%	
c–Lighthouse	40		2.4%	
I I—CIRCULATION & PARKING AREAS	24014			100%
1. Streets	17774	100%	100%	74%
(i) Total uncovered streets	17439	98%		
(ii) Total covered streets*	335	2%		
a–Through streets**	16304	100%	91.7%	
(i) uncovered through streets	16160	99%		
(ii) covered through streets	144	1%		
b–Cul-de-sacs	1470	100%	8.3%	
(i) uncovered cul-de-sacs	1279	87%		
(ii) covered cul-de-sacs	191	13%		
2. Parking	6240	26%		

I I I—OPEN SPACES	37254		100%	
A–Exterior private gardens and grounds	22384		60%	
B–Cemetery	3400		9.2%	
C–Future usable land (assumed private property)	11470		30.8%	

TOTAL LAND AREA WITHIN BOUNDARY	110600			100%
I—AREA OF PRIVATE DOMAIN = Gross Built-up Residential area with courts + Area of all cul-de-sacs + Area of all gardens/grounds + Assumed private future usable land	79431			71.8%
II—AREA OF PUBLIC DOMAIN = Total land within boundary – area of private domain	31169			28.2%

* Streets are covered by rooms, called "sabat" in Arabic.

** Through uncovered streets used by vehicular circulation and pedestrians = 10400 m². 58.5% of all streets (item 1); 63.8% of through streets (item 1a).

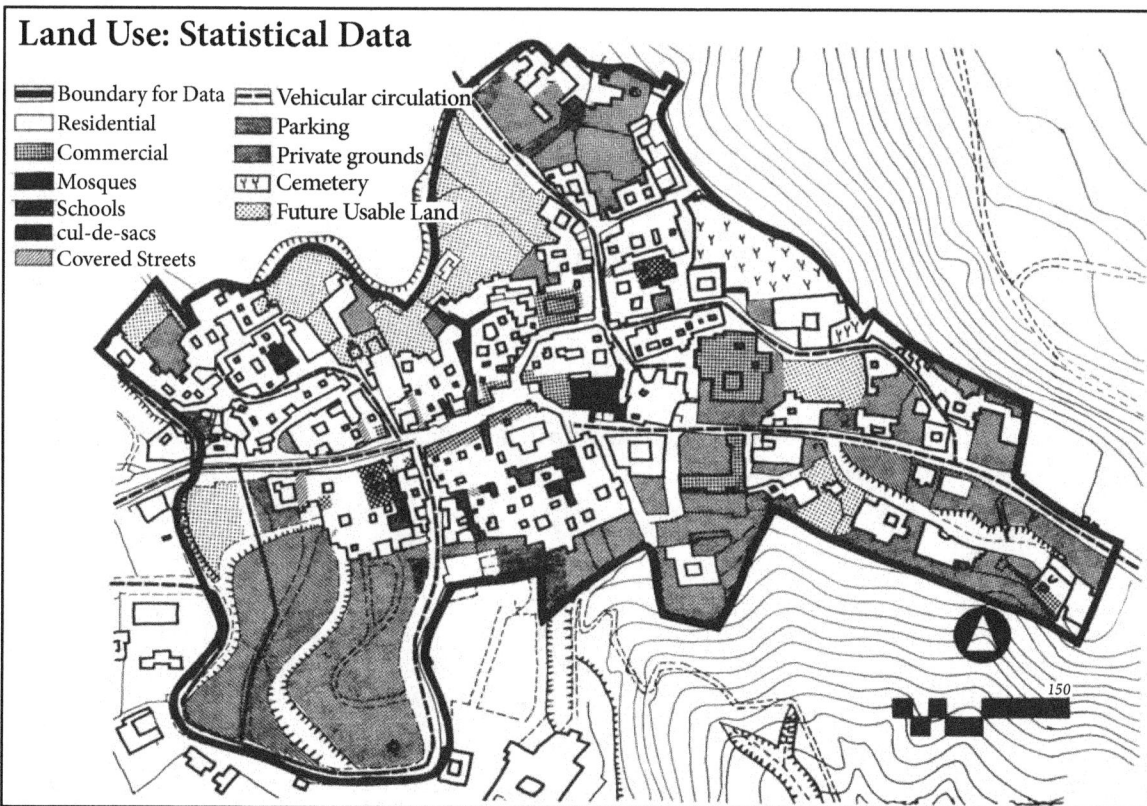

Land Use: Statistical Data

DENSITY:

The key information item which is required to calculate density accurately is the number of houses within the area used for statistical data. This information was not available, and it is impossible to calculate this accurately from the maps or air photos, due to the nature of the built form. This is because houses of many sizes are interlocked three dimensionally, in addition to overlapping with various other uses.

The following is an attempt to identify the number of optimum houses which are possible within the built form of Sidi Bou Sa'id, from which density figures are derived. The only constraint used was that the ground area of the average house should not be less than 150 m^2. The procedure is broken down into identifiable steps:

1. Ground coverage of residential built up area including courtyards = 44107 m^2.
2. From research undertaken in Tunis by Besim Hakim, it was found that the average percentage which courtyards take up from the built ground coverage is 24%,
   ∴ 24% of 44107 = 10585.7 m^2 area of all residential courtyards.
3. From the Tunis case, we also find that the average area of a courtyard—including service courtyards—and based on various house sizes, is 24 m^2,
   ∴ 10585.7/24 =441 courtyards.
4. Assuming every house has an average of 1.5 courts of this size (this is to include service courts and multiple courts which the larger houses tend to have), then:
   441/1.5 = 294 houses possible within the existing built form of Sidi Bou Sa'id.[5]
5. The average number of people/household used is 6. This figure takes into account the larger number of persons/ household in the Palaces and Large Residences, and is also corroborated by studies undertaken for Tunis.
6. 294 houses x 6 average persons/household = 1764 population within the bounded area used for statistical data.

Gross Density (using total area within boundary)

	Hectares (11.06)[6]	Acres (27.3)
Persons/unit area	159.5	64.6
Houses/unit area	26.6	10.8

Net Density (using the area of Private Domain within boundary)

	Hectares (7.94)	Acres (19.6)
Persons/unit area	222.2	90
Houses/unit area	37	15

---

[5] This figure is corroborated by using the number of private phones available in Sidi Bou Sa'id, which is 153 (based on the 1974 phone directory). From knowledge of the village and the phone service in this region of Tunisia, plus the fact that Sidi Bou Sa'id is an affluent suburb and most of the people who would have phones would be living within our bounded area. We find that the ratio of private phones to houses of 1:2 is realistic.

[6] 1 Hectare = 2.47 Acres.

SCULPTED RELIEF ON A DOOR FRAME

CHAPTER 4

SYMBOLISM AND FORM

INTRODUCTION

In this section, symbolism in the village is discussed at three different scales. The largest scale is, of course, that of the village itself—the forms and relationships of the typical houses which give the town its recognizable fabric. Also discussed at this scale are the important social and symbolic elements of the town which stand apart from the norm, such as the Mosque, the mausoleums and the cemetery. At the smaller scale are the types of entrances, the windows, the steps and the smaller built-in elements. At a still smaller seal are the types of surface embellishment such as plaster carving, stonework, tiles and simple whitewash.

ROLE OF ISLAM

The basic tenet of Islam is that there is one God and that the necessary role of man is one of submission to His will. The idea of God's supremacy is similar in Islam to that of Christianity; the great difference lying in the extent to which religious influence pervades the life of the individual Muslim and his community.

Beyond the declaration of faith, all practicing Muslims are expected to pray five times daily, to fast during the holy month of Ramadan, to give a percentage of savings to the poor, and, if possible to perform a pilgrimage to Mecca once in their lifetimes. In addition to these individual duties, Islam provides guidelines in all areas of social, economic, political and moral life.

The Muslim is made aware of his place in the world as a responsible member of a community of equals, under the benevolent guidance of God. Society is therefore ideally a place of harmony and peace, where conflict and antisocial tendencies are given no place to grow. The traditional Arab town can be understood as the expression of the Muslim's view of life and a place where each individual can live his/her life in a proper and fulfilling way.

PART I: THE VILLAGE SCALE

The essence of Islamic religion is manifested in the homogeneity of the village environment. The basic simplicity of whitewashed masonry dominates the entire village, giving it a visual harmony symbolic of the social harmony within the community. In Islam it is forbidden to put one's wealth on public display and so all of the houses are almost anonymous in the treatment of their street facades. It is only on the interior that the owner is at complete liberty to express his wealth, lifestyle and imagination. Hence, by maintaining a basic house type—the ubiquitous courtyard house (each nevertheless unique due to its interior treatment and as a growth cell of the organic structure of the village)—each man can feel the dignity to which he has a right regardless of income or class. Privacy is therefore very important to the town-dweller, and is a need which plays no small part in the character of the houses. This can be seen in the use of the low doors inset within a larger door which require a passerby to bend down in order to see in, the indirect entry which hides the inside of the house, the enclosed courtyard, the special exterior windows which allow the occupant to see out unnoticed and the high walls which surround private garden areas.

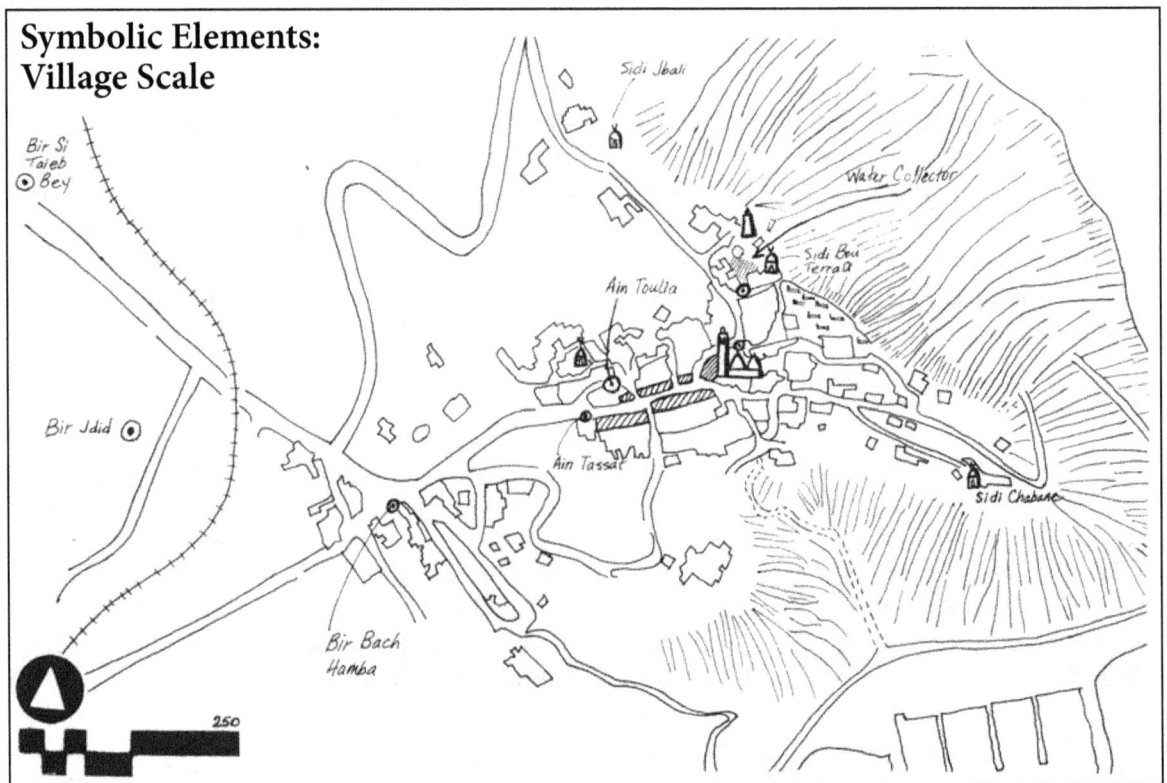

Symbolic Elements: Village Scale

SYMBOLIC ELEMENTS AT THE VILLAGE SCALE

MOSQUE[1]

As the spiritual and intellectual center of the town, the Mosque symbolizes the unity of the town's population to the faith. The Mosque is built over the mausoleum of the greatly venerated patron saint of the village, Abou Sa'id.

SOUK

The central market, or souk, is the historical center of commercial life of the town although today it caters more to tourists than the townspeople. Most of the cafes (which form the center of the social life for the men) are situated here.

MAUSOLEUMS

These are the tombs of the holy men who lived and taught in or near the village. Their graves are still highly respected by the people of the town. They are known as "Marabout" in French and "weli" in Arabic.

PUBLIC WELLS AND CISTERNS

These are historically important because, where no private wells existed, close proximity to these water sources was an advantage.

CEMETERY

The cemetery grew around the graves of various holy men. Cemeteries are of great significance to Muslims. Non-Muslims are forbidden to enter the cemetery grounds.

LIGHTHOUSE

The lighthouse occupies a place of historical significance as it was built on the site of a Ribat, or fortification, the remains of which form a base for the present day structure.

MAUSOLEUMS

The typical form of a mausoleum is a cube-shaped masonry structure covered by a cupola or dome. Often a crescent symbol or spherical marker is placed on the top to indicate its religious significance.

The mausoleum usually has a single door which is painted in a distinctive arch design: red with a green surround separated by a white line. Green is the symbolic color of the Prophet Mohammed while red symbolizes the zealous struggle for Islam.

---

[1]The Mosque and Souk elements are discussed in Chapter Six, and the Lighthouse is discussed in Chapter Two. Part I of this chapter discusses the Mausoleums, the Public Wells, Cisterns and the Cemetery.

The tomb of Sidi Bou Sa'id is the best known of the village's mausoleums. It formed the center of the growth of the village during the 18th and 19th centuries. Various other mausoleums have formed the nuclei of other built-up areas in the village.

The mausoleums of various saints and well respected individuals are greatly venerated by the people of the town. The offering of some small gift such as candles, or perfume is done in the hope of achieving some good fortune in family matters such as a good marriage or the birth of a male child.

Sidi Chabane

This is a relatively large mausoleum clinging to the top of the cliff. A cafe has been built around it with an unobstructed view towards the marina and the Gulf of Tunis.

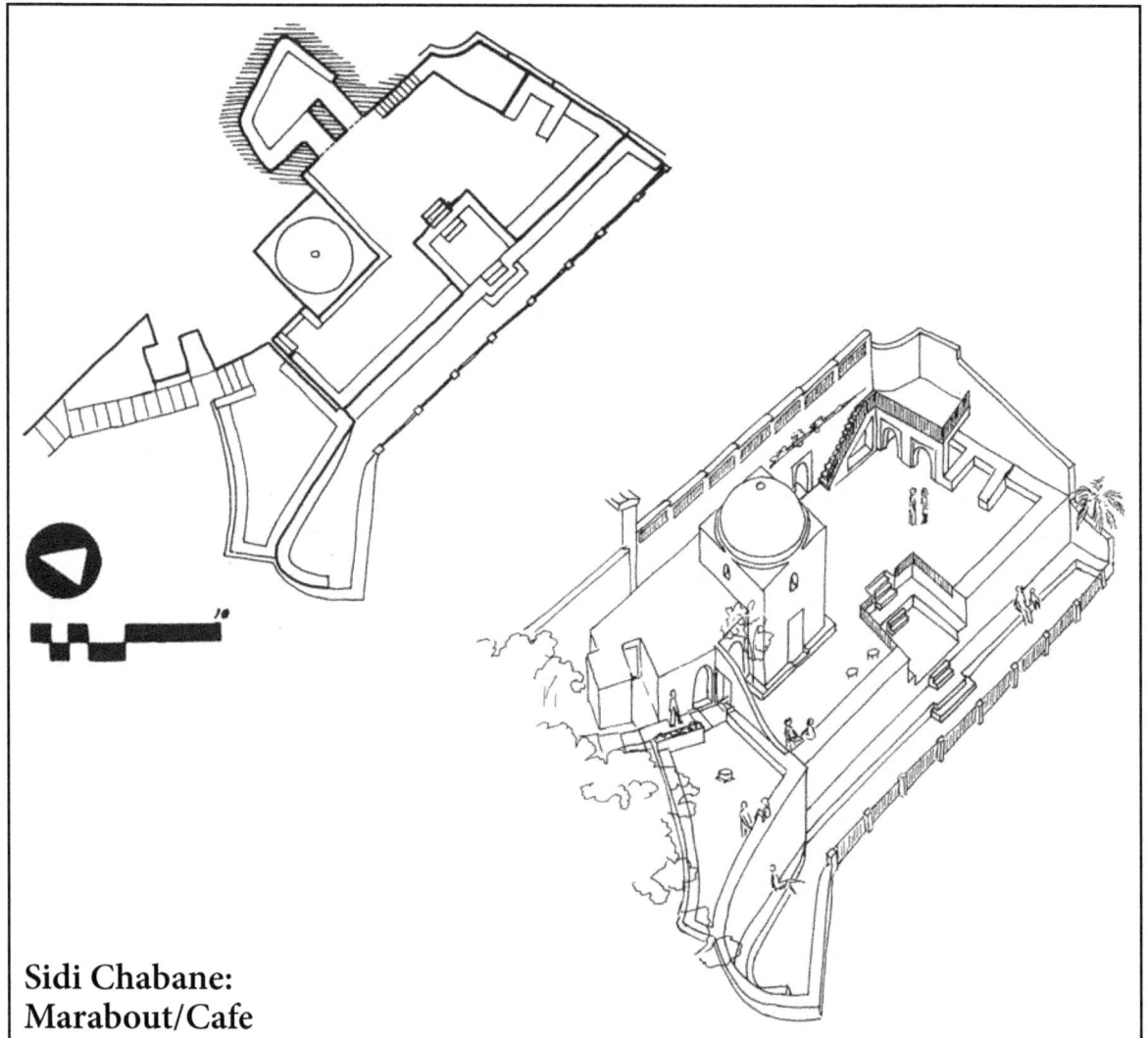

Sidi Chabane:
Marabout/Cafe

PUBLIC WELLS AND CISTERNS

Obtaining water has until recent times posed a problem for the residents of Sidi Bou Sa'id. This is because of its elevation which places it high above the water table. In ancient times, a series of cisterns were used to collect rainwater. When the town began to grow in the 18th and 19th centuries, certain sovereigns and rich Beylical ministers provided the town with public wells. Wells typically consisted of a simple rectangular stone edifice, enclosing a small reservoir which was filled from the well. Water fountains in the sides of the structure fed into watering troughs for the animals.

BIR JDID

This well, built in 1794 by Youssef Saheb et-Tabaa follows the general form. It was one of the most important wells of the town, due to the excellent quality of its water. Water from the well had to be transported up the village using donkeys. The well is no longer used, but the house built behind it for the guardian is still occupied.

BIR SI TAIEB BEY

This well is situated beside the road to la Marsa. It is a traditional type of installation, but is interesting due to the elegant facade of the water reservoir, which has a commemorative plaque. The water from this well is brackish, so it was used only for animals. The plan of the installation shows the ramp which the camels would walk down when drawing water. The well was built in 1895.

AIN TOUILA

This is probably the oldest well of the town. It is of a differing form from the others, and is situated in the heart of the older built-up area. It may have existed since Roman times. It consists of a tight grouping of four openings, the sides of which were worn into grooves by the ropes bringing up water. However, these openings were recently sealed off. Apparently the well was associated with superstition concerning ghosts which haunted the well during winter nights, appearing in frightening forms in the dark deserted street.

WATER COLLECTORS

Because of the inconvenience of obtaining water for those living in the high part of the village, a rainwater collector was built around 1848. Situated near the present day lighthouse, it consisted of a large sloping area paved in whitewashed masonry. It drained into two large reservoirs, access to which could be gained by the two large doors at the bottom of the street which leads up to the cemetery. One of these was for public use only during certain hours of the day in summer. The other supplied a public fountain called Sebil Bash-Hamba, near the Mosque, to which it was connected by an underground clay pipe.

The water needs of present day Sidi Bou Sa'id found their true solution with the branching of the water conduit which feeds the northern suburbs of Tunis; this conduit has been reinforced recently by the construction of two immense reservoirs on the hill of Amilcar.

CEMETERY

All graves in a Muslim cemetery are oriented toward Mecca in the same way that all Muslims face Mecca when they pray. Graves are marked by a masonry slab, about 50 cm by 200 cm by 10 to 30 cm in depth (about the size of the human body). Children's gravestones are correspondingly smaller.

MARKERS

A man's grave has one marker, while a woman's grave has two; one at each end. Often, man and wife may be buried under the same gravestone, in which case the marker corresponds to the most recently interred.

SIMPLE GRAVES

The simplest graves are of rough masonry construction, plastered and whitewashed in the same manner as houses. Its marking may be very simple; a piece of an old ceramic tile, a stone, or perhaps nothing at all. Most graves in the cemetery, including more elaborate ones, have a small hole or cup inset in the center, which serves as a water collector for the birds.

ELABORATE GRAVES

The more elaborate graves are set on a slightly raised platform or paved area. They are more regular and may be covered with ceramic tiles, usually in white or light pattern. Markers are of stone or marble, engraved with the name, birth and death dates, etc.

ENCLOSED GRAVES

Some families have small plots of land set aside for the graves of that particular family. A low masonry wall (about 50 cm–1 m) surrounds the area. Within the enclosure, the graves for male members of the family are on one side, and those for females on the other.

SPECIAL GRAVES

An example of a special grave is Sidi Bou Doulabi which consists of a small mausoleum covered by a cupola. People used to light candles in this cupola during their visits .

Mausoleums (Marabout) and Lighthouse

1. Marabout Sidi Chabane from adjacent private garden

2. Within Cafe of Sidi Chabane

3 & 4. Detached and attached "marabout" examples

5. "Massasa" privately donated suction operated water outlet for pedestrians

6. View of lighthouse

Public Water Wells and Cemetery

1. Bir Jdid
2. Bir Si Taieb Bey
3. View of cemetery and minaret in background

4. Example of an elaborate grave
5. Example of a simple grave
6. Enclosed grave
7. A 'special' grave

PART II: SMALL SCALE ELEMENTS

DOORS

In Sidi Bou Sa'id door types can be divided into two basic groups:
1. Small doors about 2 m high and consisting of two halves.
2. Larger doors 3 m high containing a smaller door within.

The doors are made of wood although a few are covered with copper cladding. Traditionally the smaller doors had marble frames carved with symbolic designs while the larger doors were surrounded by Arabic arches constructed of stone. A true Arabic arch followed strict mathematical equations which pinpointed the centers for two circles in contrast to the newer arches which were constructed with the use of only one center.

Door decorations, whether simple or elaborate, are made up of patterns of iron nail studs symmetrically repeated on each door half and painted black against the blue background of the doors (blue being the predominant door and window color in Sidi Bou Sa'id). Often up to 4 cm in diameter these studs originated in the days when homes had to be built for protection from invaders. Today they are still used to reinforce the structure of a door as well as to give it a certain degree of psychological strength.

To restrict the penetration of the sun and at the same time maintain privacy and air movement many doors are surmounted by air vents.

In a society where visual privacy is highly valued, doors had to be designed carefully. Thus doors open and close quickly and are as narrow and small as possible. Many doors are so narrow (50 cm for one leaf) that one has to turn sideways to enter while others are so low (150 cm) that the visitor has to bend down to enter—automatically paying symbolic homage to his hosts! Due to the narrowness of the typical streets, all doors open inwards.

Heavy iron rings for two door knockers ("halka") are usually placed at the height of a man while sometimes a third one is added lower down for children. Traditionally, it is said, the two upper knockers were allocated to men and women, and each knocker had a distinctly different sound from the other two. In this way, the occupants could tell if the person knocking was a man, woman or child.

INDEX TO DOOR AND WINDOW TYPES

DOOR TYPES

Approximate Size: 2 m x 1 m—Comprise about 75% of all doors. Some have ornamentation and/or vent above.

Approximate Size: 3 m x 2.5 m—Least common type of door. Contain a smaller inset door. Some have ornamentation.

Approximate Size: 4 m x 3 m—Most decorative and beautiful doors. Contain a smaller inset door. Stone frame. Sometimes surrounded by tiles.

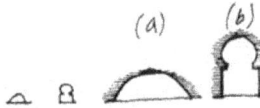

(a) archway entrance to wells

(b) through-entrance to some semi-public spaces.

WINDOW TYPES

Approximate Size: l m x 1.6 m—Simplest window
(a) Ground floor windows
(b) Upper floor windows

Approximate Size: l m x 1.6 m—Upper floor windows Types (a) and (b) with bulging curved grills.

Approximate size: variable—Only on upper floors. Facing primary streets or squares.

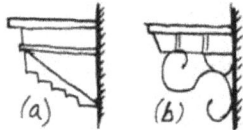

Approximate Size: dependent on window width
(a) most common canopy
(b) less common than (a). Very decorative.

DOOR EXAMPLE # 1

This is the most common type of door found in Sidi Bou Sa'id, in fact about 75% of all doors fall into this category.

The example chosen here is found in the older section of town near the Mosque. The two leafs of the door taken together measure 2.0 m x 1.0 m. For general entry only the right leaf of the door is used. This measures 2.0 m x 0.5 m and opens inward. The marble frame around the door is 20 cm wide.

This door has a very simple geometric design on it formed from nail studs. The lines of the nail studs correspond to the lines of the wooden door bracing inside.

The door has two door knockers ("halka"), one on each side, placed 1.6 m above ground.

CONSTRUCTION

The door is made up of wood planks 10.5 cm x 3.5 cm supported from behind by 6.5 cm x 11.0 cm studs spaced at 39 cm horizontally.

The marble frame partially supports the door opening. The inside structure for the door is left exposed.

USE

The door opens in two halves. Generally only the right half of the door (2.0 m x .5 m) is used. If large items need to be moved through the door then both halves are opened.

Due to the narrowness of the door when it is half open (.5 m) one has to enter sideways. Little visual contact can be established with the inside even when someone is going through the door.

As with all doors, the door knockers used are of quite heavy metal which enables the rapping to be heard more vividly.

The example illustrated was chosen because of its simple design and because of its typical size and marble frame.

DOOR EXAMPLE # 2

This type of door is found on the more elaborate types of houses and is usually highly decorated.

The arch on this door is a variation of the Arabic arch in that it is formed of only one arc (instead of two) and thus does not come to a point at the top.

This particular door is found just off the main street in the oldest section of town (see key map page 69). The effective part of the door measures 2.65 m x 1.68 m while the complete doorway without the frame measures 4.20 m x 2.80 m. The smaller secondary door—which is worked very sensitively into the design—measures 1.5 m x .65 m. The door is painted blue while the nail studs are painted black.

CONSTRUCTION

Each door is made up of 20 cm x 3 cm planks framed by 6.5 x 11 cm wooden studs spaced at 43 cm horizontally.

The metal nail studs used in the construction of the door are combined in the overall design of the decorative studs. The arch is made of stones which were cut in place and surrounded by tiles. The black and white of the arch is a traditional pattern probably dating from ancient times when the colors would have been inherent to the stones and not painted on.

USE

The regular entrance for the door is through the smaller secondary entrance. One must bend down to enter this door. The symbolic meaning of this act is said to come from Andalusia (Muslim Spain) where, by bending as he entered, the guest displayed homage to his host. As with all doors in Sidi Bou Sa'id, this one opens inwards. Opening the larger doors permits the entrance of animals and carts. The width of the door was often established by the size of these carts.

The example illustrated was chosen because its design incorporates tiles, an air vent, a black and white arch and a nail stud design.

SPECIAL DETAIL

One of the interesting details on this door is its special locking system. On the door there are three of these locks—one each for the large doors and a smaller one for the secondary door.

SYMBOLISM

There are nine different symbols on this door created by the patterns of the black metal studs. The most common one is the moon. One can also find anchor, star, cypress, cross, arcade and geometric motifs, (see page 84)

VARIATIONS

The accompanying seven photographs show how this door can be varied to give a different "personality" to different homes.

Door Examples 1 and 2

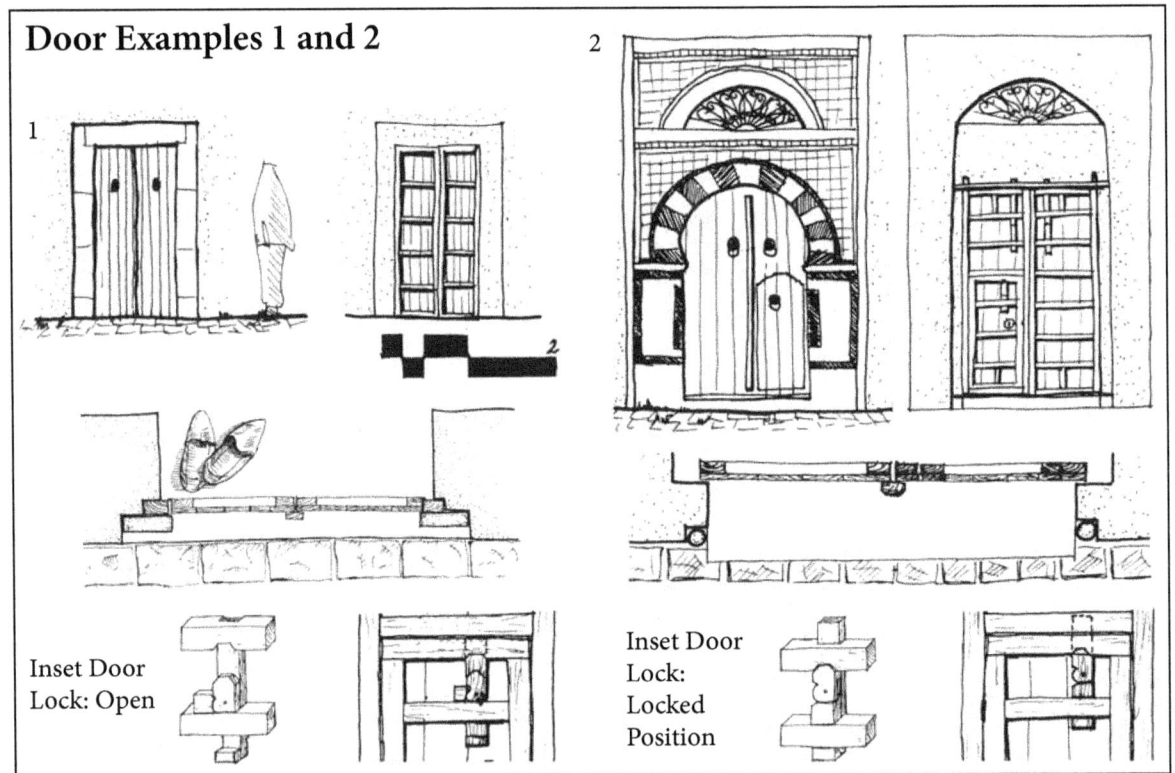

Inset Door Lock: Open

Inset Door Lock: Locked Position

Location of Door Types

Index of graphic symbols to door
and window types: see pages 65–66

Door Example 1 and Variations

**Door Example 2
and Variations**

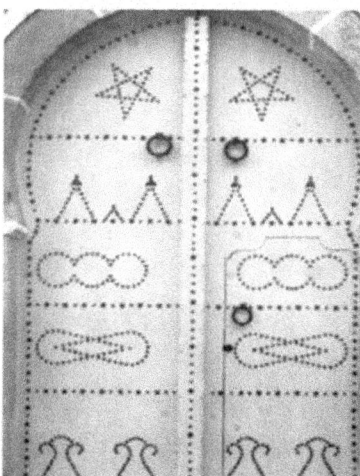

**Examples of
Uncommon Doors**

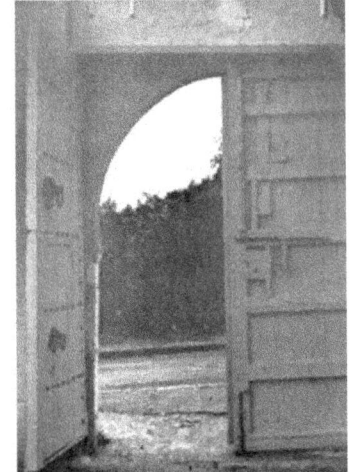

WINDOWS

Because windows are the other elements besides doors which maintain a link with the public streets, special care is necessarily taken in their design. Traditionally, for reasons of visual privacy and security, there were no windows on the ground floor. Later when windows were added, they were kept as high above the street as possible and a lattice screen called a "mushrabeya" made of wooden slats was included in addition to the metal grill.

The traditional practice of locating windows as high as possible on exterior walls did not conflict with the requirements of glare prevention in arid climates.

Windows facing courtyards and on upper storeys are kept lower to the floor and often provided with a built-in seat or ledge.

The protective iron grills on windows are a very prominent design element. Traditionally they were simple forged iron bars but because the resultant aspect was so severe the craftsmen of Sidi Bou Sa'id added gracious "S" shaped bars in the Andalusian custom. Today, these bars are approximately 1 cm square in section although the older bars have a round cross-section. On the lower floor there are usually flat grills flush with the wall with a wood screen behind. On the upper floors the grills protrude out from the wall.

All windows are glazed for days in winter when the air is relatively cool outside. Shutters are another important design element because they can totally eliminate direct solar radiation on hot summers days.

Many windows followed proportions based on the Golden Section (length : width = 1 : .618) or the more direct ratio of 2 : 1

GROUND FLOOR EXTERIOR WINDOWS

Traditionally there were no windows on the ground floor although windows now on the ground floor are usually high and screened off by a wooden lattice called "mushrabeya".

The example shown on page 74 comes from near the entrance to Dar Abdel Kaffe.

This window is covered by an ornate flat metal grill which is not as common as the "S" shaped zlabia type. It is interesting to note how the thick walls are bevelled to diffuse the incoming light.

GROUND FLOOR INTERIOR WINDOWS

Windows to the interior are less concerned with privacy than outside windows. Usually they are lower to the ground and the ledge below them forms a very useful space for keeping odds and ends.

The example on page 74 shows a fairly typical window to the interior courtyard. The grill is of the very common "S" shape or zlabia variety.

UPPER FLOOR WINDOWS

Windows on the upper floors tend to be lower to the floor than those on the ground floor. These often have built-in seating. Traditionally a wooden mushrabeya is put on the inside of the iron grill to enable the occupants to look out without being seen.

The accompanying example, on pages 75 and 77, has the typical decorative tilework around the seating and at the foot of the window.

UPPER FLOOR BAY WINDOW ("MAUCHARABIEH")

A maucharabieh is a special bay window sometimes found on the upper storeys of larger houses. It permits discrete observations of the street life below: a direct solution to the problem of retaining visual privacy for the women while allowing them to see the outside world. A maucharabieh always protrudes from the facade to permit a panoramic view of the main street or square below.

The wooden shutters and/or glazed portion is on the inside and the wooden mushrabeya lattice screen is on the outside. Both are hinged in two places and can be folded upwards for ventilation and/or an unobstructed view (see pages 75 and 78).

WOODEN LATTICE ("MUSHRABEYA")

A mushrabeya is a wooden screen used to reduce glare and at the same time act as a visual privacy shield. It is composed of 1.5 cm x .7 cm wooden strips which are rounded along one side to diffuse the incoming sunlight. The strips usually crisscross at about 45 to 60 degrees to the horizontal, and the resulting square light openings are usually 1 cm x 1 cm. Traditionally these screens were an integral part of all exterior windows—sometimes even following the curved shape of the exterior iron grillwork (see pages 75 and 78).

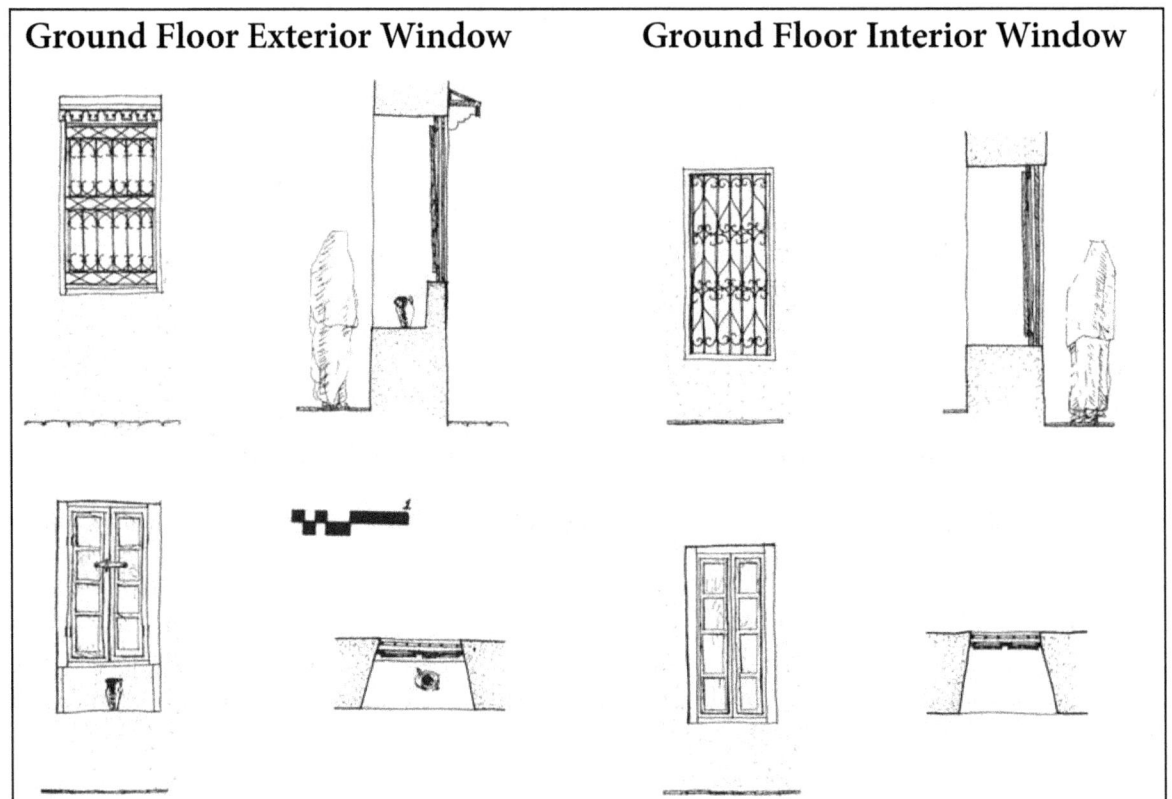

Ground Floor Exterior Window   **Ground Floor Interior Window**

Upper Floor Window

Upper Floor Window: "Maucharbieh"

Detail of Wooden Lattice

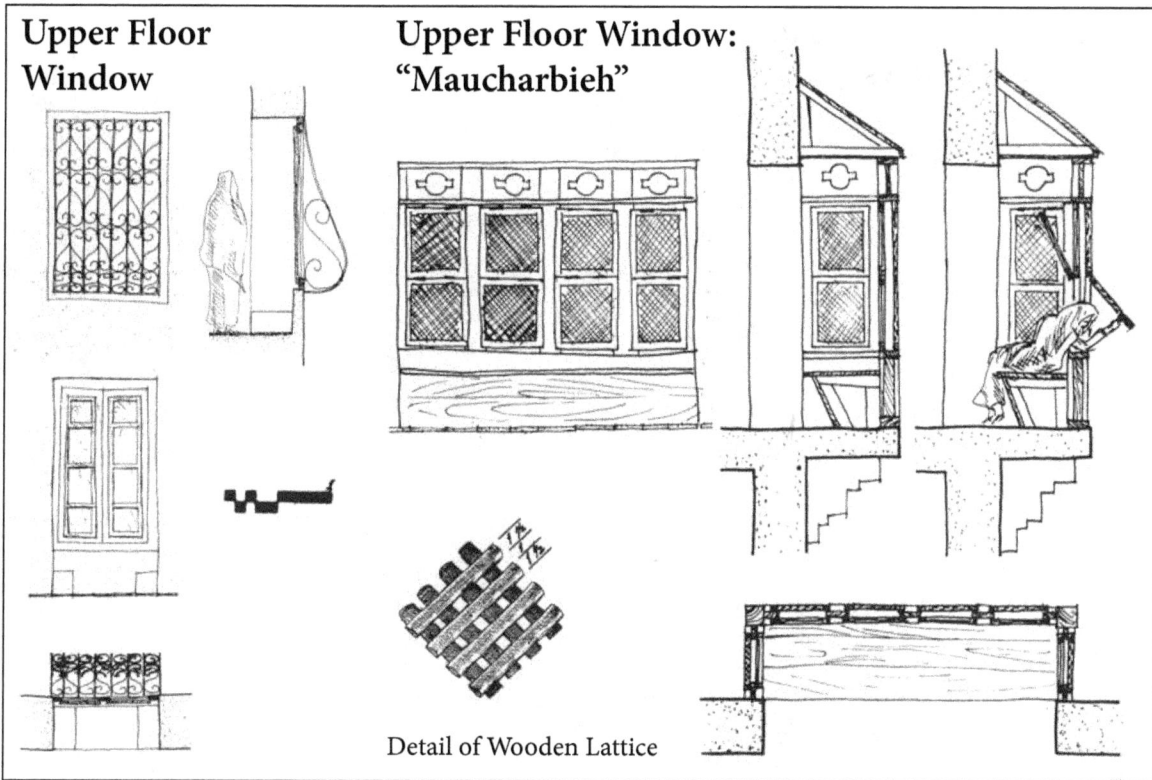

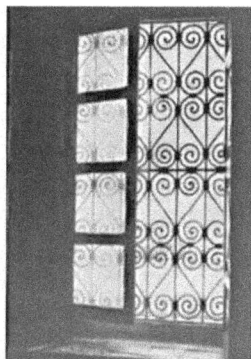

Examples of Ground Floor Interior Windows

**Examples of Ground Floor
Exterior Windows**

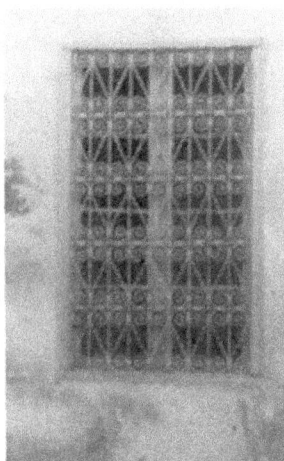

Upper Floor Windows

Far right: Window illustrated on page 75

Right: Example of upper interior window

Others: Upper exterior windows

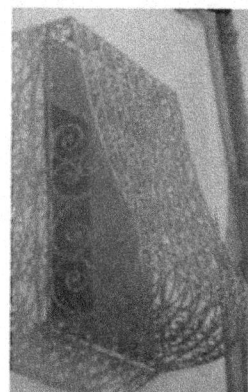

Upper Floor Bay Windows: "Maucharabieh"

Ventilation/Light: Semi-Circular Openings

PART III: SURFACE EMBELLISHMENT

BASIC PRINCIPLES

To the Western observer, perhaps the most striking feature of Islamic decoration is the complete absence of human forms. The prohibition of figural representation in Islamic art is related to the condemnation of idolatry—the fear that an image may become an object of worship. It has also been suggested that the imitation of living things is a form of blasphemy, in attempting to do what only God can do. The Islamic view is that God created man with qualities of life, knowledge, will, power, hearing, sight and speech. Since these qualities cannot be represented in an image, then any image must be false in essence, causing the viewer to turn his attention away from the important and divinely ordained attributes of humanness toward the superficial aspects of bodily form. Thus, in Islam, man maintains a dignity which elsewhere is usurped by his image, which is the tendency in modern Western society. Islamic art and decoration therefore aid in eliminating turmoil and passionate suggestions and offer instead equilibrium and peace.

With the exclusion of human forms and most other animal forms the Muslim artist is left mainly with geometric and floral designs as a basis for his decorative repertoire, in addition to writing as an art form—using the Qur'an as the primary source. The basic rules governing the use of these designs are:
    (a) no single element may be given undue prominence
    (b) the eye enjoys a general impression rather than any particular detail, conveying a feeling of harmony and unity.
    (c) symmetry counteracts the tendency toward overcrowding and unrest.
Certain advantages relative to Islamic society are apparent in this form of ornament:
    (a) it has a universal character, belonging to no single class or period in history
    (b) it allows for a large degree of creativity without becoming simply a vehicle for individual expression.

The most typical Islamic form of embellishment is the swirling plant form known as Arabesque. One flower grows out of another, without beginning and without end. This design is capable of innumerable variations, but a consistent feature is the split leaf and continuous stem. Its rhythmic forms are suggestive of endless life and the infinite vastness of God.

Other plant motifs include the palmette and rosette, chrysanthemums and abstracted forms. The geometric interlacing of bands to form intricate designs is another common form of decoration seen in this area, usually in relief work on plaster or stone. It is derived from the Arabic-Islamic designs of Morocco and Andalusia.

The frequency of Qur'anic inscriptions on the walls of houses as well as in mosques, is indicative of the extent to which Qur'anic values and law reaches into the life of the Muslim, giving direction and support in all his daily activities. The written words function as symbols in addition to the concepts they convey. Qur'anic verses are often inscribed against a background of arabesques and floral scrolls, sometimes becoming indistinguishable in form from the surrounding design—a perfect symbol of divine law merging with earthly life.

1. CERAMIC TILEWORK: TYPES AND ORIGINS

The technique of fabrication of ceramic tiles was first introduced into Tunis from Andalusia at the end of the 15th century. Andalusian immigrant artisans later installed workshops in the quarter of Qellaline in the Medina of Tunis. Tilework became popular in Tunis during the 16th and 17th centuries and was used to decorate the walls and floors of its great homes and palaces. Tilework influenced by patterns in Spain, Morocco, France, Italy and Asia Minor began to be used in Sidi Bou Sa'id in the 18th and 19th century when the village became a popular place of summer residence for many of the important people of Tunis.

TYPE I

The tiles manufactured in Tunisia in the 18th and 19th centuries typically contained floral motifs, often separated by diagonal strips which form a grid when assembled together. The top sketch shows such a tile, and a smaller scale assembly of four tiles. Each tile measures approximately 13.5 cm square.

TYPE II

The second type, a radiating floral pattern, is also a common Tunisian design. Four of these tiles combine to make up the complete design, each is 12.5 cm square.

TYPE III

The third type, called "lion's paw", may be of Spanish origin. It is used extensively in Tunisia. Its strong yellow ochre design with a center of black and white star form gives it a royal character,

Ceramic Tilework

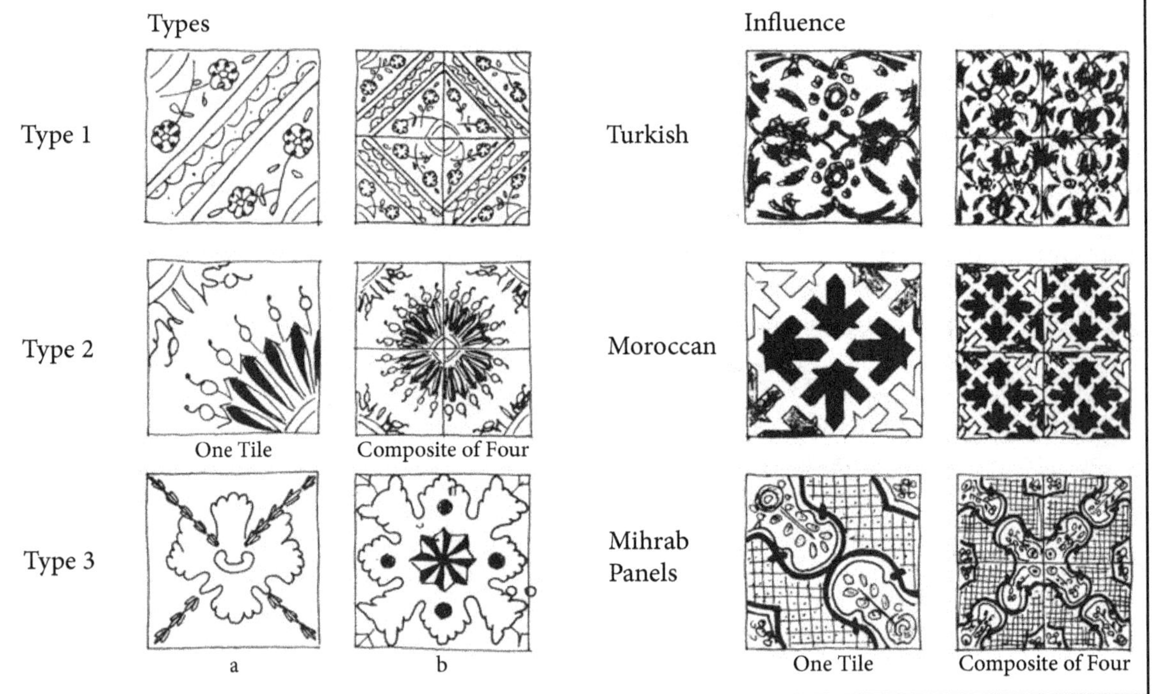

perhaps due to its association with the lion. It is used mainly as a bordering strip, with an edging of narrow (3 cm) black tiles, around doors, windows, etc. The tile measures approximately 12.7 cm.

DESIGN INFLUENCES

TURKISH INFLUENCE
These are generally floral designs which connect to form a continuous pattern of color and movement. The colors used in the example shown are blue, green and yellow (or brown).

MOROCCAN INFLUENCE
Geometric designs are a dominant feature of Moroccan ceramic work. This tile can be read as interwoven strips running in all directions, or as a swastika pattern joined together. The coloring of the tiles creates a contrasting pattern of squares, when seen from a distance.

ITALIAN INFLUENCE
Italian tiles came in a wide variety of patterns usually baroque floral designs.

SWALLOW'S WING
This type of tile is so named because two tiles together give the appearance of the coloring of swallows' wings. In French they have the more poetic name of "aile d'hirondelle". These tiles are of Andalusian/Spanish inspiration and were made in varying sizes in Qellaline in the Medina of

Swallow's Wing Tilework

Basic Tile

Tile 1

Tile 2

Composite Pattern of Two Tiles

Six Alternative Combination Patterns from
One Basic Tile

Composite of Four Tiles

Tunis. Tiles of this type found in Sidi Bou Sa'id are black and white although they were also made in green/ white and green/yellow. Several patterns can be formed by arranging these simple tiles in different ways, as shown in the illustration on page 81.

MIHRAB PANELS

Mihrab panels are large composite tile panels showing a design of vase and scroll-like plant forms enclosed inside an arch. These panels are of Turkish inspiration, and were produced in Tunis by the artisans of Qellaline. They were used in the most luxurious palaces of Tunis and other important buildings.

BIRD TILES

Many of these tiles were used in the large mausoleums of Tunis. Each one is hand-painted and thus has its own slight, interesting variations. Birds seem to symbolize the happiness and lightness of spirit prevalent in the Tunisian people and, indeed, Tunisians have a strong affection for birds as evidenced by their world-renowned birdcage.

USES OF TILES

Tiles of many types, ages and combinations find a multiplicity of applications in Sidi Bou Sa'id. Odd fragments are combined for paving steps, benches and patios. The tendency to re-use ancient materials appears in the same manner that antique columns and capitals are used where convenient in the construction of new houses. These ancient building materials are often of high quality and superior in design and interest to any newly made material. All the older tiles are hand painted, the

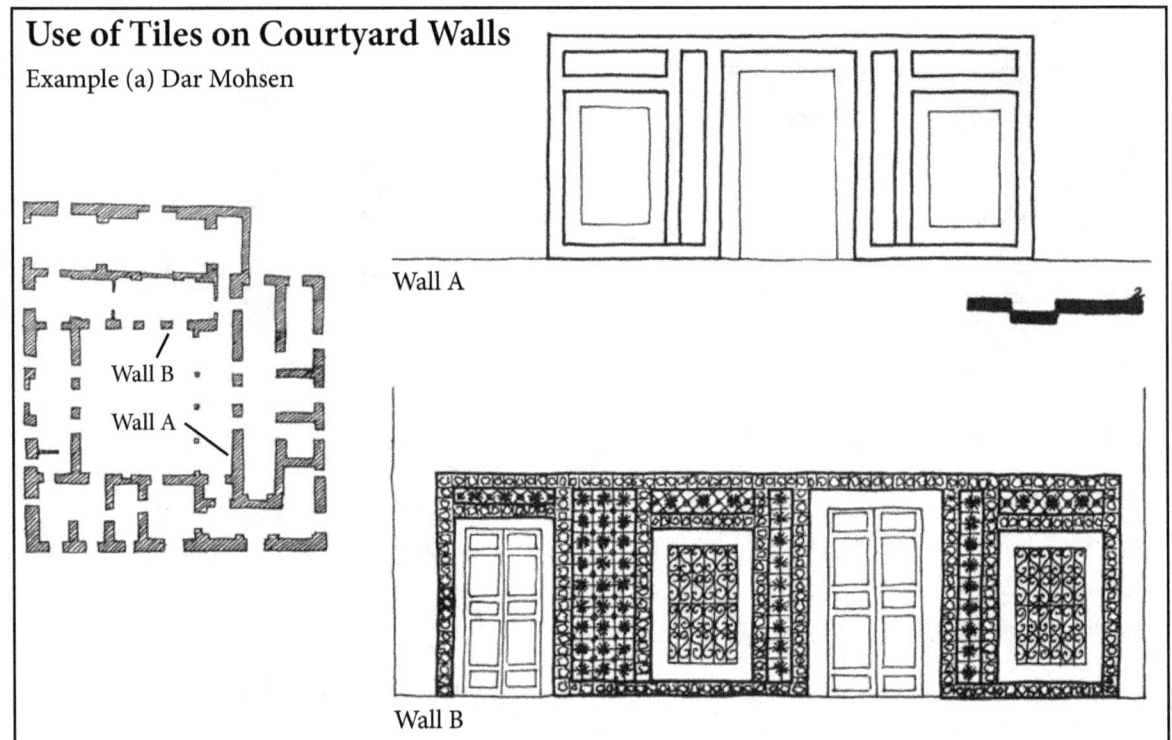

Use of Tiles on Courtyard Walls

Example (a) Dar Mohsen

Wall B

Wall A

Wall A

Wall B

individuality of each tile providing subtle variation which can be appreciated at close range. Single tiles are sometimes used on a wall, like a picture, or on a pathway or on gravestones.

Indoors, tiles are used extensively as wall panelling, sometimes covering the entire wall (Dar Dellaji), and sometimes in a strip along the base of the wall. On floors, special tiles are sometimes used in the center with a border strip of different tiles, giving a carpet-like effect. Tiles also appear on window ledges, steps and built-in benches. One of the more elegant uses of ceramic tiles is on the walls of the enclosed courtyard, as shown by the following two examples:

a) Dar Mohsen

The illustration on page 82 shows how strips of "lion paw" tiles are used to form an elegant two-dimensional framework incorporating the doors, windows and leftover spaces of the enclosed courtyard at Dar Mohsen. The result is a homogenous composition with its own rhythm and balance. The tiles used in this courtyard are of Tunisian origin.

b) Dar Ben Cheikh

Measuring 5.55 m x 6.45 m this is a more intimate courtyard than the one at Dar Mohsen (see illustration below). Its arrangement is strictly symmetrical. On the side of the entrance from the stair, two shallow cupboards are set into the wall to maintain the symmetry of the wall openings. The tiles used for panelling the walls are of Italian influence; one type is used in broad bands along the base of the wall and above door level, while another type fills the remaining spaces. The tiles used do not seem to belong to any modular system being simply arranged in whatever manner

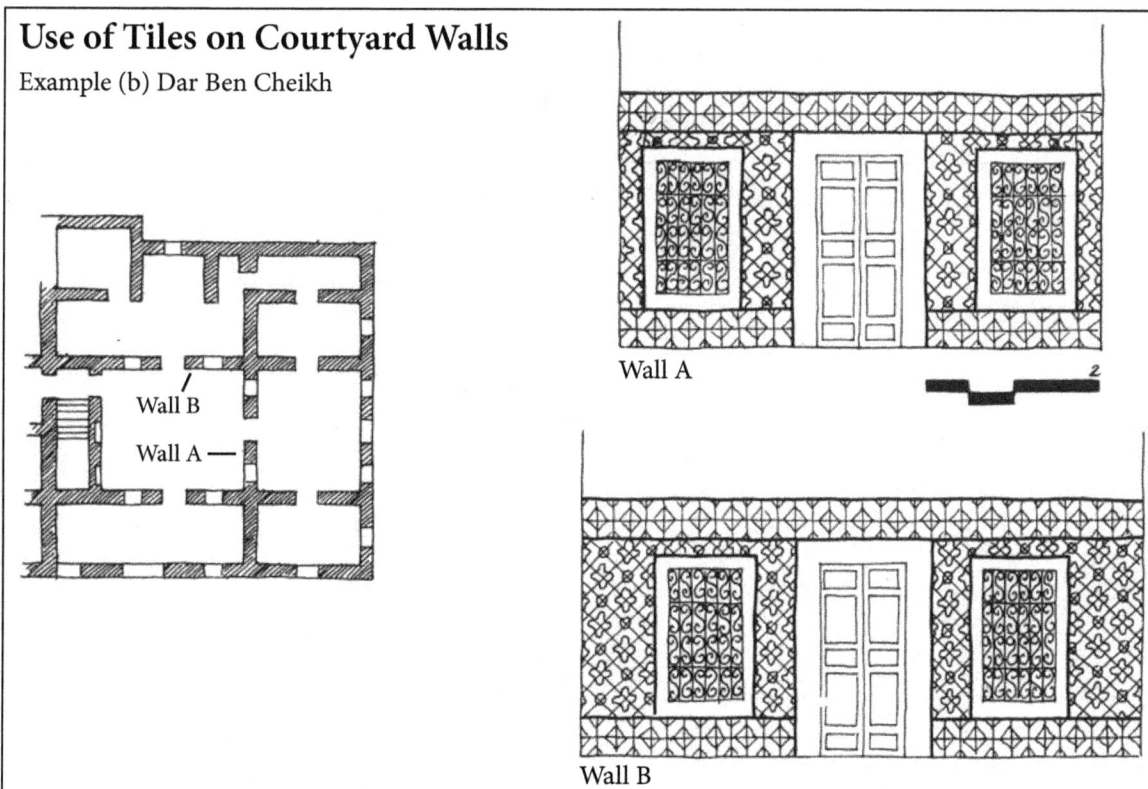

Use of Tiles on Courtyard Walls

Example (b) Dar Ben Cheikh

Wall B

Wall A —

Wall A

Wall B

gives a pleasing pattern arrangement—either horizontally, vertically or diagonally—and are simply cut off to fit the space available.

2. PLASTERWORK

The use of sculpted plaster was introduced to Tunisia by the artisans of Morocco and Andalusia. It is used to embellish areas which do not receive much physical wear such as the wall areas above tilework and the underside of vaults, cupola domes and arches.

Common design motifs used are the cypress and polygonal star shaped figures. In very elaborate buildings, plasterwork is used in many intricate patterns over the entire ceiling.

3. DOOR AND WINDOW FRAMES

Doors and windows are usually framed in stone although the most expensive houses use marble. Designs are sculpted in relief usually at the base, corners and middle of the lintel and sometimes all around. Influence is often Turkish—vase with scroll-like foliage, radiating flower forms etc. Italian influence appears in floral and baroque designs.

4. DOOR STUDDING

Metal studs are the most common exterior decoration of the doors in Sidi Bou Sa'id. This method, which was popular in Andalusia (Muslim Spain), combines various symbols to create the overall design.

At first, studs were used only along the wood framing in simple horizontals and verticals, as a means of securing the wood framing. Their only symbolic function being to emphasize the door's strength. Later, studs were used to fill in the remaining areas with various standard symbols which combined to create a pleasing effect. Some of the common symbols are as follows:

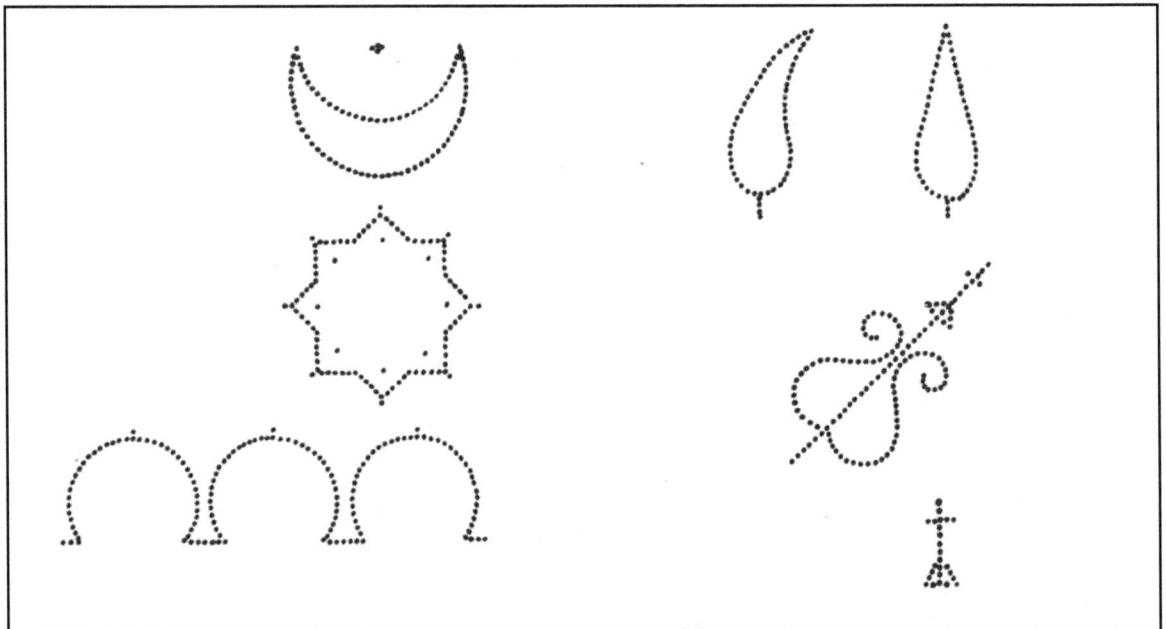

CRESCENT MOON

This symbol, which also appears frequently above the door in relief on the stone or marble frame, has religious significance. As the person must bend down to enter the low door, he is thus obliged to show his respect to this symbol. This symbol has been used in this region for at least 2000 years, as evidenced by Punic tombstones from Carthage.

ARCADES

The use of the Arabic arch in the arcades of mosques has resulted in its recognition as a symbolic element, much like the Gothic arch in Western culture.

CYPRESS

A common tree in this area

CROSS

Small crosses appear on many doors, but do not indicate any adherence to the Christian church.

USE OF COLOR

Most doors, window frames, and grills in Sidi Bou Sa'id, are painted sky blue. No doubt, this custom developed from the psychological attractiveness of cool colors in a hot climate. Door studs are usually painted black to make them stand out against the blue.

DETAIL OF A STONE WALL

CHAPTER 5

MATERIALS AND CONSTRUCTION

This chapter attempts to show how the factors of climate, materials and construction techniques have determined the built form of a traditional Tunisian town such as Sidi Bou Sa'id.

INFLUENCE OF CLIMATE

A basic tenet of this section is that construction should be an adaptation to the climate of a region and not its domination. Climate plays such an important role in construction that it is imperative to discuss in some detail how climatic factors help to influence the technologies involved. For a description of the climatic factors of Northern Tunisia see Chapter 1 of this book.

The possibility of several functions for a specific construction element cannot be overlooked. For example, walls of mud and stone are heavily constructed for obvious climatic reasons as well as to provide the structural strength necessary to support the weight of the normal vaulted masonry roofs. Roofs, in terms of structure, should be as light as possible yet in Sidi Bou Sa'id roofs are usually weighted down by a heavy layer of earth. This, it would seem, is only to increase the time lag involved in the penetration of the sun's heat. But then, when it is noticed that the second storey floor of a house also has this thick layer of earth, one is forced to the realization that the earth serves a double function of being a shock absorber as well as a thermal insulator. Indeed, without the earth, heavy footsteps could jar the vaults below; breaking the bond between the joints of the bricks and the stones in the vaults thus causing their complete collapse and even the collapse of the roof itself which is extensively used for such activities as recreation and the drying of food and clothing. Clearly the technology behind any system of construction cannot be solely attributed to climatic factors.

In terms of climatic stress, the various parts of a traditional Tunisian building are, in effect, environmental control devices. An excellent example of this is the Arab courtyard house of which Sidi Bou Sa'id has many excellent examples. (For an analysis of five of these houses see chapter 7).

The Courtyard, although constructed for privacy, security and protection from the wind also serves as an environmental control device: its high walls create shade and the large surface area of the inner walls and court area serve to draw heat from the house during the day and radiate it to the sky at night. The materials used in constructing courtyard houses—stone, masonry and earth—have high absorption qualities which delay the heat from entering the rooms adjacent to the court until evening. Through the night the heat radiates into the sky and by morning the house is cool again.

By trapping the cool night air the narrow streets of the village act somewhat like the courtyards of individual houses. Heat gain is also reduced during the daytime by the fact that the surface area of the building facades along the street are kept to a minimum. Surface treatment is also an important thermal regulator. Windows, for example, are placed high up on exposed walls and reduced both in size and number primarily for reasons of visual privacy. However, this treatment also satisfies ventilation requirements and prevents most heat, dust and ground glare from entering the building. Also, since light colored surfaces reflect large amounts of solar radiation, most of the surface areas in Sidi Bou Sa'id are painted either white or in very pale tones.

Although the temperature often drops to 0 degrees C in the region around Sidi Bou Sa'id during the months of December, January and February, none of the climatic technologies of the village have been designed to deal extensively with this problem. This is because the period of coldness is much shorter than the lengthy hot-dry period. However, the lack of techniques to reduce or eliminate moisture penetration in the masonry walls (such as damp proof coursing) and the reliance upon simple coal braziers for heating individual rooms, etc., all serve to make parts of the ground floor of a typical traditional Tunisian house quite uncomfortable during the winter months.

INFLUENCE OF MATERIALS AND CONSTRUCTION TECHNIQUES

To fully understand the construction techniques of vernacular Tunisian architecture it is necessary to examine the influences of particular materials, structural requirements and building forms.

The Tunis region lacks large forests of construction quality timber but it does have an abundance of rocks, quarried stone, clay and sand. This situation has led to masonry being used for almost all walls and roofs while wood is used for scaffolding, some supports, formwork, doors and windows. The lack of a material with any degree of tensile strength has required that large spaces be spanned with materials used in compression. Because a one—or two—dimensional roof structure would not be capable of spanning such spaces, three-dimensional arches, vaults and domes have been utilized. The lateral thrust of these arches and vaults led to the use of thick walls and buttresses and since the spans were limited by the capabilities of the masonry, the rooms became cellular elements in a structural organism. These elements can grow freely, thus permitting the expansion and contraction of the village form without disturbing the unity of the whole.

The expression of the vaults and domes can be controlled by exposing the roof form, covering it or flattening it (to achieve a roof surface for recreation, the drying of food and clothing etc) Hence it can be readily seen that some of these methods of enclosing space are also some of the influences of the final built form.

It could be said that the complete absence of modern steel and concrete has led to some very straightforward but ingenious solutions to the problems of providing shelter in Sidi Bou Sa'id.

MATERIALS

This section concerns itself with the natural and fabricated materials that were used in Sidi Bou Sa'id.

1. STONES

a) Re-used Stone: This has the advantage of being already cut.

b) Quarry Stone : Abundantly available. Generally a good building quality type of limestone. Brittle texture allows it to be easily broken into any size desired.

2. CLAY

Clay is used for the manufacture of rectangular bricks, tubular bricks, locking bricks, conduits and drainpipes. Clay is found in all areas of the country but the pure quality clay is found only at a substantial depth. There are two types of clay used in Tunisia: red or grey clay which is used for high compressive strength bricks, and white clay which is used for general purposes. White clay turns red when baked.

PROCEDURE FOR MAKING BRICKS

When the raw clay is brought to the baking site it is dumped along with a quantity of water into a large (2 m – 3 m in diameter) basin dug into the earth. White clay and red clay are often mixed together. The clay is mixed by a worker trampling it with his feet until it reaches a kneading state. At this point it is ready to be moulded into bricks using a wooden mould which accommodates two bricks at a time. The standard size of a rectangular brick is 10 x 25 x 4 cm. The bricks are moulded directly on the ground and left to dry in the sun for 48 hours during which time the brick maker sprinkles fine sand or ashes on the wet bricks to protect them from drying too rapidly and cracking. After the bricks are relatively dry any lumps are trimmed off and the bricks are stacked prior to baking.

The baking oven is approximately 6 m high by 3 m in diameter with about nine-tenths of its bulk underground. In the center of the oven is a star shaped grill below which is a ring of arches forming the firebox. This is fuelled through a small opening at the base of the oven which is accessible by a ramp. The bricks are stacked on the grill to allow for their maximum surface exposure and the proper drawing of the fire. The oven is fuelled with palm branches and olive wood. The baking lasts for 36 hours and on its completion the oven and bricks are left to cool for ten days before being removed.

POTTERY TUBULAR BRICKS

Fabricated on a pottery wheel and baked, pottery tubular bricks are 20–25 cm long and about 5 cm in diameter. In wall constructions they are used like standard bricks except that there is only one row every half meter (approximately 1 cubit).

POTTERY LOCKING BRICKS

Commonly seen in Roman ruins in Tunisia, pottery locking bricks are fixed end to end with lime mortar and used to form barrel vaults and domes.

POTTERY CONDUITS AND DRAIN PIPES

These are approximately 30 cm in length and 10 cm in diameter and are turned on a pottery wheel and baked. The exterior is often glazed.

3. LIMESTONE

—Natural Lime: This is mixed with earth and used for the construction of walls, terraces and roofs.

—Cooked Lime : Known as "chaux grasse" in Tunisia, this is used as a masonry bonding material (lime is a basic ingredient of cement) and as the major ingredient of whitewash. Dyes are often added to give it a desired color.

4. GYPSUM

Generally called plaster, gypsum is used either raw or semi-cooked. Gypsum hardens immediately with water but as it dries has a swelling action. These qualities make it an ideal material for the construction of vaulted roofs.

There are two types of gypsum:

—White gypsum which is pure quality and used in the smooth finish plaster walls and ceilings.

—Grey gypsum which is of a lower grade and used primarily as mortar.

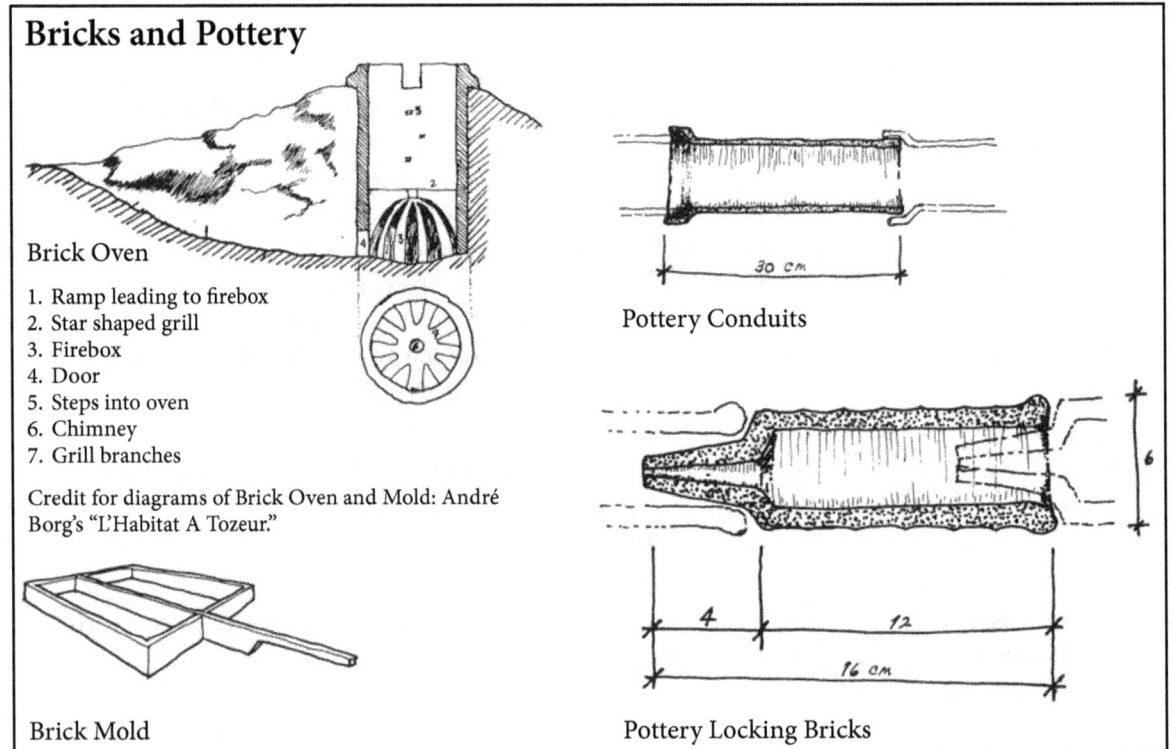

Bricks and Pottery

Brick Oven

1. Ramp leading to firebox
2. Star shaped grill
3. Firebox
4. Door
5. Steps into oven
6. Chimney
7. Grill branches

Credit for diagrams of Brick Oven and Mold: André Borg's "L'Habitat A Tozeur."

Brick Mold

Pottery Conduits

30 cm

Pottery Locking Bricks

4   12

16 cm

5. WOOD

The principal trees of Tunisia are the olive, eucalyptus, date palm and cork/oak species. Timber from these trees was used in the construction of scaffolding, formwork, tie-rods, window frames, doors and occasionally for the construction of intermediate floors.

6. IRON

Tunisia has good deposits of iron ore. In Sidi Bou Sa'id iron is used mostly for fabricating window grills, tie rods and the large square grills which are sometimes used over courtyards for security purposes.

7. MARBLE

Used in Tunisia since Roman times for small columns and finishes in palaces. A later usage was for flooring for which it was cut into tiles 35 cm x 35 cm.

CONSTRUCTION

BUILDING PROCESS

When a Tunisian family of average income decided to build a new home or extend its old one it first hired a "master mason" (amin al-bannaya) who was usually the head of all the other masons for that particular district. The master mason then discussed the requirements of the project with the client, sketched a rough plan on the ground and, after its approval, contracted for the building to be built. If need be the plan was drawn accurately on paper, using rule and compass.

In the construction of a palace or of a house for a member of the bourgeoisie the "master stone cutter" (amin al-nakkasha) assumed the functions of both architect and job captain. In such a construction project the master mason became a consultant to the master stone cutter.

Also involved in the construction of wealthier homes was the "well master" (amin al-biyara) who acted as a soils expert to determine the location of drinkable water and the suitability of the soil for construction. Because of the importance of a well in upper class homes he was always the first expert to be consulted before finalizing site selection or the commencement of construction.

The process of construction for a palace or bourgeois house was as follows:
1. Digging of the well, cisterns, and basement.
2. Installation of conduits and the building of the foundation walls.
3. Erection of the upper walls
4. Construction of the vaults, ceilings and terraces.
5. The surfacing of the courtyard and the flooring of the rooms.
6. Installation of doors and windows.

Certain symbolic practices begin and end the building process. It begins with the recitation from the Qur'an, then the sacrifice of a sheep and the distribution of its meat to the workers on the site and neighbors.

When the house is completed, all the craftsmen, workers and others who took part in the construction are invited by the owner to a "hafla" or party where he will have the occasion of entertaining his guests and distributing bonuses as food, clothes and money. Only after this ceremony, will the owner move his furniture and begin residence.

FOUNDATIONS

The master mason determined the necessary width and depth of the foundations (the depth usually being 1–4 m). In his book *Palais et Demeures de Tunis* (1967), Revault explains the procedure for constructing foundations as follows:

> The execution of these foundations was generally confined to groups of ten to twenty workers (two or three for the average income house)…On a bed of mortar made of earth and lime (about 20 cm thick) they tamped sand and gravel and small to medium stones…including scrap and damaged pieces of conduit. Meanwhile, the master stone cutter, depending upon the rhythm desired, chants with a slow drumming tempo … When they reached 50 cm from the grade surface they began constructing the walls using more regular stones.

WALLS

Flat stones bonded with an earth and lime mortar were used to level the top of the foundation walls before the construction of the upper walls. To prepare this mortar the lime was added and mixed several times by workers who wrapped their feet and legs with rugs and goat hides to prevent burns.

The stones were laid in a double row according to size, the master mason relying on his helpers to carry the stones and pick the properly sized ones for a particular row. The larger stones were always laid first, followed by a row of irregular stone followed by a levelling course of brick or flat stone. The two rows were tied together with an infill of rubble.

The finished wall was generally 50–80 cm in thickness and occasionally it was decreased in width towards the top. Except for the occasional kitchen divider and some brick-infill doorway walls, all walls of traditional Tunisian construction are load bearing. Load bearing walls produce the narrowest possible span and simplify the task of spanning in masonry to manageable dimensions. Two methods of construction were possible when a man built a house adjacent to another. First, if the neighbors were on friendly terms, it might be agreed that one wall of the existing house would serve as a support wall for the roof or the floor and ceiling vaults of the new house. Second, if the neighbors were not on friendly terms, then a new wall against the existing wall would have had to be built. Because of the reinforcement provided by the old wall, the new wall was usually reduced in thickness from about 60 cm to about 20 cm. This thinner wall was constructed of bricks and/or flat stones. The reason for this thinner wall is that the most difficult forces to contend with are not the vertical but the horizontal forces resulting from the thrust of the vaults.

ROOFS

The lack of suitable tensile materials and the inherent constraints of masonry led to the development of sophisticated vault, dome and arch systems to solve the problems of spanning the seemingly infinite variety of spaces arising from the various requirements of traditional architecture.

Walls

60 cm | 20

Existing | New

New wall built adjacent to existing wall

50 – 80 cm

Typical Load Bearing Wall

70-80 cm

Wooden "Tamping" Mallet

a

Existing | New

b

Existing | New

New structure built adjacent to existing wall
(a) independent support for roofs
(b) partially dependent on existing wall for roof support

Wall

80 cm | 30

Foundation

Foundation Treatment:
Increased wall thickness to avoid point loading

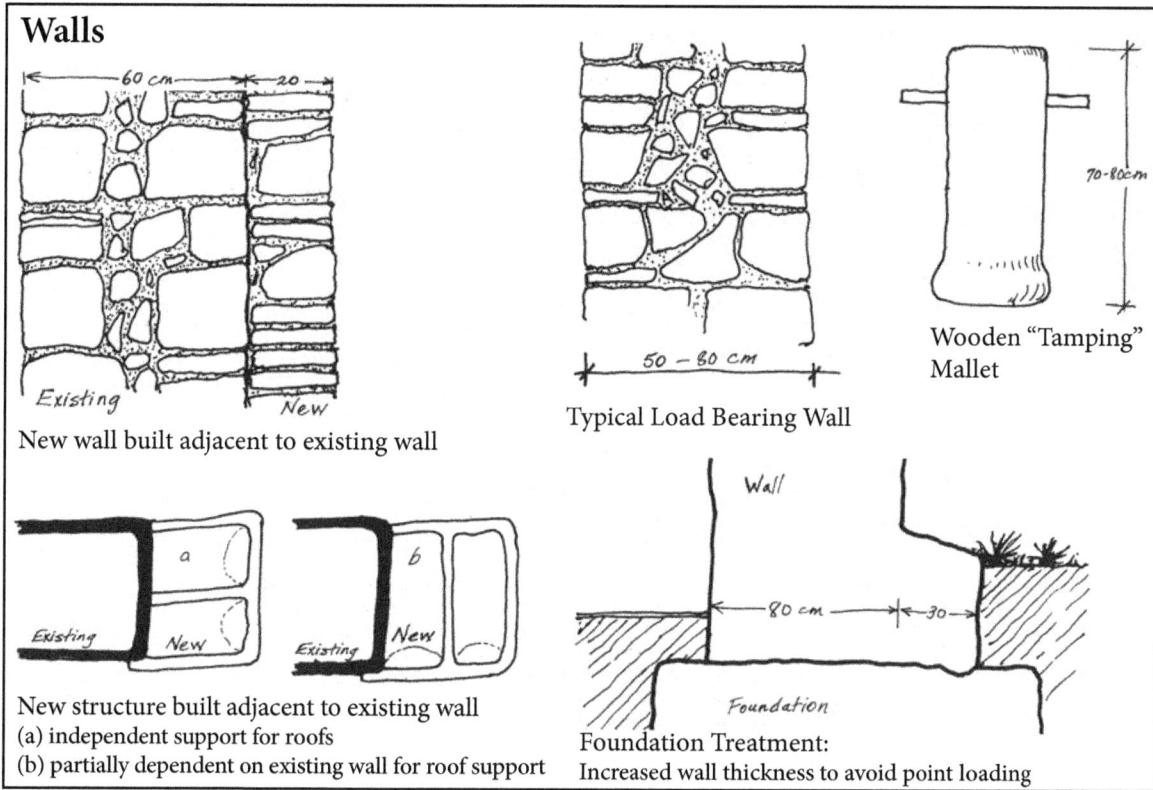

In Sidi Bou Sa'id the most commonly used vaults were barrel (simple) vaults, cradle vaults and groin vaults. Other vaults used to a lesser extent included the cloister vault and the cupola vault. The spans of these vaults were typically in the range of 1.5–4 m. They were always composed of brick except for the cupola vault which was constructed of pottery tubes.

The use of these basic vault shapes allowed for multiple combinations and interconnections including a groin vault extending into two or three barrel vaults or a series of six to nine parallel groin vaults.

The Mosque Complex at Sidi Bou Sa'id contains many examples of possible combinations and interconnections (see floor plans and sections of the Mosque in Chapter 6).

The various manipulations of the basic techniques of vaulting enabled the builders of Sidi Bou Sa'id to roof almost any shape of space whether a square, rectangle, rhombus or trapezoid. The degree of vault curvature is directly related to the distance between its supports because the less the degree of the curvature the greater the forces pushing outward. The sum of the vault thrust and its dead load must not project a resultant point above grade.

The construction of a vault began with a single row of brick being laid flat at the springing point. The main layer of bricks (what is seen from beneath) was handset without any type of support or framework other than a gypsum mortar bond which was mixed fresh for each brick. Each time a brick was laid the hand was held for a minute or two until the mortar set. As a guide for ensuring the proper curvature of the vault the mason fixed a string on a pole at the center of the arc and

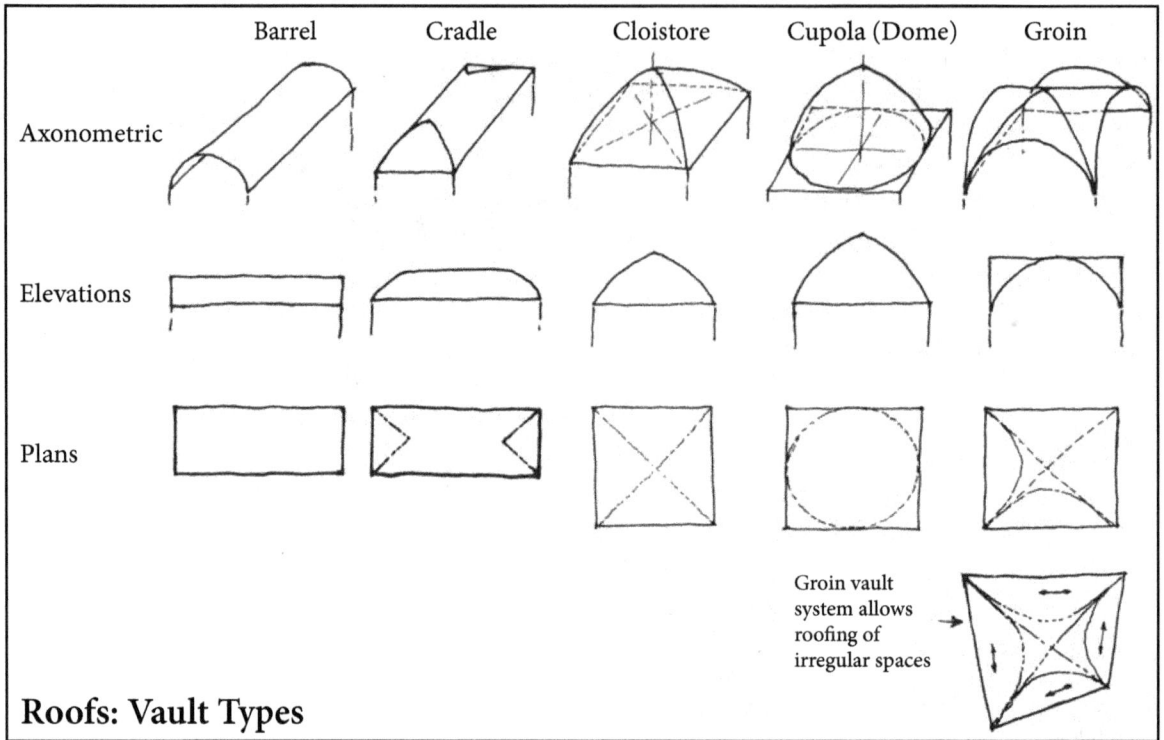

Roofs: Vault Types

Vault Details

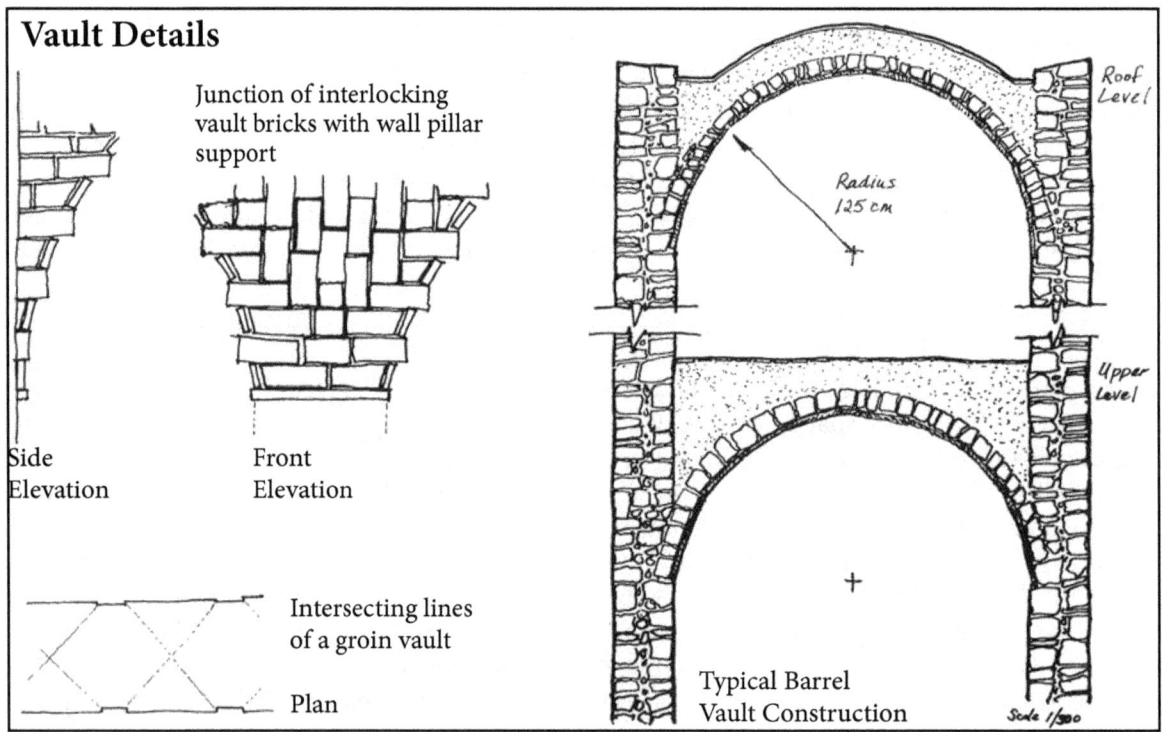

Junction of interlocking vault bricks with wall pillar support

Side Elevation

Front Elevation

Intersecting lines of a groin vault

Plan

Typical Barrel Vault Construction

Vault Details

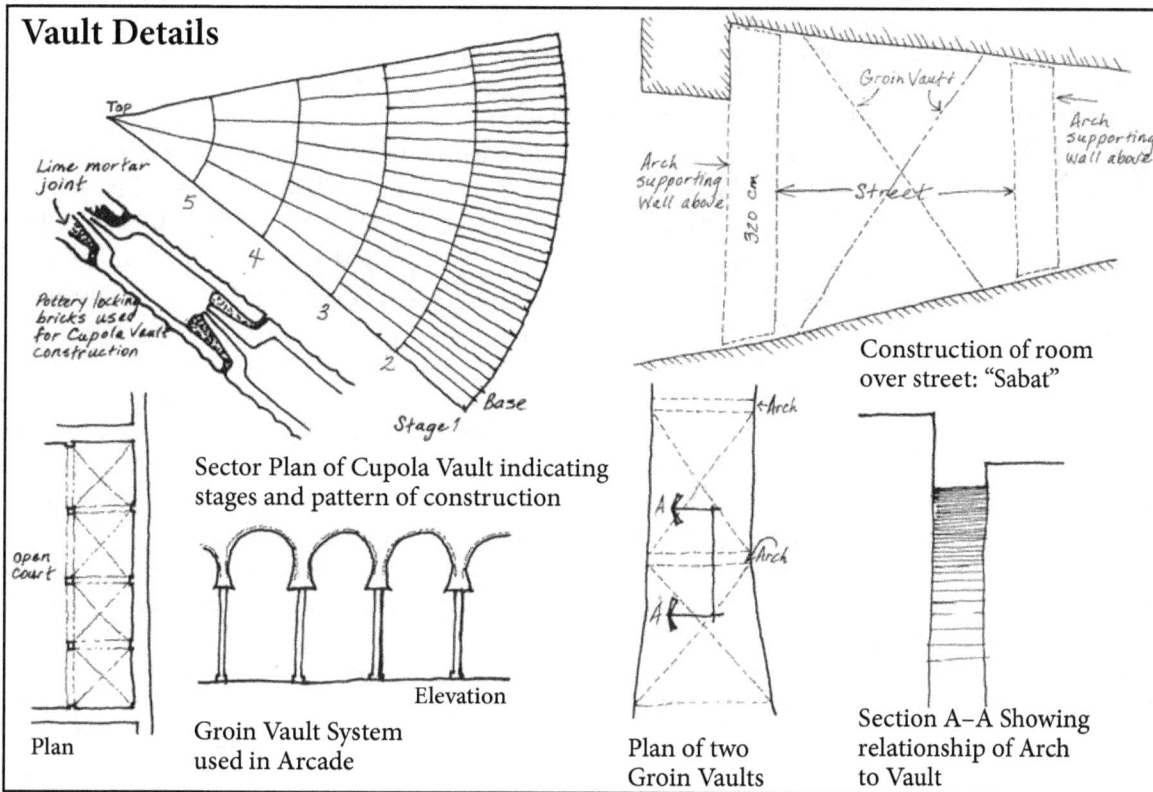

Sector Plan of Cupola Vault indicating
stages and pattern of construction

Construction of room
over street: "Sabat"

Groin Vault System
used in Arcade

Plan

Elevation

Plan of two
Groin Vaults

Section A–A Showing
relationship of Arch
to Vault

then tied the other end of the string around the wrist of the hand with which he laid the bricks. The degree of curvature of the vault was thus automatically governed by the length of this string.

The bricks have little structural significance of their own but rather act as a form for the load bearing vault of stone and mortar which was built at the same time and which was sometimes doubled or tripled to increase the strength of the arch. The vault was covered with a layer of compacted sand or earth to a depth of 15–60 cm. The walls were then extended another 70–80 cm beyond the base of the vault to form a rain gutter. Next, a 2 cm layer of lime mortar was spread on the top of the vault to act as a water sealant and later painted with a lime whitewash.

In the barrel and groin vaults the bricks were always laid parallel to the direction of the span while in the cradle vaults the bricks were laid perpendicular to the span. The bricks in these vaults were normally laid with a staggered bond although occasionally one sees the herring-bone pattern (which is actually more typical of recent constructions).

One of the most interesting details of the groin vault and its derivatives is found at the interlocking of the arch bricks with the supporting pillars or walls. At the base of the intersecting circles, the interlocking bricks were very pronounced but as each of the four intersections curved up into the vault they began to form the smooth shape of the vault. Without this brick locking pattern the vault would have lost its structural stability. A groin vault can project from a wall or one to four of them can project from a single stone pillar.

Unlike the groin vaults, cradle and cloister vaults do not have a pattern of interlocking bricks as their structural stability is gained through their inherent form.

CONSTRUCTION OF A CUPOLA VAULT (DOME)

A cupola vault was probably constructed by first laying a ring of interlocking pottery tubes on a pendentive circular base. As the mason laid the subsequent rows he gradually leaned them inwards, occasionally stopping to reinforce them with a layer of lime mortar as they became unstable. This process of stacking and plastering the tubes in rows of decreasing diameter continued until the cupola vault was completely closed at the top. As in the simpler vaults, a secondary skin of mortared stone was laid to give the vault its structural stability.

ARCHES

Arches also played an important role in vaulting systems. In the Mosque of Sidi Bou Sa'id, for example, they were used to support the large cupola vaults and at the same time to act as dividers for the adjacent cloister and groin vaults. Arches were also used as dividers to separate vaults of differing heights and to terminate the sides of groin vaults in an arcade construction.

Arches were also used over streets to buttress the facades of facing buildings. Similarly arches were used to support a room over a street—called a "sabat" in Arabic. This is a traditional example of the modern concept of "air rights".

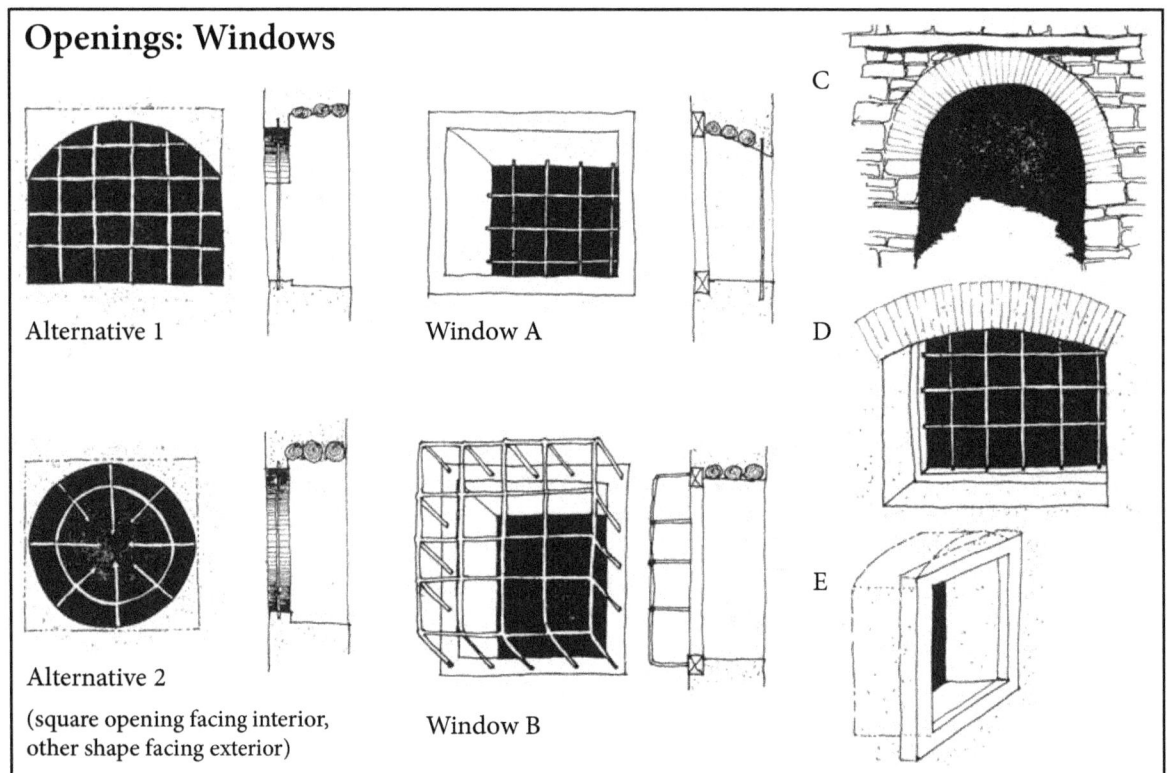

Openings: Windows

Alternative 1

Window A

C

D

E

Alternative 2

(square opening facing interior, other shape facing exterior)

Window B

Another common structural element found in Tunisia is the wooden tie rod. Usually made of oak they have been found to last up to 400 years with little noticeable deterioration.

The "Skaf luha" (an Arabic term signifying a flat ceiling constructed of wood—not unlike a wood joist floor system) is a rare, expensive type of ceiling due to the fact that the wood had to be transported from distant forests or imported, before being hand cut and carved. The usage of this ceiling type and its level of decoration signified the owner's affluence.

WALL OPENINGS

This section examines traditional Tunisian methods of creating openings in a wall without compromising its structural stability.

The simplest method of constructing lintels for doors and windows was to cast spanning poles into the wall above the opening and then cover them with a layer of bricks on a mortar bed. This concept can be found in the small openings used for lighting and ventilating kitchens and livestock rooms. Some minor variations of this basic technique are shown by the accompanying diagrams. As one can see, the major lintel of wood is still present in windows "A" and "B" although the exterior adds a certain aesthetic form to the opening. Diagram "C" shows an archway for a door where the wood pole is the structural element and the arch has no practical purpose. Diagram "D" shows an arch which has been left exposed to show its pure structural shape. Diagram "E" shows a structural arch which, in complete contrast to window "A", has an inset rectangular opening.

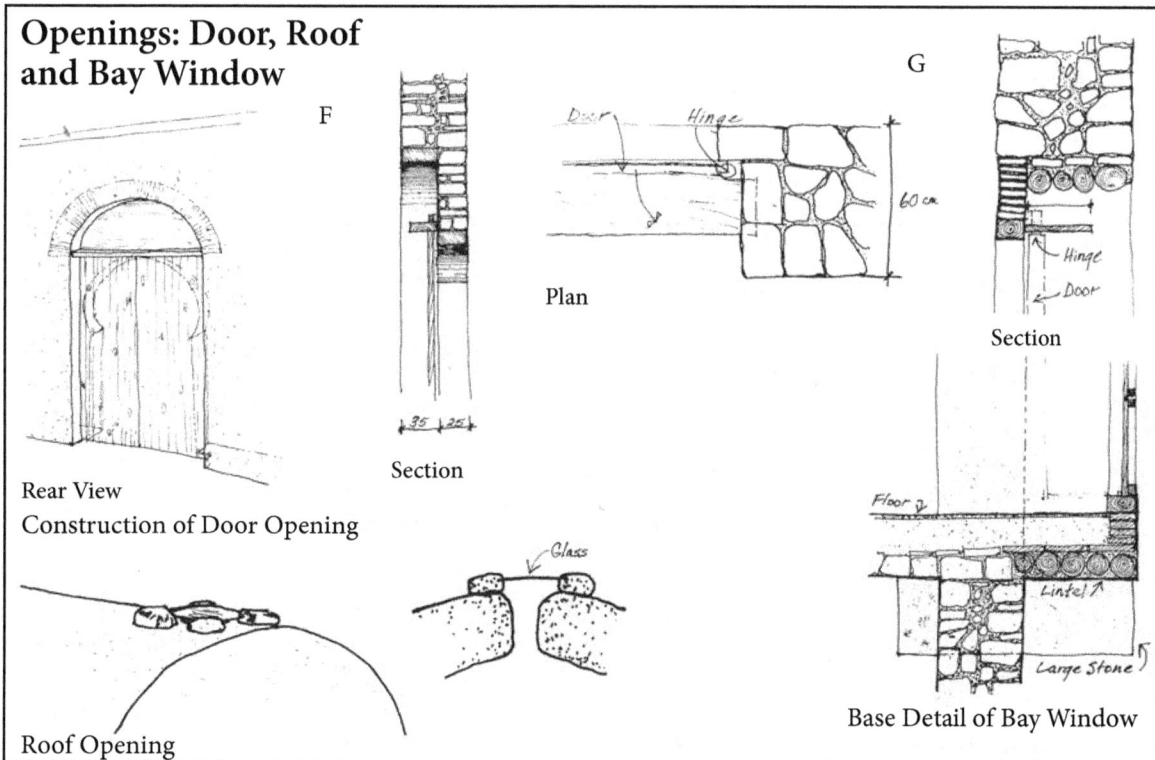

Openings: Door, Roof and Bay Window

F

Rear View
Construction of Door Opening

Section

Plan

G

Section

Roof Opening

Base Detail of Bay Window

Door openings are just a further development of simple window openings constructions. Sketch "F" illustrates the structural elements of the doorway. First is the front lintel, squarely cut from a piece of wood, and supporting only the width of the wall above. This acts as the head of the door jamb. Second are four poles supporting the remaining width of the wall. On top of these poles is a layer of bricks which creates a full surface for the stone masonry. Close to the top of the opening is a wide board supported by the masonry on either side of the door opening. As can be seen in Diagram "G" the door is hung on hinges consisting of heavy wooden pins which project through the top and bottom of the door into cup shaped recesses in the stone sills.

Another characteristic method of spanning door openings in the region was by means of double arches in which the major arch always spanned a greater width than the finished opening. At the springing point of the major arch was a thick board spanning the inside opening. This board, coupled with a minor exterior arch, formed the jamb for the double doors. The major arch was often constructed of brick, or sometimes, of fitted stone.

ROOF OPENINGS

Two kinds of openings are occasionally found in the vaulted roofs of Sidi Bou Sa'id. The first is found in the poorer houses and consists of a small rectangular hole covered by a pane of glass mounted on four masonry stubs. In the large cloister vaults of Dar Thameur several small (15

Typical Roofscape

cm square) openings are seen, their function likely being for ventilation, lighting and aesthetics. Presently roof openings are glazed, although originally they were left open.

FINISHES

Depending on the wealth of the owner, exterior finishes can vary from magnificent sculpted plaster to lime whitewash on a lime and sand mortar. Windows and doors are usually painted a sea blue color to protect the wood from decay and to add the element of color to the otherwise plain facades.

The interiors of the houses were often quite elaborate. Ceramic tiles were used for the floors and some of the walls of wealthier houses. Generally walls were plastered smooth and painted with a lime whitewash. The quality of the finishing on the ceilings and walls was usually directly related to the owner's wealth; varying from simple whitewash to elaborate plasterwork.

The floors were finished with glazed or unglazed clay tiles. Marble tiles are more recent. The tiles were always laid on a 10 cm base of earth and lime and then set with gypsum and sand mortar.

"Skaf Luna" or flat wooden ceilings were usually left exposed—their owner's affluence being signified by the elaborateness of their painted decor.

MISCELLANEOUS

Cantilevered window balconies are quite common in the Tunis region. These were constructed by casting two large rectangular stones into the wall to form a support for a lintel of wood poles covered by a layer of bricks. The final floor of earth and tiles was built on top of this. The balcony enclosure was constructed completely of wood (see chapter 4).

Private cisterns and wells are found only in the wealthier homes of Sidi Bou Sa'id. Usually located beneath the courtyard, the cisterns were filled during the winter rains—the water being used primarily for purposes of household and personal hygiene while wells were reserved for drinking water. At the end of the construction of a house the cisterns were covered with earth and terraced to complete the surface of the courtyard.

The accompanying diagrams show an access mouth to a typical cistern. Next to this is a convenient basin used for miscellaneous purposes.

Because of the loose sandy soil in this region, a special technique was developed for the construction of wells. The project begins with the construction of a circular wooden ring with a number of heavy wooden teeth fastened to its underside. The diameter of this ring is about 1.5 m which is the minimum space in which a man can effectively work. Once the proper site has been selected, cut stones are laid on top of the ring to form the base of the cylindrically-shaped well. As a worker digs away the earth in the center and beneath the ring, the ring slowly starts to settle. As this digging and settling process continues, more stone is laid until the walls of the well are completed. The mouth of the well is then finished with corbelled layers of stone.

LOSS OF TECHNOLOGY

The traditional techniques of construction are quickly dying in the Tunis region, indeed, there are only a few master masons with a complete knowledge of traditional construction techniques in the whole area. It seems that many of the younger competent masons have gradually left for the major urbanized areas of the country or to other countries such as Italy and France where wages are higher and work is more plentiful.

Traditionally, trades were handed down from father to son and their mastery was perfected through years of apprenticeship.

In the last few years, masonry construction has begun to be taught in various technical schools but, without the experience of the master masons the emphasis has usually been on modern techniques. With these, young graduates go to work under construction contractors and build accordingly.

Several attempts were made by various architects over the last fifteen years or so to reintroduce the traditional techniques of construction. Even though there are continuous attempts to design buildings responsive to the country's traditional built forms (vaults, domes, arcades, courtyards etc.), the traditional techniques seem difficult to retain and are therefore threatened with extinction.

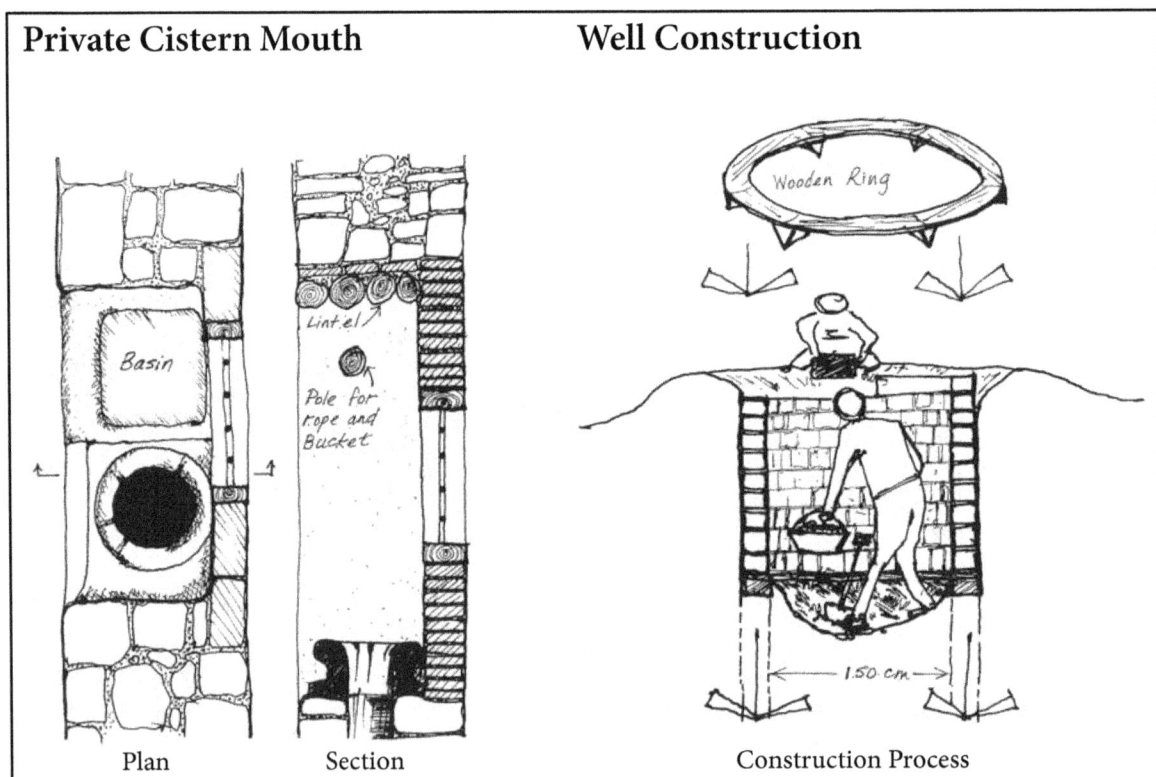

Private Cistern Mouth

Basin

Lintel

Pole for rope and Bucket

Plan   Section

Well Construction

Wooden Ring

1.50 cm

Construction Process

Construction Details

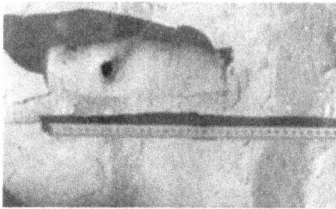

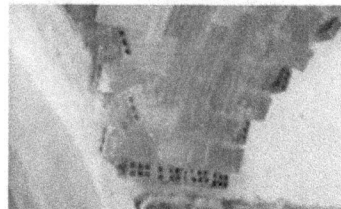

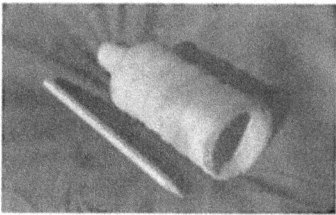

FORMAL RECEPTION CEREMONY IN VILLAGE SQUARE, 1975

CHAPTER 6

THE VILLAGE CORE

THE SOUK

GROWTH OF THE SOUK

The Souk of Sidi Bou Sa'id developed along the major road leading up to the old main entrance to the Mosque and around the square fronting on the Mosque. This is the typical location of a souk in an Arabic-Islamic town as it allows the integration of shopping and marketing with the daily cycles of prayer.

The former women's entrance to the Mosque became its main entrance in the late nineteenth century when the old entrance was converted into the cafe presently known as the Cafe des Nattes. The tea and coffee served in the cafe are prepared in the area previously used to gain access to the Mosque courtyard.

In the old days the necessities of life were provided by an open vegetable market on the site of the present square, and small shops on either side of the main street which sold meat, shoes, leather and cloth. Other amenities such as a sweet shop, a bread shop and a coffee shop were added as the town grew in size.

Today the main square serves as a market, an outdoor cafe on weekends and in the summer, and each August as the site for some of the functions of the "Kharja" (see chapter 2).

Unfortunately, Sidi Bou Sa'id's attractiveness to tourists has directly contributed to the changes of much of the Arabic character of its souk, for with the heightened influx of tourists in the early 1960's, requests to clean up the core of the town next to the square resulted in the relocation of the vegetable market, butcher shop and fish shop to their present location in the basement of the Magasin General in the more recently built lower town. The shops that remained were not sources of undesirable smell and sight and included the two major cafes, a barber shop, three small grocery stores, a vegetable shop, a doughnut shop and a sweet shop. In addition, the original shopping strip on both sides of the main street was extended and new shops catering mainly to tourists and consisting of a number of boutiques, jewelry shops, carpet and tapestry shops were opened.

ACTIVITIES OF THE SOUK

The operation and character of the cafe, square and souk varies greatly from day to day and from season to season. During summer, there is a large influx of tourists and residents from Tunis. This brings an unusual amount of activity to the area filling the square with people. For these occasions, chairs and tables stored in rooms adjacent to the square are arranged outside.

In summer the souk is open from 7:00 a.m. to 8:00 p.m. but very little happens in the morning until 9:00 a.m. when bus loads of tourists arrive on the scene. Any selling activity dies down at sunset when most people go to the cafe and the square for a quiet coffee or mint tea.

During the winter, the volume of people is reduced and it is only on weekends that the cafe and square come to life again. Like the houses of Sidi Bou Sa'id the small street front shops forming the souk are designed primarily for use in a dry climate. In periods of rain the shops are usually closed and the tourists run to the shelter of the Cafe des Nattes.

Abutting onto the shops on both sides of the street are typical Arab houses with high walls and rooms open only onto the interior courtyard. Two storey houses with the top floor above the shops overlooking the street are the only ones with windows on the exterior walls. For most of these houses, entrances are off a cul-de-sac or side street. Only the ones situated in the middle of a long block have their entrances off the main street, in which case their interior courtyards are always carefully shielded from public view.

The souk in typical Arabic towns provide a major source of income to the people who operate the small street front shops. These people are usually inhabitants of the town or its immediate outskirts. The tourist souk in Sidi Bou Sa'id is not typical in this respect, for although it is operated by a few residents of the village, a large number of shops are operated by people living outside the town, and in some cases these people own and operate more than one shop. A few shops in the souk of Sidi Bou Sa'id are owned by the municipality and rented for use as boutiques, etc., while others are owned by the owners of the houses immediately adjacent.

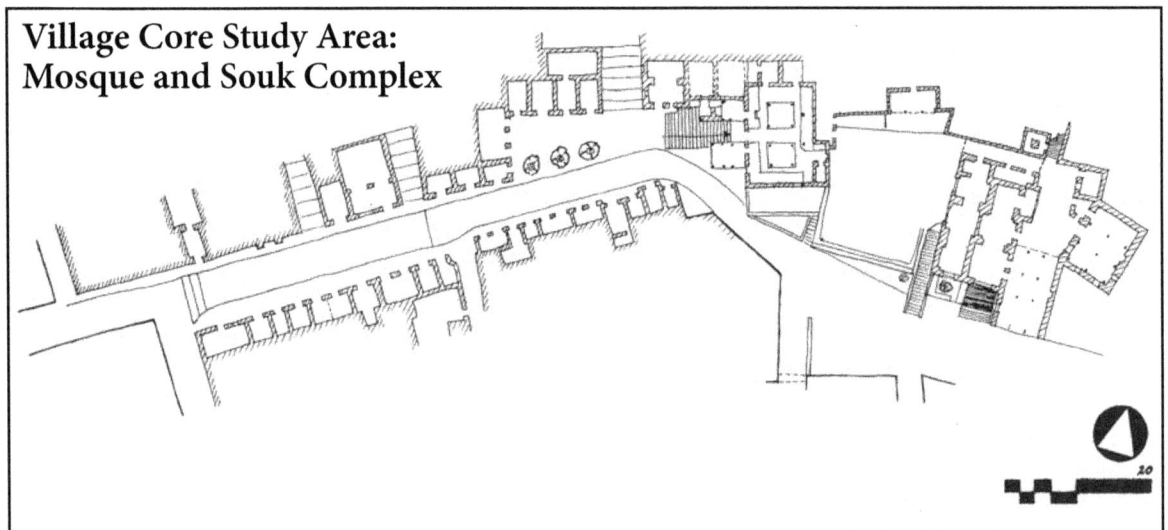

**Village Core Study Area:
Mosque and Souk Complex**

It may be said that tourist souks such as the one at Sidi Bou Sa'id are important for two reasons: firstly to generate badly needed foreign exchange and secondly to provide an outlet for the intensive artisan industry.

Bargaining allows a proprietor a greater chance of making a profit than he could expect under a fixed price system. This is obvious as soon as one enters the Cafe des Nattes, for instance, where the prices of drinks are not fixed and one can easily be expected to pay several different prices for a cup of tea. However, the prices of such food items as vegetables, meat, etc., are fixed in the souk although they are slightly higher than those in Tunis or at the Magasin General only a few hundred yards away.

Even though women are allowed to work they have not yet begun to take part in the mercantile activity of the souk at Sidi Bou Sa'id. All shops are operated by men and the only part which women play is in the purchasing of clothes and food.

THE MOSQUE

FUNCTIONS OF THE MOSQUE

Although the noon hour prayer on Fridays should, whenever possible, be performed in attendance at a Mosque, it is permissible for a Muslim to perform the five daily prayers wherever it is most convenient. It is always required to cleanse the hands, face and feet with running water before praying.

The five prescribed daily prayers are:

SALAT AL-FAJR: The dawn prayer between the break of day and sunrise.

SALAT AL-ZUHR: The noon prayer when the sun passes the meridian.

SALAT AL-'ASR: The late afternoon prayer

SALAT AL-MAGHRIB: The prayer immediately after sunset

SALAT AL-'ISHA: The prayer after sunset and before retiring to sleep.

The English word "mosque" is a corruption of the Arabic word "mesjid" meaning "place of prostration". The most conspicuous features of the mosque are the "minaret", the "mihrab" and the "minbar". These serve respectively for the call to prayer, the direction of Mecca, and the platform for the Friday sermon. They parallel the roles of the "muezzin", the "imam" and the "khatib".

The duties of the muezzin are to call the people to prayer from the minaret. The imam on the other hand has a much more important role, for he is the leader who stands in front of the assembled believers to ensure unison in the movements of the prayers. In performing his duties the imam faces the mihrab at all times. This is a niche set into the main wall of the mosque on a line radiating from the spiritual center of Islam: Mecca.

The minbar is a rostrum for exhortation and preaching. Characteristically it is a projection at right angles to the main wall, often adjacent to the mihrab, with steps leading up to it. The Khatib speaks from the minbar. Because the sermon by the Khatib is only given at the time of the noon prayers on Friday the minbar is sometimes fitted with wheels so that it can be pushed into a recess when not in use.

Certain other features of a mosque deserve attention. The lack of an altar or special sanctuary and the limited furnishings are probably the first things to strike the Western visitor. Sometimes one can find a colonnade running at right angles to the mihrab and often the building is covered by a soaring dome. Decorations are limited to light fixtures, inscriptions from the Qur'an and mosaics depicting geometrical or floral motifs. Usually there is a large "sahn" (court) outside the mosque which is used for prayer on crowded occasions and when the outside climate is comfortable.

PHYSICAL ENVIRONMENT

MOSQUE COMPLEX

The mausoleum and zawiya of Sidi Bou Sa'id form a complex of buildings adjacent to the central square of the village that cannot go unnoticed. Although the architecture is similar in technology and materials to the rest of the village, the four whitewashed domes and the minaret towering above the adjacent buildings set the Mosque apart in a special manner.

The functional part of the Mosque is composed of a series of intimate interior and exterior spaces.

The vistas of the Bay of Tunis and the twin peaks of Djebel Bou Kornine are framed by the Arabic arches of the colonnade in the open prayer court and can be viewed equally as well from the

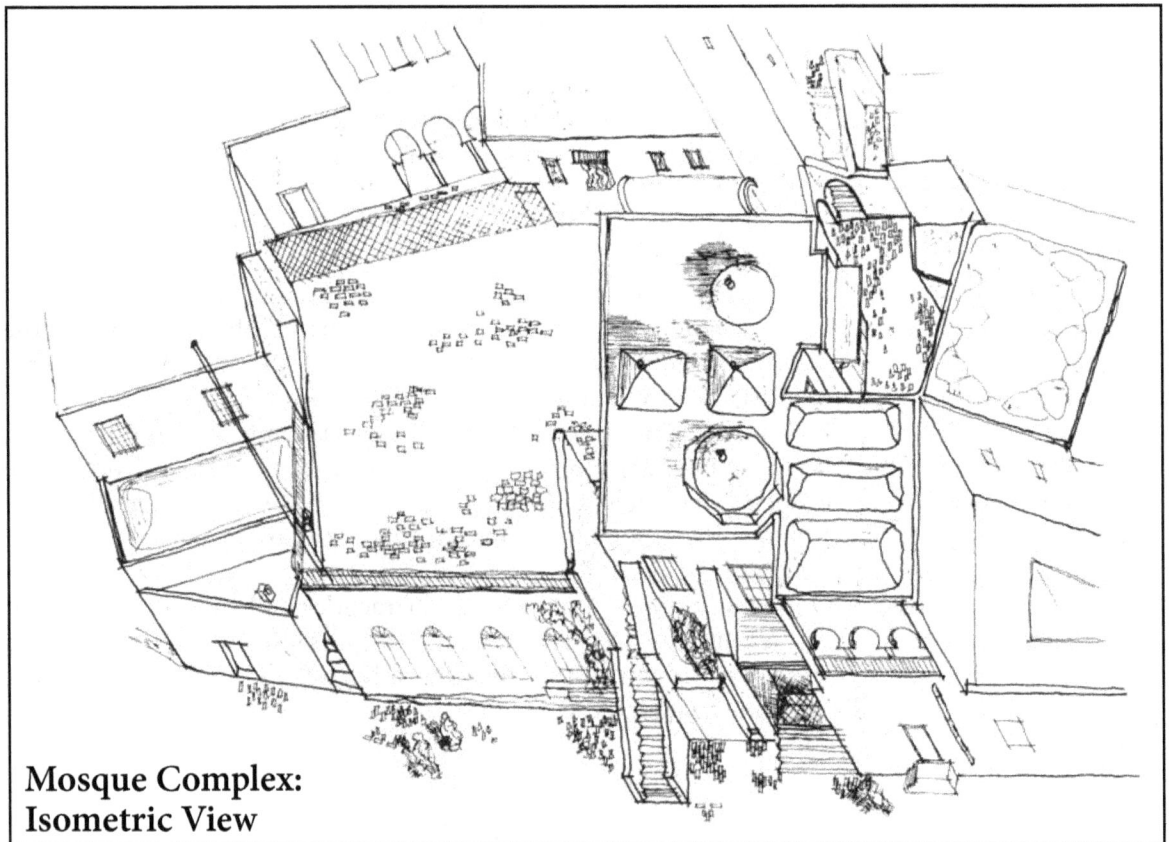

**Mosque Complex:
Isometric View**

Mosque Section and Minaret

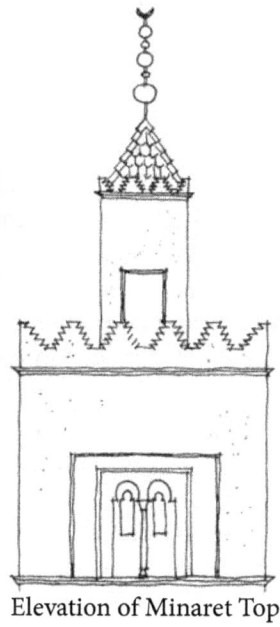

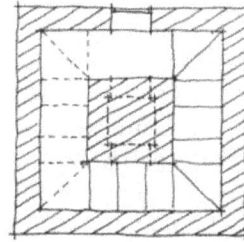

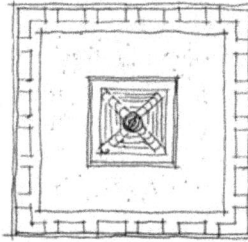

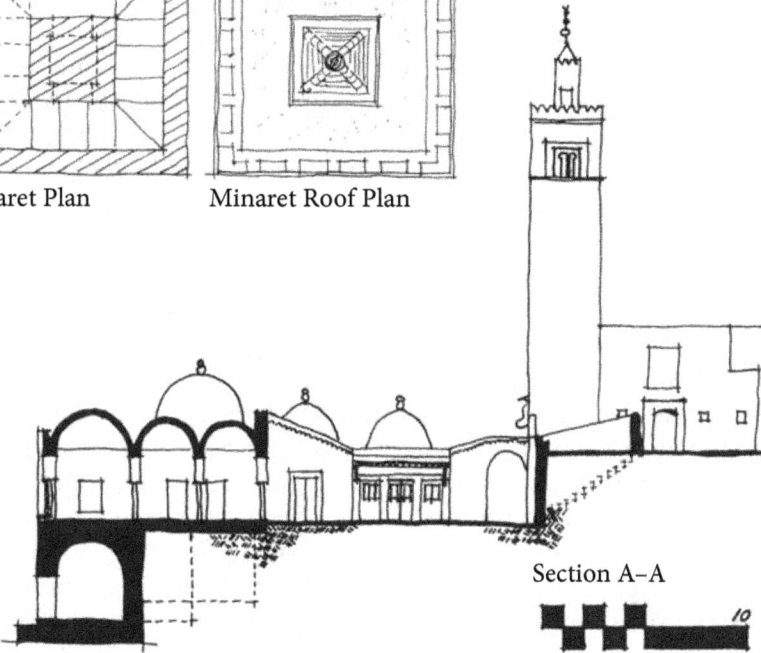

Minaret Plan

Minaret Roof Plan

Elevation of Minaret Top

Section A–A

Mosque Plan

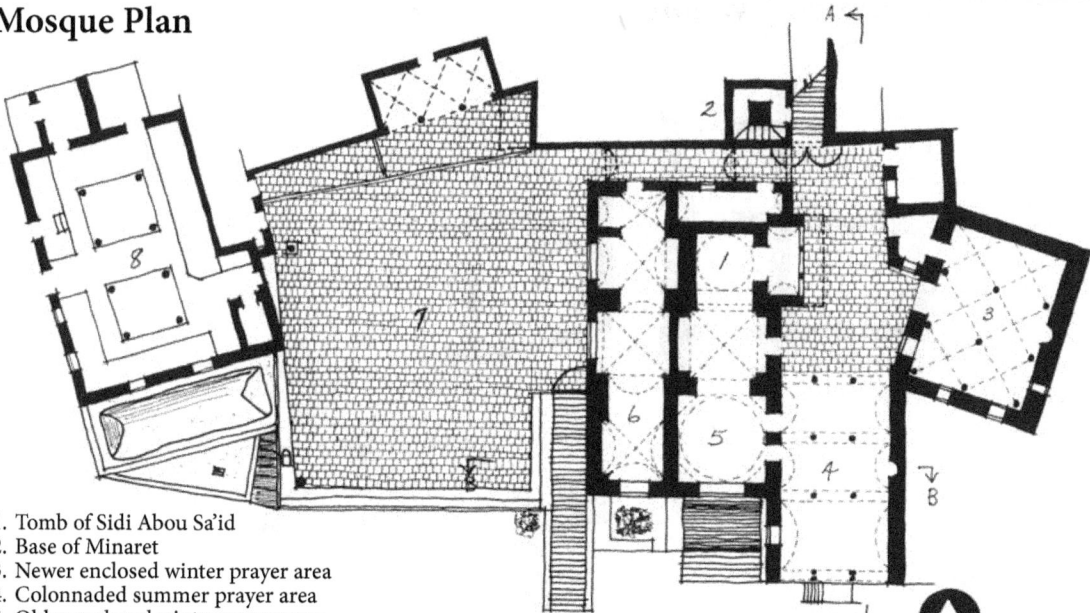

1. Tomb of Sidi Abou Sa'id
2. Base of Minaret
3. Newer enclosed winter prayer area
4. Colonnaded summer prayer area
5. Older enclosed winter prayer area
6. Tombs
7. "Sahn": open air raised plaza
8. Cafe des Nattes

Qibla

large open court of the sahn. These views are possible because of the careful attention paid to siting the building on the slope, which has a grade difference of 9.5 meters over its width and 5.8 meters between street level and that of the prayer court. The idea of having a view is somewhat unique to the mosque of Sidi Bou Sa'id for it is the common practice in Arabic-Islamic cities and villages that the mosque be inward looking and almost totally abutted onto by adjacent buildings.

The way in which the physical structure of the Mosque had been integrated with its neighboring buildings is a good example of the mixed land use so common in Arabic-Islamic towns. This integration developed in a natural way due to the steeply sloping site, a flexible attitude towards land use and an imaginative technique of massing the buildings to provide for the necessities of privacy, access, natural lighting and structure. It is quite a delight to notice how the mosque, the cafe, the shops and dwellings abutting the souk combine to make such visual and functional harmony.

The materials and methods used in constructing the Mosque do not differ from those used in the rest of the village. The structure is load bearing masonry, stuccoed on the exterior and whitewashed. For the most part the interior is also whitewashed although there are limited amounts of adornment and glazed tilework in the major enclosed prayer space and around the mihrab and the tomb of Abou Sa'id. Just about every type of vaulting is utilized in the structure of the building: intersecting barrel vaults on columns, barrel vaulting, domes on pendentives, domes without pendentives, groin vaulting and cloistered vaulting.

As it exists today the entrance to the Mosque is neither dominant nor distinguished. This is because the grand stairs which lead up from the main square to the Cafe des Nattes at one time served as the major ceremonial entrance, opening where the present cafe stands onto the open

Mosque Section and Elevation

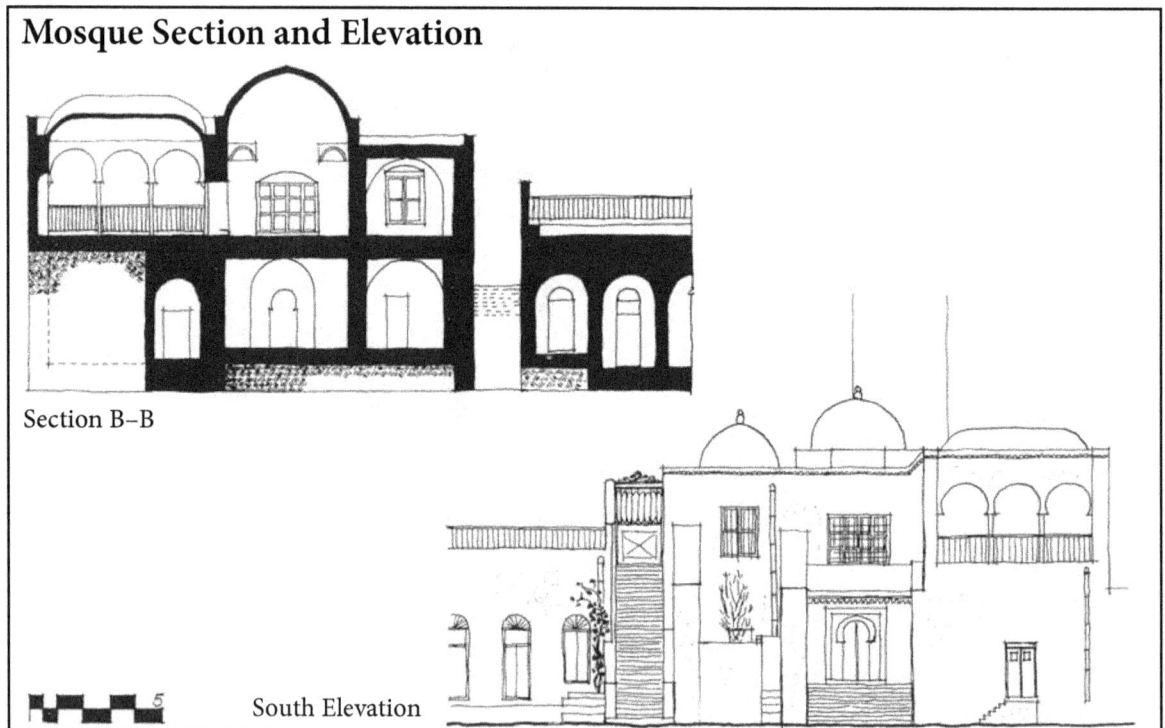

Section B–B

South Elevation

terrace. This entrance way served as a stronger link between the village square and the Mosque proper than the present side entrance composed of a narrow flight of stairs.

An interesting fact about the Mosque of Abou Sa'id is that its two mihrabs do not point in exactly the same direction. This is possibly due to the constraints imposed on the site by adjacent buildings. It would seem, however, that the mihrab of the newer, enclosed winter mosque is closer to the true direction to Mecca than that of the older summer prayer area—the former being approximately 6 degrees from the true direction to Mecca (which is 22°56' 46" South of East), while the latter is about 22 degrees off. Nevertheless both of these orientations fall well within the traditional allowable deviation from the true direction to Mecca.

The columns in the Cafe des Nattes and in the roofed summer prayer area of the Mosque are painted with spirals of red and green; red symbolizing the zealous struggle to spread Islam and green being the color of the prophet Mohammed's cloak.

SOUK AND SQUARE

The souk of Sidi Bou Sa'id consists of a series of small shops located on both sides of the main pedestrian street from the steps separating the pedestrian and vehicular area to the main stair at the foot of Cafe des Nattes.

To accommodate the change of elevation along the street, shops were grouped together and set on a series of steps each one consisting of two or three shops. Street front shops were either single storey building or two storey building with ground floor shop and second storey living quarters.

The size and shape of the shops were directly related to the material and skills available at the time of their construction. Stone was used for constructing bearing walls usually about 0.6 m thick and non load bearing walls about 0.4 m thick. Single vaults of brick construction was the usual method of roof construction, double vaults or cross-vaults being used for larger spans.

Where a second floor occurs, the top of the vaulted roof is filled with stone or brick and leveled to establish an even surface for the second floor.

The pedestrian path leading from the main entrance at the foot of the hill at Sidi Bou Sa'id terminates at the major nodal point at the foot of the stairs of the Cafe des Nattes. From here two other pedestrian linkages connect the square to the rest of the village. The accompanying sections show the general relationship between the square and the enclosing buildings.

SOUK ANALYSIS: SHOP SIZES

Shops can be categorized into three classes:
- (a) Small shops
- (b) Medium shops
- (c) Large shops

(a) SMALL SHOPS

These are minimum space shops only providing space within the shop for the storage of small quantities of merchandise and for access of a single person to view items for sale. These shops can only function in good weather conditions since all items are displayed on the open door and insufficient space exists for the process of bargaining so necessary for the purchase of any item. Shop size is usually about 1.5 m x 1.5 m with a maximum ceiling height of 2.9 m.

(b) Medium Shops

The size of such shops are adequate to provide sufficient space for the storage and display of merchandise along the wall and for movement of two persons for examining what is being offered for sale.

Merchandise on sale is usually displayed on the doors and walls on the street front with the process of bargaining occurring immediately outside the door or on the street.

The approximate size of such shops is usually 2.5 m wide by 4 m long with a .5 m wide system of shelves along three walls.

(c) Large Shops

Usually two medium-size shops are linked together by eliminating the common load bearing wall and replacing it with an arch to carry the two roof loads of the barrel vaults.

These shops have two exterior doors allowing for easy circulation within the shop.

Although merchandise is displayed on the open doors and exterior walls most of the merchandise sold is stored within the shop. The process of bargaining thus taking place inside the shop.

Shop size is about 3.5 m x 6 m with roof height of 3.5 m to 4 m.

SHOPPING STREET

The method of advertising and the process of bargaining are the two key ingredients in the sale of an item. Since the pedestrian street is where the majority of the shops occur the width of the street is important both to prospective buyers and to salesmen.

No two people can be separated by more than 4 m if they are to be able to discern each others facial expressions and carry on a conversation. This distance is important since within it a salesman can

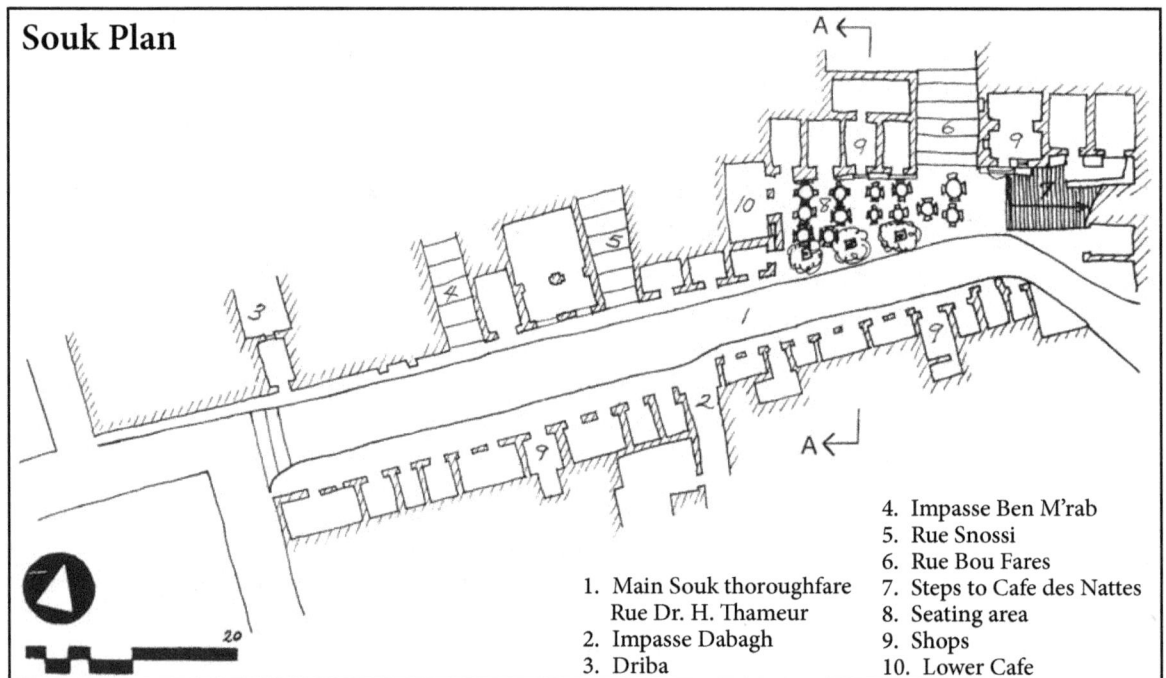

Souk Plan

1. Main Souk thoroughfare Rue Dr. H. Thameur
2. Impasse Dabagh
3. Driba
4. Impasse Ben M'rab
5. Rue Snossi
6. Rue Bou Fares
7. Steps to Cafe des Nattes
8. Seating area
9. Shops
10. Lower Cafe

tell whether a person is interested in an item or not by listening to remarks about what is displayed and by reading the facial expressions resulting from the effect of his advertised products.

The pedestrian street of Sidi Bou Sa'id falls within the 4 m limits explained above and therefore functions efficiently for the purpose of the souk.

SQUARE ANALYSIS

SIZE AND ENCLOSURE

The size of the square falls within the limits set out in footnote 2, on page 21 of Chapter 3 for recognizing familiar faces. Within this limit people in a space can relate to each other visually.

Together with size the second most important factor for the design of a square is the degree of enclosure. This is very important to provide a sense of place so necessary for encouraging people to pause and sit in a square. The enclosure around the square of Sidi Bou Sa'id is very subtly achieved because of the three major pedestrian routes leading from it. Except for the main pedestrian path leading to the square, there is complete visual enclosure of the square. This is achieved on the other two exits from the square by curving the path so that one cannot see beyond 20 m from the square. As previously discussed in Chapter 3, visual enclosure is dependant on the level of the eye and the horizontal and vertical angles of vision. Since the square along its longest diagonal measures only 25 m, and the height of the building measured in this direction is approximately 8 m, the view of

Souk Section and Elevation

North Elevation

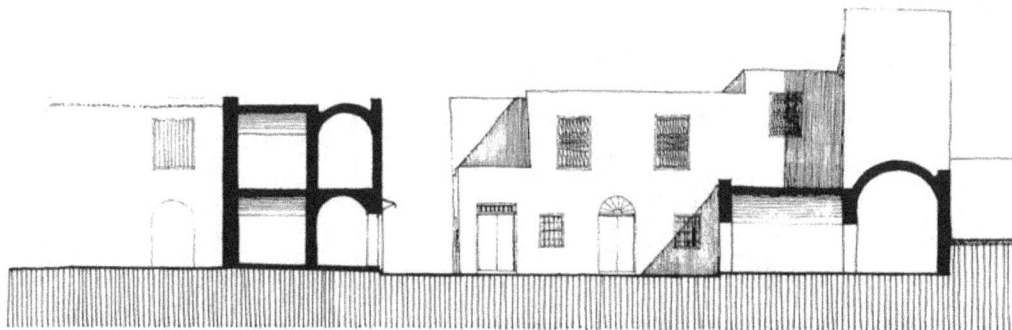

Section A–A

the eye is completely enclosed by the buildings. This sense of enclosure is further increased when a person sits at a table.

FUNCTION

The square takes on many different characters depending upon the time of day and the number of people present. Certainly it is at its most vibrant and exciting on a Friday night or Saturday in the summer when residents of Tunis and tourists visit Sidi Bou Sa'id to have coffee and relax. The only lighting provided at night is from the lights of the lower Cafe and the Cafe des Nattes supplemented by a small quantity of electric street lighting and, if the time of the month is right, moonlight. These lighting conditions coupled with the size of the square provide a pleasant environment for a relaxing evening. On a day or night when only a few people visit the square, its special circumfusion is lost.

SEATING

The aim of the seating layout in the square is to allow as many people as possible to sit down without obstructing major access routes or creating a formal atmosphere.

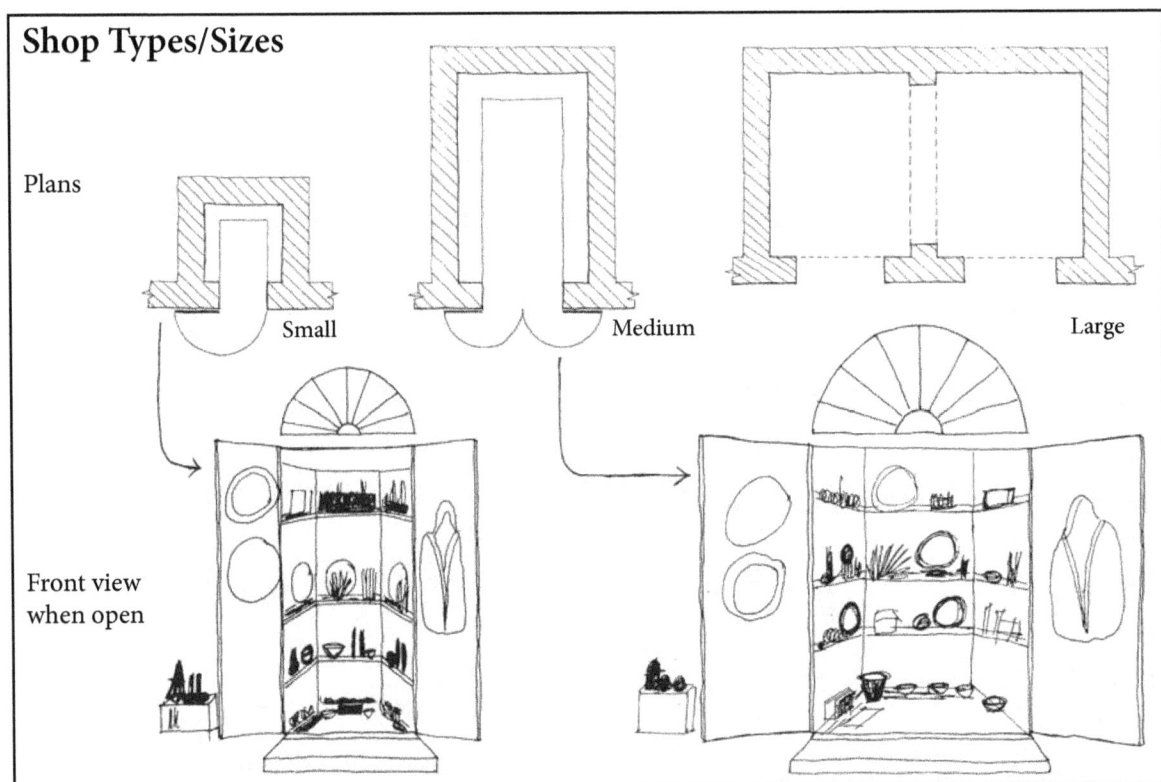

Shop Types/Sizes

Plans

Small

Medium

Large

Front view when open

Souk and Mosque

Top: Looking from Main Souk thoroughfare toward steps of Cafe des Nattes.

Right: Entrance to mosque and zawiya adjacent to minaret base.

Bottom: Three domes over Zawiya of Sidi Bou Sa'id.

CAFE DES NATTES

The prominent location of the Cafe des Nattes is primarily due to the fact that it was originally the communal space at the top of the main stair leading to the Mosque. When the door linking this space to the larger courtyard of the Mosque was sealed, the cafe was extended by constructing two covered decks at different levels on either side of the steps.

The difference between the Cafe des Nattes and other cafes of similar size lies not only in its plan but in its method of seating patrons, which consists of providing 1 meter high solid concrete pads covered with straw mats. The enclosed section of the cafe sits on a foundation of stone and its roof loads are transmitted to the ground by exterior stone walls and interior columns supporting wooden main beams and roof joists.

CAFE ANALYSIS

USE

The Cafe, although primarily used as a coffee house, is often used for a variety of special occasions because of its prominence in the town. The layout is not conducive to the provision of entertainment other than the traditional "malouf" which is easily staged on one of the central pads with the audience gathered around them on the outer seating pads.

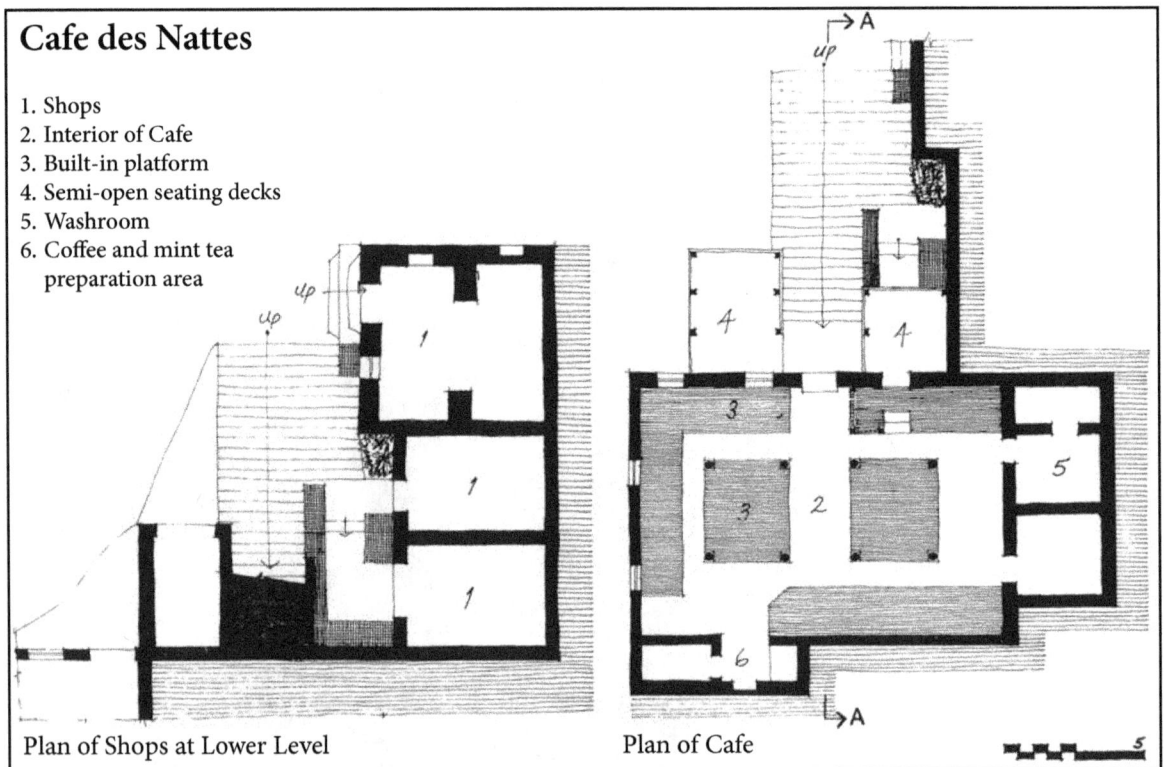

Cafe des Nattes

1. Shops
2. Interior of Cafe
3. Built-in platform
4. Semi-open seating decks
5. Washroom
6. Coffee and mint tea
   preparation area

Plan of Shops at Lower Level   Plan of Cafe

One of the most important features of life in the Cafe is the nightly card playing which can start anytime after 6:00 p.m. and continue until 1:00 a.m. Conventional tables and chairs are provided for the card players in the spaces between the pads and in the courtyards.

SEATING

Seating in the Cafe is provided by straw mats mounted on built-in platforms approximately one meter high. A customer is required to remove his footwear before mounting the sitting area if he plans to place his feet on the mats. There is a choice of two sitting positions. Usually if a customer is staying for only a short time he will sit with his legs hanging over the edge of the pad, while, if he is staying for a long time, he will remove his shoes and sit cross-legged. A third method of seating is provided by conventional tables and chairs which are made available in various parts of the cafe.

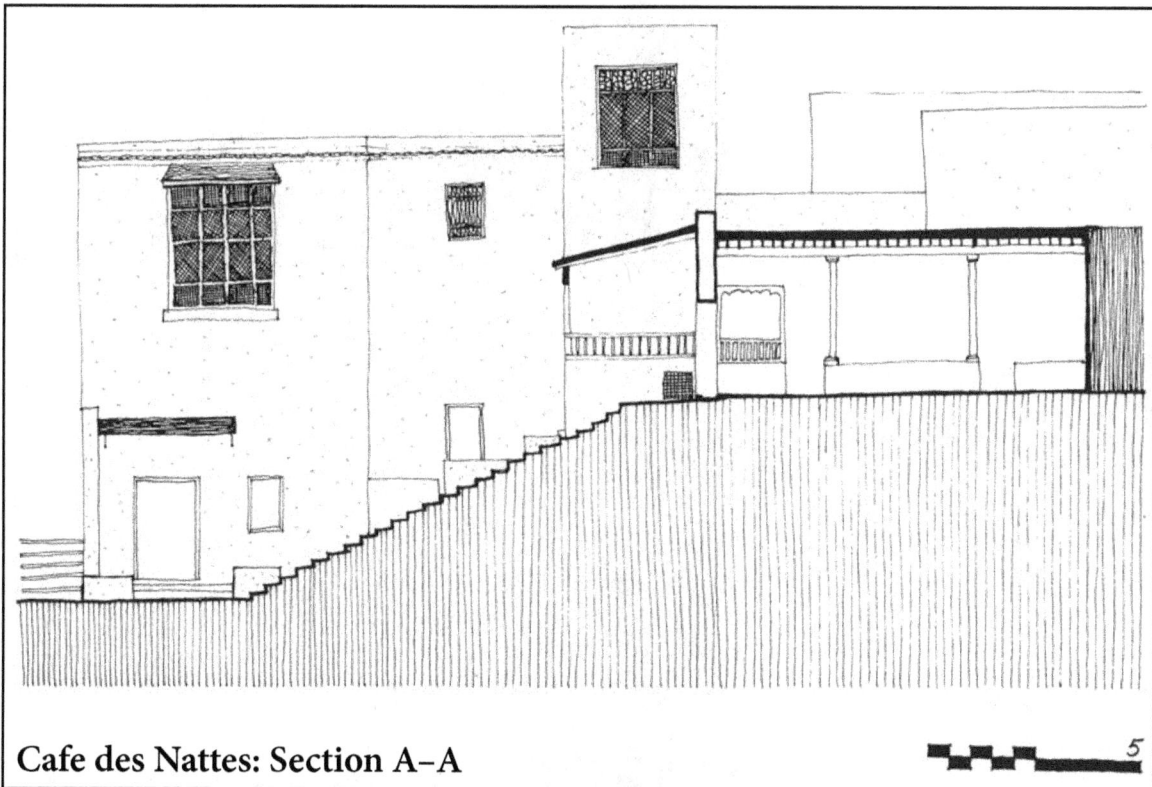

Cafe des Nattes: Section A–A

**Cafe des Nattes
and Village Square**

VIEW OF NEIGHBORING HOUSES FROM MINARET

CHAPTER 7

HOUSES

INTRODUCTION

Homes in Sidi Bou Sa'id vary from extravagantly ornate to impoverished. Of the grander homes, a few, remain intact as such, some as subdivided high rent apartments, some as crowded housing for the poor and still others as commercial or public facilities. Many of the medium scale homes remain as single living units owned by rich Tunisians for use as summer residences or as rental units (generally rented by Europeans). Homes originally built by the poor for themselves mainly kept that identity, unless bought in clusters and renovated to the more elaborate tastes of the rich. Some large, dilapidated homes are sometimes rented on a long term lease for the price of renovation thus reinitiating them into the upper echelons of Sidi Bou Sa'id society.

The house types studied in this chapter include two of major importance, two of modest and one of humble. We have attempted to record their uses and alterations through time in order to draw attention to the changes in community, lifestyle, decoration and technology which have taken place in the village. Although the examples chosen do not represent a complete catalogue of house types in Sidi Bou Sa'id they do form a sound basis for the study of traditional Arabic housing of this region.

The chapter begins with a sample of "Design Elements" from the primary zones of a typical house, regardless of its size. This is followed by highlighting the organizational principles which make a courtyard house function as a regulator of temperature. The five houses are then discussed and analyzed using a common format. The chapter ends with a comparative overview of the houses.

House Location Map

1. Dar Thameur
2. Dar Et-Toumi
3. Dar Cahen
4. Dar Abdel Kaffe
5. Dar Mrad

Dar Mohsen

TRADITIONAL ARAB HOUSING: TUNIS REGION
A SAMPLE OF DESIGN ELEMENTS

ENTRANCE

1. Driba (دريبة): A primary entrance vestibule or private lane. Allows "skifa" to be further removed from the street.

2. Skifa (سقيفة): A secondary entrance corridor or lobby with entry doors placed so that no one can see directly into the courtyard from the outside. Used in conjunction with a driba or another skifa. "Dukkana" (دكانة) or built-in bench is usually provided in the first skifa. Traditionally the male owner or occupant of the house received casual visitors or salesmen in the first skifa.

3. Ruqba (رقبة): A small unroofed space occurring at the end of a driba, at the junction of a driba and a skifa or at the junction of two skifas. Sometimes the location of a well.

COURT

4. Wust al-dar (وسط الدار): Private open courtyard in the center of the house. It could have a gallery "burtal" on one, two, three or four of its sides. It sometimes has a small water pool and/or fountain at its center. In rich houses a "majin" (ماجن) or cistern is built under the courtyard for collecting rainwater from the roofs.

5. Burtal (برطال): A colonnaded gallery off of a main courtyard, giving importance and sometimes sun protection to the main room, and/or giving access to services or stairs

6. Dwiriya (دويرية): A secondary courtyard in a service area joined to the main courtyard by a corridor. One of its sides is sometimes roofed by a "Burtal Dwiriya" (برطال دويرية) giving protection to a well. The Dwiriya is sometimes connected to the Makhzen the major space for storing bulky provisions, which is also accessible from the street.

ROOMS

7. Bit trida (بيت طريدة): The most common room type. It usually has no wall recesses. It occurs in rich and modest houses.

8. Bit bel-Kbu u mkasar (بيت بالقبو و مقاصر): The primary room in a rich or middle class house. It is usually located opposite the entrance and could have a colonnaded gallery in front of it.
The room is divided into:

- a central alcove called "Kbu" (قبو) where there is usually built-in seating and elaborate wall and ceiling decorations. It is used as the primary living area where close relatives or friends are received.
- two small rooms symmetrically located on each side of the kbu and called "maqsura" (مقصورة) (singular). They are used as bedrooms.
- two opposite alcoves used for built-in beds and/or storage. The built-in beds could occur on one or both sides, and are usually framed with a decorative wooden structure and called "Hanut Hajjam" (حانوت حجام), literally translated as 'Barber's shop'. The reason is because they look like the decorative fronts of barber shops found in Tunisia.

SERVICE

9. Matbkha (مطبخة): Kitchen   10. Kommaniya (كمانية): Pantry   11. Mihad (ميحاض): Toilet

Design Elements

Entrance

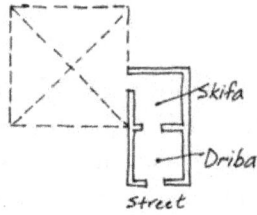
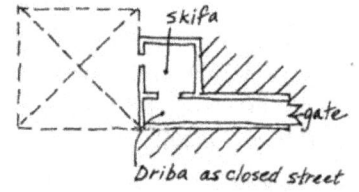

Courts

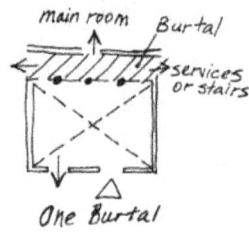
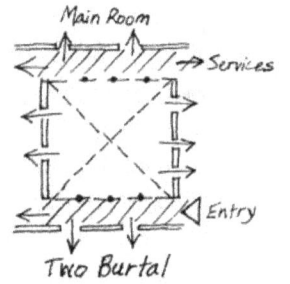

Rooms

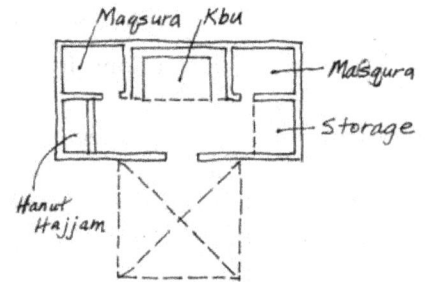

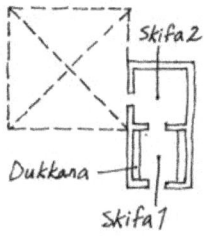

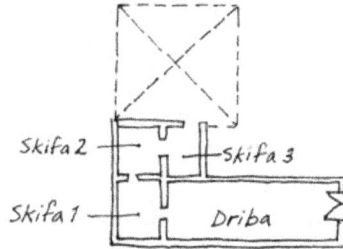

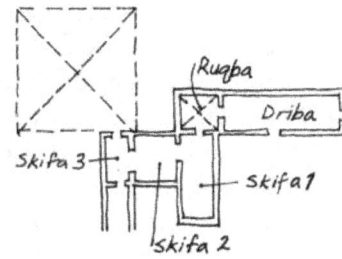

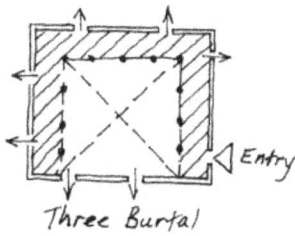

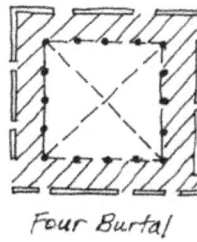

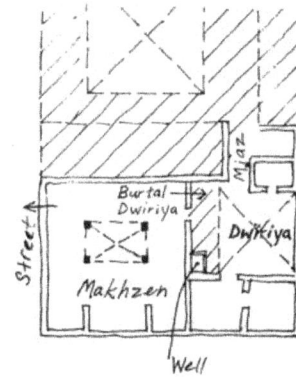

Service

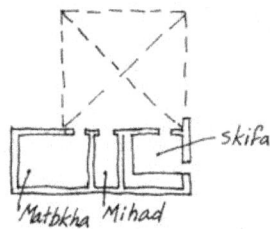

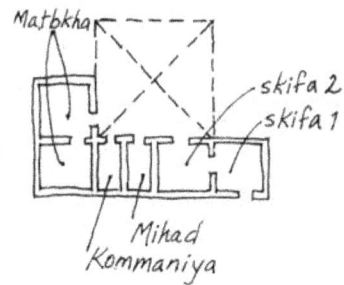

THE COURTYARD AS A TEMPERATURE REGULATOR

The courtyard of a house works best as temperature regulator when:
- The height is greater than the width (sketch 1, opposite).
- The higher the walls in relation to the width of the courtyard the greater the amount of shade that will be provided (sketches 2 & 3). Lateral distance of shade on courtyard surfaces for all five houses studied are indicated for the summer and winter solstices in the chart below.
- The courtyard acts as a reservoir for cool air which flows down from the roof at night and provides extra wall surface to reradiate heat from inside (sketches 4 & 5).
- High walls hamper air circulation in the courtyard thus preventing the dissipation of the cool night air collected near the ground. They also protect the courtyard from occasional uncomfortable windy conditions (sketches 6 & 7).
- Vegetation is often used to increase the amount of shade in a courtyard. Unless such planting is extensive it will not make an appreciable difference in the amount of radiant energy received by the walls (sketches 8 & 9).
- In Arab houses windows to the outside are placed high on the wall, mainly for privacy. The courtyard windows however are placed low to the ground. Cross ventilation of a room can be obtained by allowing hot air to escape to the street and be replaced by cooler air from the courtyard (sketch 10).

$L = H \cot \theta$

Where: L = Lateral Distance of shade on courtyard surface.
H = Height of courtyard
θ = 75° (Summer Solstice in Sidi Bou Sa'id).
28° (Winter Solstice in Sidi Bou Sa'id).
cot 75° = .27
cot 28° = 1.88

Name of House	Courtyard Height (H)	Lateral Distance of Shade	
		Summer Solstice	Winter Solstice
Dar Thameur	5.5 m	1.5 m	10.3 m
Dar et Toumi	5.5 m	1.5 m	10.3 m
Dar Cahen	4.2 m	1.1 m	7.9 m
Dar Abdel Kaffe	5.0 m	1.4 m	9.4 m
Dar Mrad	3.9 m	1.1 m	7.3 m

Lateral Distance of Shade Created by Courtyard Walls, on the Summer Solstice (June 22) and the Winter Solstice (December 22).

Courtyard as a Temperature Regulator

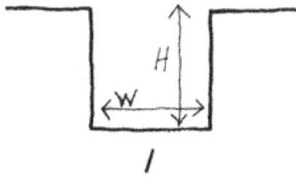
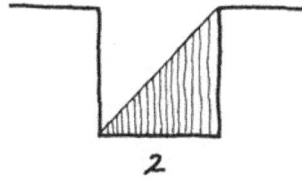
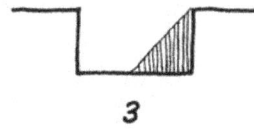

1

2

3

Night   DAY

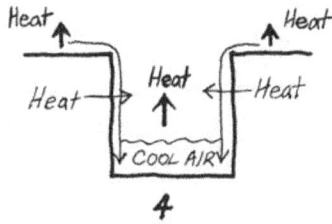
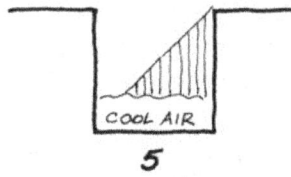

4

5

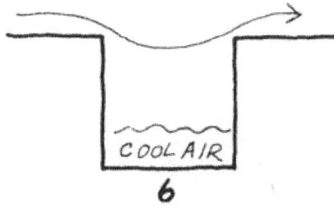
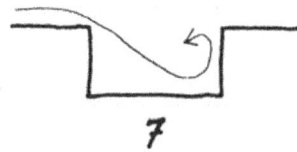

6

7

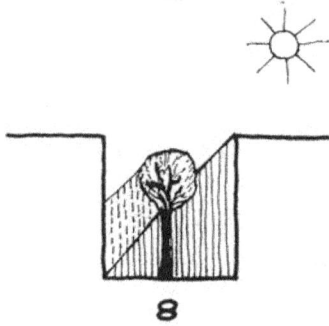
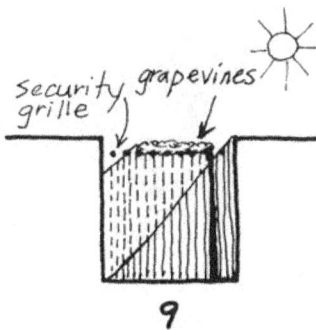

8

9

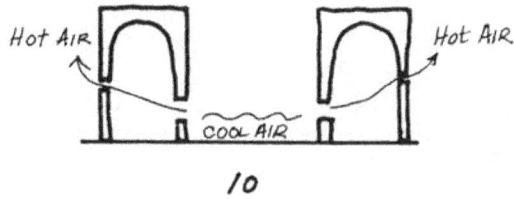

10

DAR THAMEUR

Construction Date: circa 1820

Classification: a rich man's summer house   **Designer/Builder:** unknown

Original owner: Bey Mahmud bin Ali   **Present owner:** Thameur Family

Occupants: the artist Ben Zarrouk and his wife occupy the house full time while the Thameur Family occupies it only part time.

History: The privileged site at the foot of the Zawiya Mosque was chosen by Bey Mahmud bin Ali (1814–1824) as the site of his summer residence. This residence (ca. 1820) was originally quite small but, over the years, has been gradually enlarged by the acquisition of smaller neighboring residences and the addition of a second storey over part of the main level.

In the middle of the last century, the enlarged palace was bought by a rich Tunisian family, the Thameurs, from the Princess Zoubeida, the Bey's daughter.

Because of the Bey's simple tastes, the palace was originally only sparsely decorated although its style and design was considered in the late 19th century to be a symbol of almost inimitable luxury. When the Thameurs bought the palace they paved the original bare courtyard with marble and covered its walls with decorative clay tiles. The Thameurs also added the partial second storey with its reception room which could be entered by a set of private stairs on the patio-side of the house.

Although today the house has been divided into four apartment units, the main floor, including the courtyard, remains the summer residence of the Thameurs.

SOCIO-CULTURAL

Past users of the main house include Bey Mahmud bin Ali, his family and entourage while his guests and unmarried sons would have lived in the upper apartments. Present user of the main house is the Thameur Family while the artist Ben Zarrouk and his wife use the upper apartments.

Privacy: The house is turned in onto its courtyard and has no ground floor windows except on the south side which is visually protected by a steep slope to the water. On the north the courtyard and main house are protected by the height of the upper apartments.

Security: A high degree of security is afforded by iron grills on all windows and over the secondary court on the east side of the house. Guards used to be posted at the stable entrance and at the main driba.

ENVIRONMENT

Land Use: Except for a small garden on the south side of the house, the whole site is occupied by the building.

Vegetation: The garden contains grass, shrubs and olive trees although there is no vegetation in the courtyard.

Views: From the house there are splendid views of the mountains and the Gulf of Carthage while the views in the upper apartments take in Tunis and the Mosque.

Natural Lighting: Because the major windows face south the house escapes the hottest sun in summer but gets the maximum benefit from the sun in winter.

Humidity: Humidity levels are good in the upper apartments and unknown in the main house.

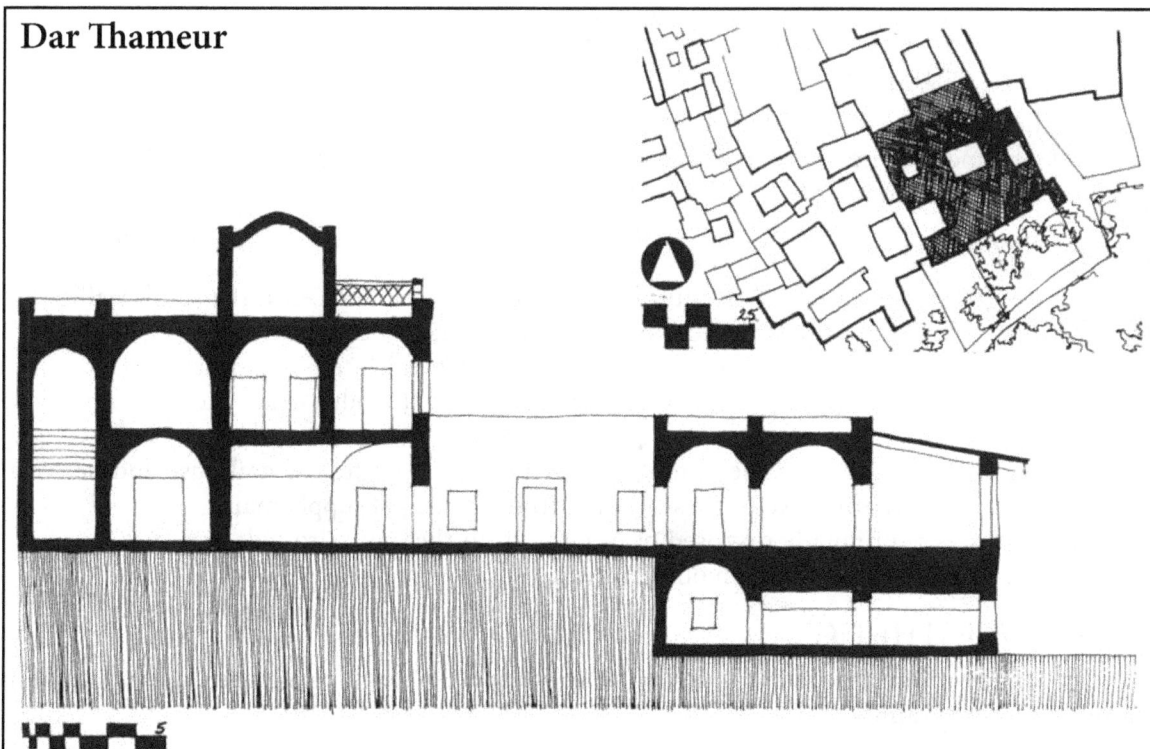

Dar Thameur

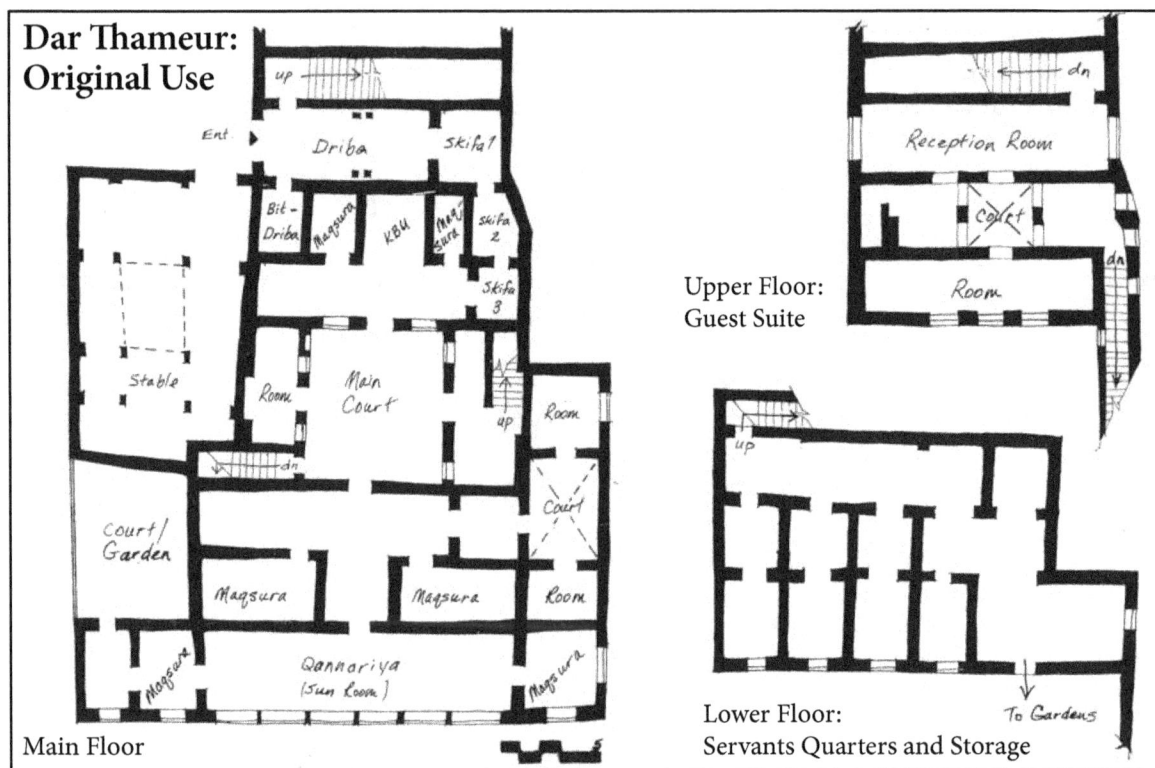

Dar Thameur: Original Use

Main Floor — *Ent., Driba, Skifa1, Bit-Driba, Maqsura, KBU, Maqsura, Skifa 2, Skifa 3, Stable, Room, Main Court, Room, Court/Garden, Maqsura, Maqsura, Room, Court, Maqsura, Qannariya (Sun Room), Maqsura*

Upper Floor: Guest Suite — *Reception Room, Court, Room*

Lower Floor: Servants Quarters and Storage — *To Gardens*

TECHNOLOGY/SERVICES

Construction Type: Load bearing masonry structure with brick vaulted roofs. Exterior finish is lime and sand mortar finished with a lime whitewash whereas the interior finish is lime mortar or ceramic tile or earthenware tile.

PRESENT CONDITION:

Main House: There is evidence of structural failure of courtyard walls and the south wall of the main court is bulging and needs reinforcing. There are cracks in the lintels of several doors and windows and the brickwork of the courtyard is beginning to deteriorate somewhat.

Upper Apartments: Although some of the finishes are deteriorating due to age there is no evidence of structural failure.

Water Service: Originally from the cistern collected from rainwater for daily use and personal hygiene. Drinking water from wells. Present water from municipal supply mains.

Sewage: Wastes were originally disposed of in pits within the main grounds and gardens of the house. Today they are fed to the main public sewer.

SENSUAL/AESTHETIC

From the exterior, Dar Thameur has an anonymous appearance which allows it to blend in with the rest of the community.

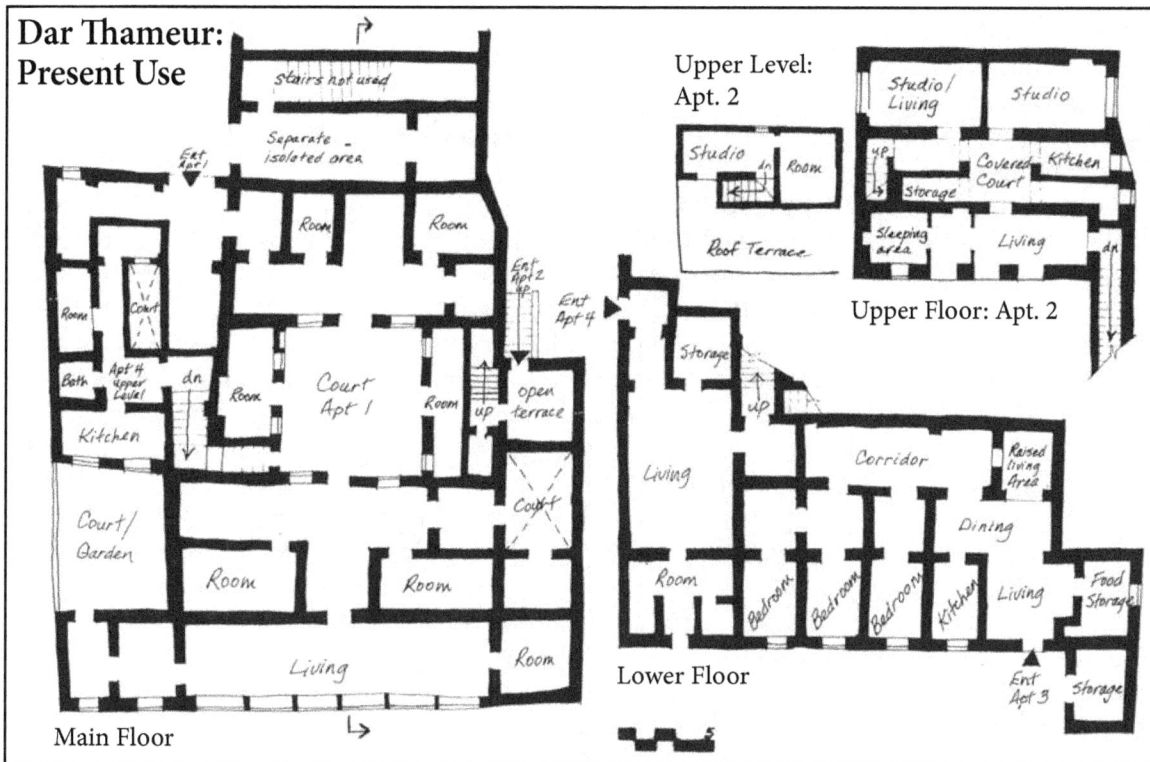

Dar Thameur: Present Use — Main Floor; Upper Level: Apt. 2; Upper Floor: Apt. 2; Lower Floor

Of the four apartments the Zarrouk apartment has all the original floorings of black and white marble tiles and the original wall tiles of the "tiger paw" design. Because of three large windows overlooking the courtyard and the Bay of Tunis the front of the apartment has an open, airy feeling. A sense of openness is also evident in the two rooms at the back due to their proportions and large windows.

It was not possible to enter the main house of Dar Thameur although it was possible to see the tilework and flooring of the courtyard placed in by the first Thameurs. There is no vegetation in the courtyard and there is no protective screen over it. This is the main apartment of the complex.

A third apartment has been built in the previous storage rooms. Although the old brick vaults have been painted white the rooms still feel dark, damp and cave-like. The floors are paved with stone slabs. The rooms facing the garden all have windows making them very personal spaces.

The fourth apartment is to one side of the rest of the house, and more recently renovated. It is an 'open air' house as its partially covered courtyard serves as the circulation/corridor space. In the part which belonged to the Thameur's main residence the walls are covered with beautiful tiles. In the later additions the walls are left plain and the floors are covered with "swallow's wing" tiles. Because it is made of various sections of the original house, this apartment is not a complete, well-defined unit as the others are.

DAR ET-TOUMI

Construction Date: circa 1850
Classification: a rich man's summer home   **Designer/Builder**: unknown
Original Owner: Cheikh Ech-Cherif   **Present Owner**: M. Albrecht
Occupants: paying hotel guests
Alterations: renovated in 1931 to transform original house from a summer residence into a hotel.
History: built during the same period (mid 19th century) as Dar Mohsen (present Municipality offices of Sidi Bou Sa'id), both summer residences marked the village extensions—Dar et-Toumi towards the east and Dar Mohsen towards the west (see location map on page 120) . Prior to 1831 the palace of Mahmud Bey and the residences of his secretary general and personal body guard were located on the site. Cheikh Mohamed ech-Cherif el-Gorchi chose this location for his summer residence as it was adjacent to the Zawiya-Mosque, a holy place he liked to frequent.

Inherited by Cheikh ech-Cherifs son, after his father's death at the turn of the century, the home was abandoned and left to decay. Tahar ben Hassen ech-Cherif sold the property to his maternal uncle, Mostafa et-Toumi giving the home another name. The present owner, M. Albrecht from Switzerland, bought the building in 1965, calling it 'Hotel Dar Zarrouk' after the restaurant section of the hotel situated opposite.

The home had no upper stories except a small area used as a retreat. Renovations to Dar et-Toumi were done in the traditional approach of rich city dwellers—i.e., not fearing the addition of new elements but using great care, evident in the adaptation, evolution and originality. Fortunately for the building M. Albrecht has executed much of his renovation in a like manner. Throughout its history Dar et-Toumi, although much altered was never enlarged.

SOCIO-CULTURAL

Past Users: (1) Cheikh ech-Cherif, his family and entourage, (2) Cheikh et-Toumi, his family and entourage.
Present Users: hotel staff, director and guests.
Privacy: Maintained by a high retaining wall along the lower terrace and dense plantings in the garden. Windows of the ground floor reception room detract from privacy. The family quarters are protected by gardens and a driba from the reception area. The degree of privacy is good.
Security: Iron grills on all windows, heavy wood bolts on all doors. Main gate of iron grillwork. Terrace retaining wall is steep enough to deny access on that side of house. No fence around open garden. Security measures appear to be sufficient.

ENVIRONMENT

Land Use: Site has been formed into three terraces: highest one is occupied by stable, middle one is occupied by main house and lowest contains garden.
Vegetation: Extensive planting (bushes and flowers) on south side of house. Grape vines wrap around a trellis in courtyard.
Views: South, to gardens, Gulf of Carthage and Hammam-Lif. West, minaret of Mosque complex.
Natural Lighting: Generally good in all parts of building. Trees on south side of building reduce solar penetration in summer.

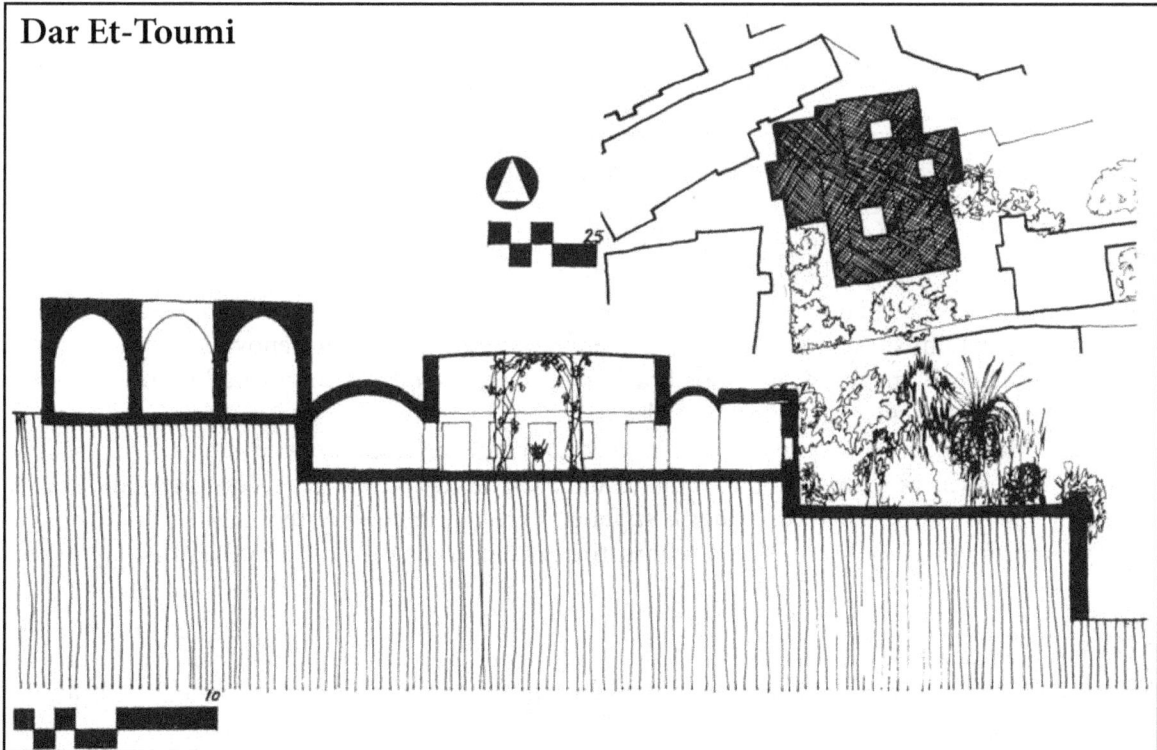

Dar Et-Toumi

Dar Et-Toumi: Original Use

1. Druj
2. Driba
3. a. Bit al-Driba
   b. Bit Diwani
4. Makhzen
5. Rwa
6. Skifa
7. Bit u Mkaser
8. Dwiriya
9. Matbkha
10. Bit el-Khdem
11. Bit
12. Wust el-Dar
13. Bit Diwani
14. Mjaz
15. Bit Bel Kbu u Mkaser
16. Mak'ad
17. Mkaser

Original use plan after
Revault, J., 1974.

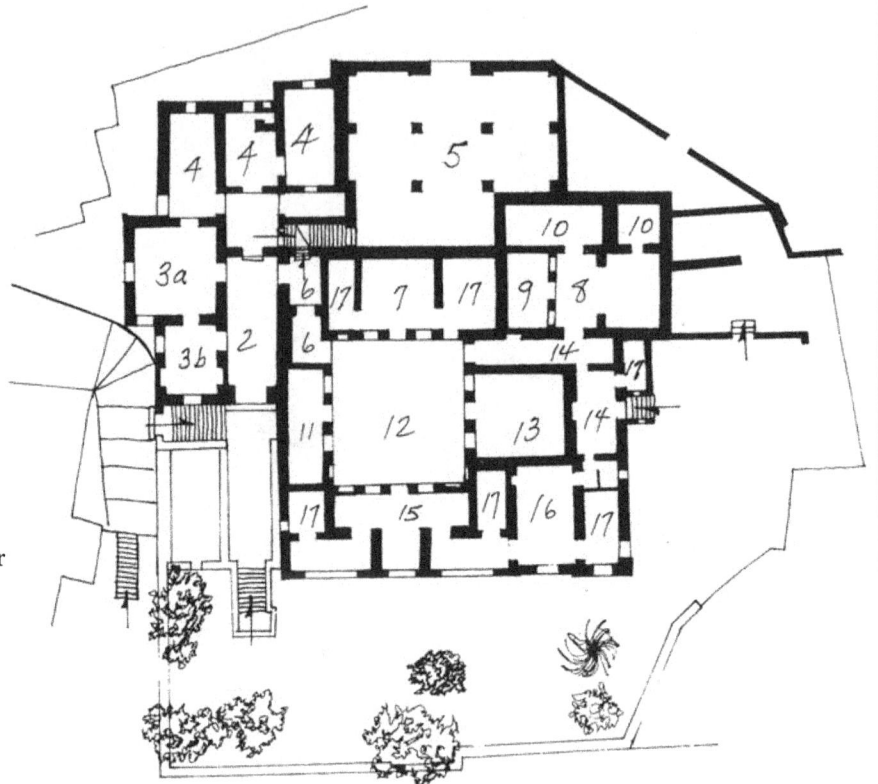

Humidity: Building seemed slightly damp on the inside. Possibly caused by much of courtyard being covered and shaded.

TECHNOLOGY/SERVICES

Construction Type: Load bearing masonry walls with masonry vaults (50 cm + for original). Stable has masonry columns with masonry groin vaults. Walls added during renovations are non-load bearing masonry (8 cm thick). Exterior finish is lime and sand mortar covered with whitewash. Interior finish is cement stucco with clay tiles.
Present Condition: No evidence of leaks or structural failure. In excellent repair.
Water Services: Cistern, collecting rain water from roof, under courtyard. Accessible by an opening on north side of courtyard. Today water is supplied by the municipal system.
Sewage: Originally disposed into pits within the garden area. Today it is linked into municipal system.

SENSUAL/AESTHETIC

Space: Dar et-Toumi still gives one the image of a grand Arabian summer home. The beautiful gardens and grand entrance lobby speak of the richness of its past. The character of the building

Dar Et-Toumi: Present Use

1. Stairs
2. Entry Hall
3. Salon
4. Reception
5. Office
6. Kitchen
7. Storage
8. Garage
9. Courtyard
10. Bedroom
11. WC
12. Ironing
13. Second Court
14. Laundry
15. Corridor

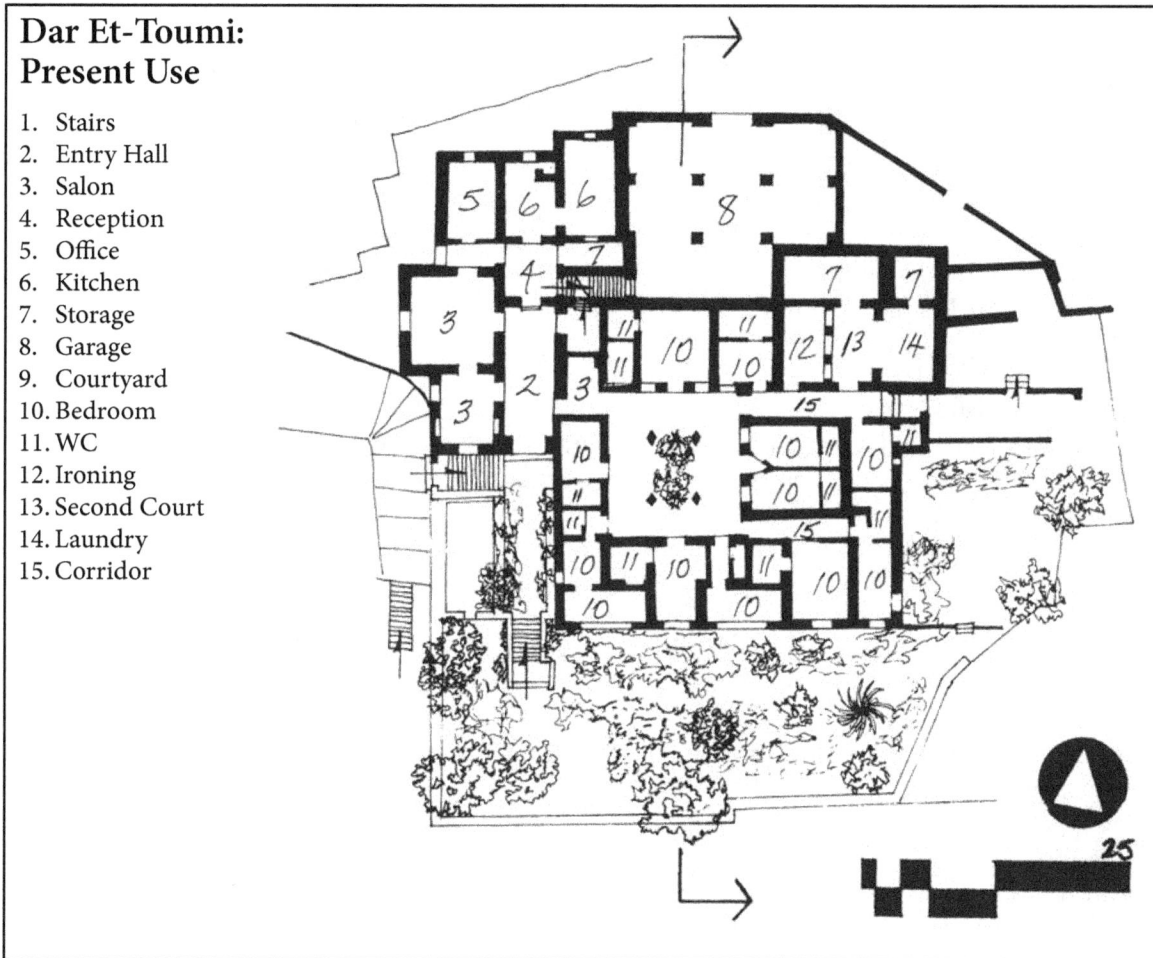

has been maintained by retaining as much of the original decoration as possible in wall and floor tiling, vaulting and stonework.

In the larger rooms which have been subdivided, the grand scale has been maintained by utilizing the original vaults. In small corridors where the height would have been too great, traditional wood joist ceilings have been used to be in keeping with the rest of the building.

A semi roof of corrugated iron has been added in the courtyard giving it an enclosed feeling quite uncommon to an Arabic courtyard. Standing in this courtyard one does not feel that one is outside. This is the one departure from the traditional Arabic use of space.

Color: The original tiling of Dar et-Toumi has been retained where possible. These tiles add greatly to the character of the building. The main lobby still has its original earthenware tiles while the courtyard is paved in white marble. In other places where the floor has been replaced, broken blue and white tiles have been set in concrete to add color. The wall tiling in the courtyard is very well preserved providing a pleasant contrast to the dull colors of the flooring, and the sandstone frames of the doors and windows. In places the relief carving has been highlighted with black paint.

DAR CAHEN

Construction Date: Original part before 1831; additions circa 1920
Classification: a year round residence (modest)   **Designer/Builder**: unknown
Original Owner: Lasram Family   **Present Owner**: Baron D'Erlanger (Jr.)
Occupants: Paul and Martin Cahen
History: Original portion of Dar Cahen, now a sewing room and child's bedroom, was part of Dar Lasram which was built for Cheikh Mohamed Lasram and his family. Dar Lasram and its surrounding buildings were bought by Baron D'Erlanger (Sr.) in about 1900. Sewing room and bedroom of Dar Lasram became part of a self contained flat in 1920.

SOCIO-CULTURAL

Past Users: Possibly servants of Dar Lasram (old section).
Present Users: Professional French family, Mr. and Mrs. Cahen.
Privacy: South side protected by extensive gardens. Courtyard overlooked by houses on north side. Major entrance is through large garden.
Security: Iron grills on all windows. Iron brace on main door. No grill over courtyard.

ENVIRONMENT

Land Use: House occupies a corner of the previous palace Dar Lasram, facing onto large gardens at the edge of the town. Site slopes from NE to SW. Northwest corner of house touches the adjacent building.
Vegetation: Large gardens overgrown with cacti, olive trees and bushes. Medium size orange trees in courtyard.
Views: Lake of Tunis from child's bedroom and sewing room. Garden and Bay of Carthage, from living room window.
Natural Lighting: Daylight is not adequate in master bedroom and the rooms on the east of the house. Courtyard receives adequate sunlight. Old section catches afternoon sun.

Dar Cahen

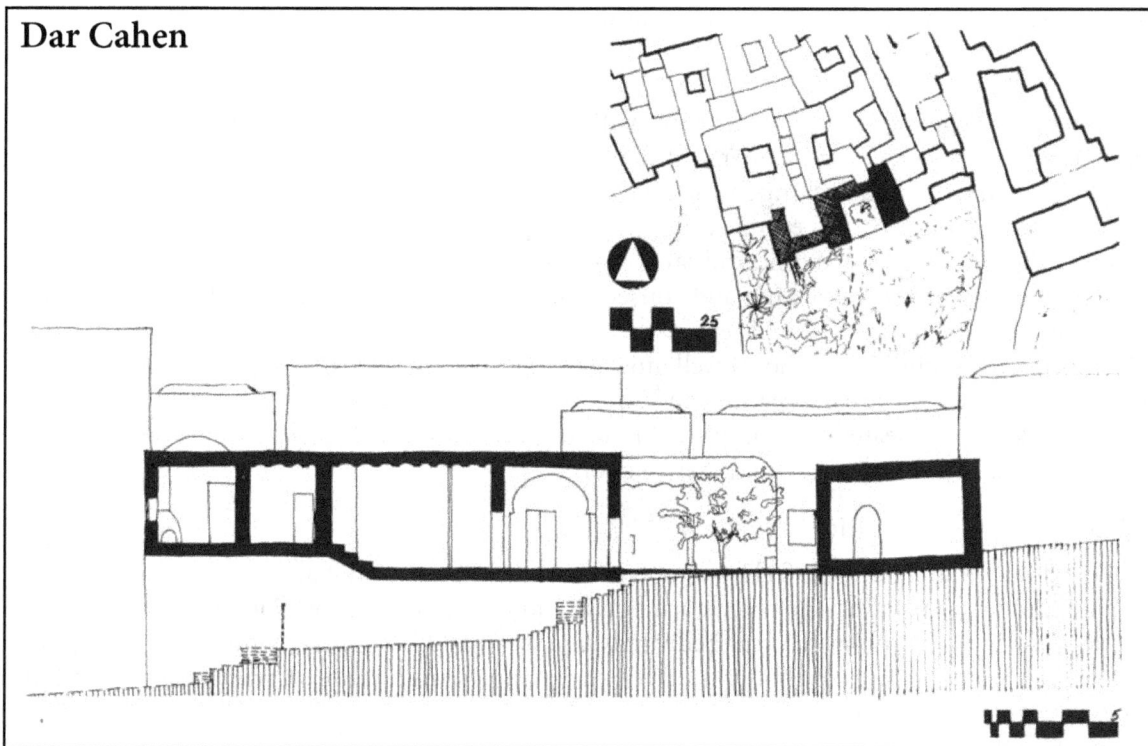

Dar Cahen

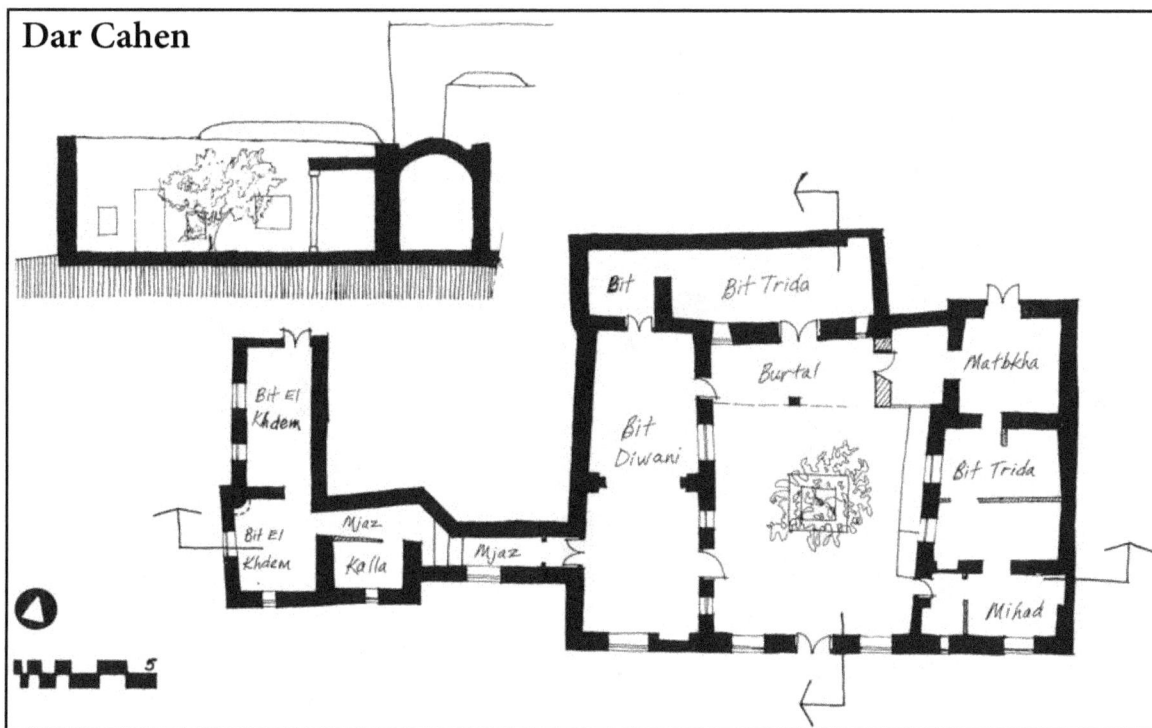

Humidity: Fair, some moisture creep in walls during winter.

TECHNOLOGY/SERVICES

Construction Type: Load bearing masonry with jack arches (shallow brick vaulting between steel joists at approximately 75 cm centers) in newer section. Load bearing masonry vault in sewing room. Wooden joists and decking in child's room.

Interior finishes: stucco and ceramic tile.

Exterior finish: whitewashed lime and sand mortar.

Present Condition: Some cracking and consequent leaking at south end of western wall in living room. House in reasonable state of repair.

Water service: Originally from local well, now from municipality.

Sewage: Originally disposed in garden and street, now flushed into municipal system.

Heating: Originally heated by a fireplace in old section. Presently kerosene heater in old section and a centralised hot water system in new section.

SENSUAL/AESTHETIC

Space: the courtyard gives the feeling of openness and coolness, and it acts more as a garden than as a traditional courtyard. The rooms are not spacious but are comfortable in winter as well as summer. Some of the rooms, such as bedrooms, are small and have small windows

Color: most of the color in the house is derived from applied decoration. There are no colored tiles except for those in the courtyard.

DAR ABDEL KAFFE

Construction Date: Circa 1765
Classification: Modest summer house   **Designer/Builder:** Unknown
Original Owner: Unknown   **Present Owner:** Abdel Kaffe
Occupants: Summer: Abdel Kaffe. Winter: Gill and Catherine
History: Dar Kaffe was built as a modest summer residence about 200 years ago on the site of an old Roman Villa. The owner lived in the rooms on one side of the courtyard while his wives lived in the rooms on the opposite side. To the west of the house was a large garden overlooking Dar Mohsen towards Tunis. The garden contained many Roman relics from the site on which it was built. In 1906 the house and the adjacent garden was bought by a French Colonialist who did a lot of renovations and added rooms to the top of the house.

SOCIO-CULTURAL

Past Users: Modest Tunisian family. French Colonialist family. In the original house the men occupied the west side and the women occupied the remainder.
Present Users: Winter–French corporant. Summer–upper middle class Tunisian family who use the complete house.
Privacy: House looks inward to courtyard except for windows on west side. (Privacy was sacrificed for view). House is cut off from public by garden and foliage. South wall is shared.

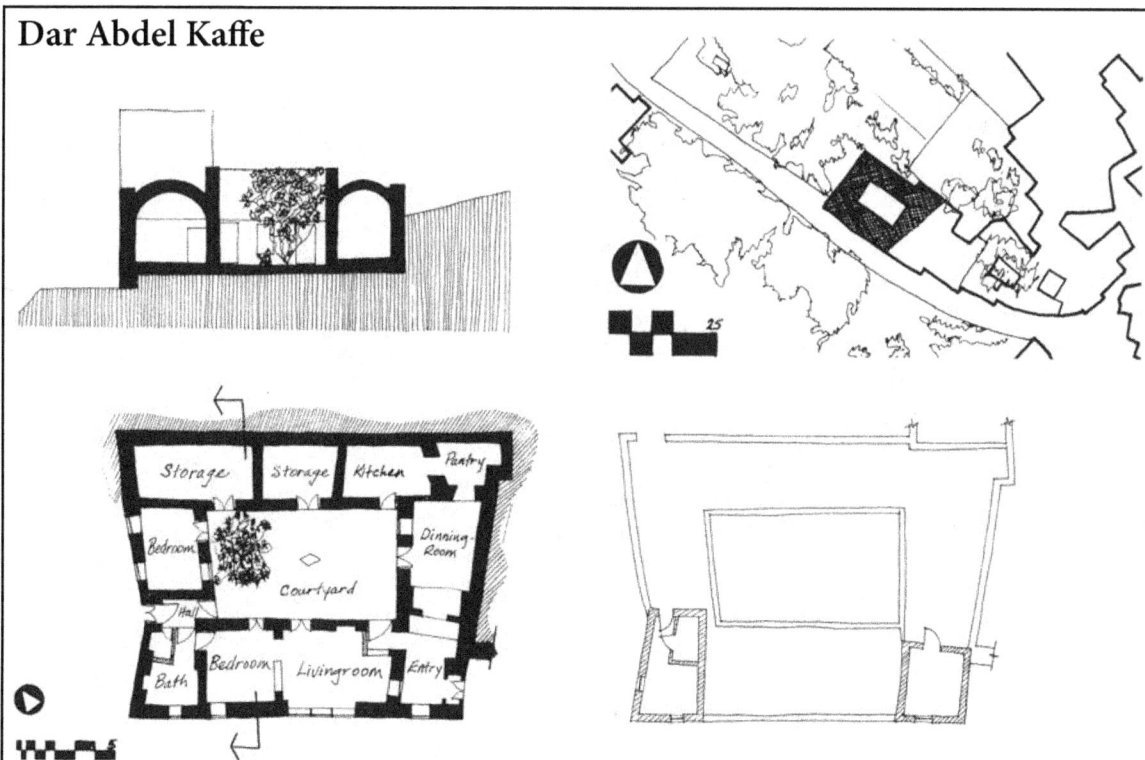

Dar Abdel Kaffe

Security: Iron grills on all windows. Heavy wooden bolts on exterior door with iron braces. Wrought iron gates inside wooden doors. Iron grills over courtyard. Degree of security excellent.

ENVIRONMENT

Land Use: House built on southwest corner of lot sharing the wall of a neighboring house. East wall built into the hill. Rest of site is occupied with sloping gardens.

Vegetation: Numerous olive trees and low bushes in garden. Grape vines on north side of courtyard.

Views: West to the lake of Tunis from men's quarters.

Natural Lighting: Day lighting good in all parts of house except for east side (embankment). Sunlight does not enter house except in men's quarters in late summer. The courtyard's two storey extension provides shade in the summer.

Humidity: Poor. Moisture creeps up all walls in winter due to lack of damp-proof coursings.

TECHNOLOGY/SERVICES

Construction Type: Load bearing masonry with masonry vaults.

Exterior finishes: stucco.

Interior finishes: Ceramic tile and stucco.

Present Conditions: No evidence of structural failure. Leaks in kitchen roof. In reasonable repair.

Water Services and Sewage: Presently municipal supply.

Heating: None, except that provided by one gas heater.

SENSUAL/AESTHETIC

Space: The rooms give the impression of being large and cool, reinforcing the information that it was built solely for a summer residence. Privacy within the house is poor, the sleeping area is part of the living room.

Color: The large amounts of tiling and its variety provides relief from the whiteness. Most of the rooms use a great deal of blue tiling which gives the impression of coolness in the summer.

DAR MRAD

Construction Date: unknown
Classification: a modest year-round dwelling
Designer/Builder: unknown
Original Owner: (?) Mrad
Present Owner: Brahim Ben Mrad.
Occupants: Alain Chandler and Noël Stremdöerfer
History: unknown

SOCIO-CULTURAL

Past Users: unknown
Present Users: upper level: Alian Chandler; lower level: Noël Stremdöerfer. At present each level of the house is being used as a self-contained bachelor flat.
Privacy: Protected from road on north side by neighboring house. No windows on west side facing other house. East side protected by vegetation. South side protected by cliff. Apartment directly underneath cannot be seen into, and cannot see into the upper apartment.
Security: Iron grills on all windows. Heavy wooden bolt on main door. Broken glass along roof parapet. Iron gate and concrete wall preventing entry to lower apartment from the road or upper apartment. No grill over courtyard.

ENVIRONMENT

Land Use: House occupies small lot on edge of cliff. Terracing used to support house. No level property.
Vegetation: None within the courtyard. Lot of vegetation surrounding the property but none directly on it.
Views: The Gulf of Carthage and the Lake of Tunis can be seen from the living room of the upper apartment.
Natural Lighting: Day lighting good except in kitchen and bathroom of both apartments. The living room of the upper apartment gets very good sunlight during the winter.
Humidity: Moisture creeping through the walls from the embankment causes the humidity in this house to be very high.

TECHNOLOGY/SERVICES

Construction Type: Load bearing masonry walls. Masonry vaulted roofs. Dome over entry. Tiles in living room.

Present Condition: Living room roof is leaky. A lot of moisture creep in walls. Broken pipes in upper bathroom make it unusable. Poor drainage in the courtyard.

Water Services: Water supplied by municipality.

Sewage: Municipality-pumped to main sewage system.

Heating: Fireplace in the living room and a gas heater in one of the bedrooms.

SENSUAL/AESTHETIC

Space: The living room of the upper apartment gives a very false impression of spaciousness because of its length and large windows facing the sea. The actual width of the room is only 2.25 meters. At one end of the living room is a small semi-closed in dining area with a sitting platform. Possibly this was the traditional alcove for a large bed, called in Arabic "Hanut Hajjam". This is a very pleasant and intimate space. The kitchens and bathrooms of both apartments are too small to be adequate for the everyday requirements of its occupants.

Color: There are no colored tiles. The only color in the house is in the upholstery of the cushions.

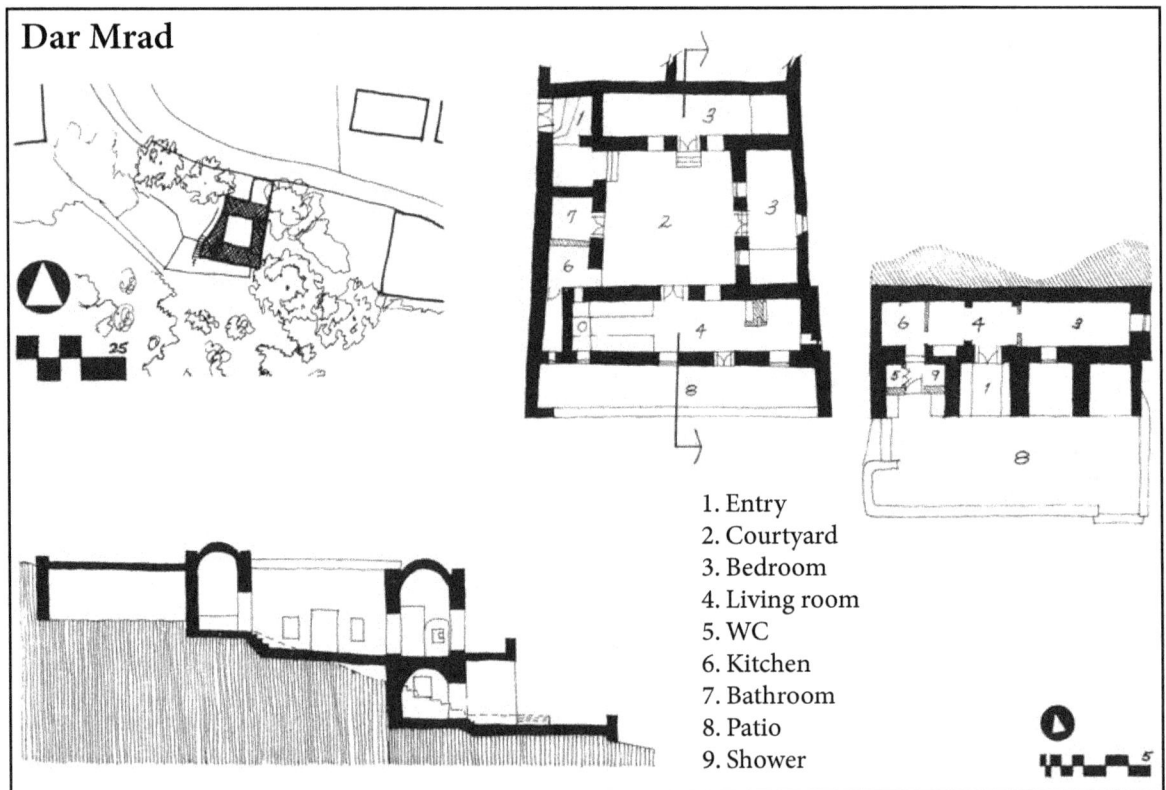

Dar Mrad

1. Entry
2. Courtyard
3. Bedroom
4. Living room
5. WC
6. Kitchen
7. Bathroom
8. Patio
9. Shower

A COMPARATIVE OVERVIEW OF THE FIVE HOUSES STUDIED.

Within Sidi Bou Sa'id the various space requirements for contemporary needs are provided by the renovation of existing buildings. From the study and knowledge of the town in general, we find that the larger homes have been adapted to more diverse uses e.g., Dar Thameur to apartments, Dar et-Toumi to Hotel, as compared to the small modest houses which are now used primarily as single rental units (except for Dar Mrad which includes two units).

In both groups the location of the buildings are on generally sloping sites affecting the planning of the houses. Fortunately the slopes face south or west receiving adequate sunlight, particularly in the winter. The only house studied which is on a flat site is Dar Cahen. All the homes are primarily single storey with later additions on the upper storey, e.g., Thameur, Kaffe. Gardens are always a part of the rich home grounds, and were added to Dar Kaffe when it was purchased by French colonialists in 1906.

Each house incorporates a courtyard forming its core, and every bordering rooms faces onto it. The richer house courtyard sometimes have grape vines. Two of the modest homes have fair sized trees in their courts. It is possible that large plant life such as trees were more common in the modest homes as they did not have gardens. The finishes in the courts of the rich homes are more elaborate with decorative tiles. Modest courtyards tend to be less decorated.

Cisterns for collecting rainwater are only found under the courtyards of the rich homes, and access to them was through a decorative well-type opening niched into one of the walls around the court.

Per cent area of the court to main floor is more stable in the smaller homes being approximately 22%, whereas in the larger homes it varies from about 10% to 24%.

The richer houses such as Dar et-Toumi and Dar Thameur have visual access to picturesque views. In the former the women's rooms have the better views of the garden and sea, whereas the men's rooms overlook the street. In Dar Thameur the men's rooms have a view of the courtyard and the gulf of Hammam-Lif. In Dar et-Toumi ground floor windows look outward: This is unusual and was made possible only because visual privacy is protected by gardens with much foliage. Dar Thameur has no ground floor windows because of the surrounding streets. Its main orientation is toward the sea and its windows face that direction and the courtyard.

In the smaller and modest houses, Dar Kaffe, Mrad and Cahen, the men's area is not so well defined nor are the rooms so numerous or elaborate. Dar Mrad like Dar Thameur has its views into the courtyard or toward the sea. The main windows on the ground floor of Dar Kaffe (in the men's rooms) face the street. This exception was made because of the fantastic view of Tunis and its lake from that area. Dar Cahen which is composed of sections built at different periods, has most of its windows facing the courtyard. A number of the windows look into the gardens, but the two courtyard wall openings are kept permanently closed.

The interior finishes vary greatly between the classes of homes. In the richer ones more marble is used for window and door frames, while ordinary stone is used in the modest homes. Tiles, colorful and patterned are used extensively in the richer homes. The only modest house which has any amount of tiling is Dar Kaffe. Exterior finishes for all classes of housing is of a lime and sand mortar finished with a lime whitewash, enhancing the anonymity of the houses from the streets, making it difficult to distinguish between rich and modest houses.

"GOD IS BEAUTIFUL AND HE LOVES BEAUTY."

A SAYING OF THE PROPHET MOHAMMED.
ARABIC CALLIGRAPHY BY ISMAIL HAQI, DATED 1942.

CONCLUSIONS

There is a lack of knowledge with regard to the factors that shaped traditional towns and villages such as Sidi Bou Sa'id. The outcome of this study is a contribution towards filling our knowledge gap and a step in rectifying that situation. However, a word of warning: If the lessons of this work are to be truly beneficial then such environments must not be approached only for their picturesque qualities or as a trove of three-dimensional forms to be pilfered without a full understanding of the building processes and cultural framework from which they first emerged.

It is perhaps appropriate here to highlight some of the reasons why "modern architecture" has often failed to create physical environments of the quality of Sidi Bou Sa'id. In addition to the impact of the rapid rate of technological and social change in the 20th century we must also identify the following factors:

1) The growth of architectural skill in the past was from the bulk of the built environment towards the top[1], i.e., monuments, yet Schools of Architecture have historically emphasized the activities and values of the small elite. A consequence of this is seen in the importance given to "Style". This is obvious in our study of architectural history which views buildings as outward looking works of art to be admired from certain locations. Usually it views the architect's skill as being primarily an applied decorative function with the planning and organization of the building being relegated to a mere adherence to stylistic determinants.

2) The development of the Beaux Arts system of architectural education simply perpetuated and formalized the approach mentioned above.

Although the modern movement has freed itself from various aspects of the Beaux Arts system, particularly by emphasizing functional organization, its intellectual food and nourishment is still based on the previous situation.

---

[1] Constantinos A. Doxiadis, *Architecture in Transition,* Oxford University Press, New York 1963. See chapters 4: 'Architects and Architecture' and 6: 'Return to a Universal Architecture'.

This state of affairs is perpetuated by the delivery systems of architecture which are not geared to solving the housing and urban problems faced by most countries today. These systems were primarily created to respond to architectural needs in terms of delivered completed products and not responsive to delivering processes which, in aggregate, create the products required.

Centuries of continuous development created the village of Sidi Bou Sa'id as we see and enjoy it today. To appreciate fully the lessons it provides I have chosen to break the environment of the village into components which can easily be transformed into usable design criteria. To make such an exercise as fruitful as possible I have chosen to rely to a large extent on the recent work of Christopher Alexander and his associates as published in *A Pattern Language*.[2] Of their 253 patterns, I have identified 92 which are embodied in the built environment of Sidi Bou Sa'id—42% of these are of the "proven usable" category (marked by two asterisks), 45% are of the "very reliable" category (marked by one asterisk) and the remainder 13% are considered to be sound but need further verification. Of the total identified patterns in Sidi Bou Sa'id, 27% relate to the Village scale and 73% to the Building scale and related Construction details.

Although most of Alexander's patterns are potentially useful for many cultures they are primarily addressed to the problems of building and urban design in the United States and Canada. I am pleased that Alexander's work so closely corroborates the discovery of my study group that Sidi Bou Sa'id contains lessons directly applicable to the North American context.

Before listing the patterns embodied in the physical structure and form of Sidi Bou Sa'id, we should be aware of the following generalities:

THE COMPONENTS OF THE BUILDING PROCESS

In the Arabic-Islamic culture the built environment was primarily shaped by a building process consisting of three components:

1. A vocabulary of specific building design elements which was understood by all users and builders. A sample of these elements from Tunisia is presented in Chapter 7.

2. An elaborate set of building guidelines primarily addressed to the conflicts arising from building activity at the dwelling group scale. Developed within the first 2.5 centuries of Islam and based on religious values and ethics, these guidelines have evolved gradually with experience and precedents.

3. Architectural style and ornamentation. This component has been applied to the facades, major entrances and courtyards of major public buildings and to the courtyards of houses of the very wealthy. The roots and philosophy of architectural style and ornamentation were basically the same across the Islamic world although regional variations did occur depending on the availability of building materials, the characteristics of local climate and the attitudes of the local religious school of law, the "madhhab".

---

[2]Christopher Alexander and others, *A Pattern Language: Towns, Buildings, Construction*. Oxford University Press, New York 1977.

PRIMARY PLANNING ELEMENTS

1. The Courtyard Building. This is the basic module used for housing and public buildings. The ratio of building area to plot is 1:1 with the courtyard taking approximately 24% of the ground coverage. Usually the building is one or two storeys in height but sometimes three.
2. The Street System. The streets are of two types:
   a) the through street , which was considered a public right of way and had to be wide enough for two packed camels to pass.
   b) the cul-de-sac, which is considered to be the private property of the people living off of it.
3. Elements Above the Street. These are primarily:
   a) the room bridging the street, or "sabat" in Arabic.
   b) the buttressing arches spanning between walls on either side of the street to strengthen the walls and prevent building collapse.
4. The Site. The steepest slopes of the hill and the areas prone to landslides created the natural boundaries of the village.
5. The Mosque. This acted as the primary growth pole from which the village grew outwards in three directions. Because the people wanted to hear the call to prayer from their houses, the minaret acted as a magnet to keep the buildings within the call to prayer radius of 250 meters as a preferred location, and also within the maximum tolerable walking distance of 800 meters.

CRITERIA ROOTED IN ISLAMIC VALUES

1. Privacy. The visual privacy of the family, particularly its female members, is highly regarded. Protecting this privacy is the entrance lobby ("skifa"), the interior courtyard ("Wust al-Dar") which is protected by law from visual penetration due to neighboring structures, and other measures.
2. Beauty Without Arrogance (see the calligraphy on page 142). Although the interiors of private houses could be decorated to the highest levels of sophistication, the exteriors were traditionally plain and simple, with the exception of the doors.
3. Building design decisions must not harm neighbors or the public. This was one of the primary principles followed by builders. Judges used this principle to determine if an owner or builder had violated his rights and prescribed judgement accordingly.
4. Interdependence. The concept of interdependence was used as an equilibric mechanism to settle disputes over the common use of walls, cul-de-sacs, drains, waste water etc.

These and other criteria were fully developed in Islamic countries by about 900 A.D. I have covered all of this material in detail in my forthcoming book on the subject.[3]

The ground is now prepared to examine patterns as they are embodied in Sidi Bou Sa'id.

---

[3] Besim S. Hakim. *Arabic-Islamic Cities: Building and Planning Principles,* London, 1986 (manuscript completed in 1979). Paperback edition with a postscript and additional content published October 2008. See also reference to other publications in footnote 1, page viii.

VILLAGE SCALE[4]

1. The projected population for 1976 was to be about 5000 people. Alexander found that communities of 5,000–10,000 people can exercise the most effective local control (12 COMMUNITY OF 7000 *).

2. The historic area (used for studies of the Built Form Systems, see chapter 3) is 270 m across and 500 m in length (14 IDENTIFIABLE NEIGHBORHOOD **). This area can accommodate up to 1800 people without overcrowding and is clearly an identifiable neighbourhood relative to the rest of the community, yet it takes up only 35% of the total community area.

3. All buildings are within the four storey limit recommended for human habitation (21 FOUR-STOREY LIMIT **). In fact the bulk of the buildings are only two storeys and yet a gross density of 160 persons/Hectare (65 persons/acre) or a net density of 222 persons/Hectare (90 persons/acre) has been achieved.

4. The primary car parking areas are within the old village. These total 6240 square meters and are only 5.64% of the area of the old village, well within the maximum 9% recommended by Alexander. (22 NINE PER CENT PARKING **).

5. Sidi Bou Sa'id is an excellent example of a preserved sacred site. The decree of 1915 was an important instrument in preserving the physical identity of the village. The annual "Kharja" reinforces the reality of preservation, (24 SACRED SITES *).

6. Visual and physical access to the water is abundant, and there are stunning views from certain locations in the village. Development is also kept well away from the shore line. (25 ACCESS TO WATER *).

7. The man-made and natural environments provide the necessary settings for the complete human life-cycle, with the exception of comprehensive employment opportunities. (26 LIFE CYCLE *).

8. The souk and the cafes form an ideal activity node at the heart of the village. (30 ACTIVITY NODES **).

9. Rue El-Hadi Zarrouk forms an active promenade with a catchment area extending beyond the boundaries of the old village. Its two nodes are the village square and the Sidi Chabane parking area. (31 PROMENADE **).

10. Diverse public demands for night-time activity are primarily provided for by the two cafes on the village square.(33 NIGHT LIFE **).

11. There is a complete household mix in the village due to the characteristics of its socio-cultural milieu and its physical fabric. (35 HOUSEHOLD MIX *).

12. Although the village is made of large building clusters, the most effective clusters are those which share a common access. The effect of the clusters is particularly enhanced by the cul-de-sacs, which are jointly owned by the people whose access to their houses is from it. (37 HOUSE CLUSTER **).

---

[4]For the purpose of facilitating further related research, I have indicated in brackets for each pattern its equivalent number and title as it appears in Alexander's book, including the number of asterisks: 2 for the "proven usable", 1 for the "very reliable", and none for the others.

13. Housing and shops are always mixed. The souk is composed of shops on the ground level with housing on the upper levels.(48 HOUSING IN BETWEEN **).

14. The village has a number of preconceived and 'unplanned' gateways to its various precincts. The latter are usually the outcome of the use of "sabat"s (room over access) and buttressing arches. (53 MAIN GATEWAYS **).

15. Cars are only allowed to use 58% of the streets within the village boundary. Since the frequency of cars is low and 42% of all streets are for pedestrian use only, children have the freedom to explore the streets in safety. (57 CHILDREN IN THE CITY).

16. There is adequate provision and variety between noisy areas and quite backs, providing contrast and relief, e.g., (a) between noisy through streets and quite cul-de-sacs, (b) between major pedestrian routes and the less frequented branches, (c) the cemetery and other edges in the village also act as quiet backs. (59 QUIET BACKS *).

17. None of the squares in Sidi Bou Sa'id exceeds Alexander's findings of a maximum recommended width of 14–21 meters (45–70 feet). (61 SMALL PUBLIC SQUARES **).

18. The village is built on a small hill, and its highest elevation is near the lighthouse; the top of which is open to the public. (62 HIGH PLACES *).

19. The tomb of the saint, Sidi Abou-Said, is reached by a succession of open and confined spaces. (66 HOLY GROUND *).

20. Forty per cent of the streets within the boundaries of the old village are solely for pedestrians. These streets create a network of connecting paths which even young children under the age of five can safely explore and play in.(68 CONNECTED PLAY *).

21. The small, intimate cemetery is surrounded by a low wall which symbolizes its sacredness. (70 GRAVE SITES *).

22. The small squares and "fina"s (enlarged cul-de-sacs) are frequently used as neighbourhood playgrounds and sports surfaces.(72 LOCAL SPORTS *).

23. The souk is made of small shops, the smallest being only 2.25 m^2 (24 ft^2). Some of the shops are rented while the others are owner-operated.(87 INDIVIDUALLY OWNED SHOPS **)

24. The village square is used as a street cafe whenever the weather permits. A relaxed, informal environment is created by the flexible seating arrangements and the opportunities to watch people strolling, laughing and talking. (88 STREET CAFE **).

25. The large number of built-in benches, raised platforms and other similar amenities encourage outdoor relaxation, particularly during the hot summer afternoons, (94 SLEEPING IN PUBLIC).

BUILDING SCALE

26. The village as a whole can be viewed as a single building composed of smaller components such as the mosque complex, the souk/square complex and the housing clusters. (95 BUILDING COMPLEX **).

27. The major parking lot is partially shielded from view by trees, embankments and buildings. Its pedestrian link to the main street is partially protected by a "sabat". (97 SHIELDED PARKING*).

28. The inherently complex street layout is given clarity and a perceptual orientation by various 'anchorage' features: the minaret, the slopes, the view to the sea etc (98 CIRCULATION REALMS **).

29. The Mosque Complex is easily identifiable at long and short range by its prominent features such as the minaret and domes. (99 MAIN BUILDING *).

30. Sixteen per cent of the total land area of the old village is made up of streets. Fifty-eight per cent of these streets are used by infrequent vehicular traffic. The intimacy of these streets for pedestrians is enhanced by the fact that their width-to-height ratios are usually 1:1 or, occasionally, 1:2 (100 PEDESTRIAN STREET **).

31. All doors and windows are derivatives of basic archetypes and are unified by size, proportion and color. This tends to clarify the orientation and location of the buildings with respect to the street system. (102 FAMILY OF ENTRANCES *) .

32. The east-west axis of the village and its south orientation along the slope of the hill, assisted by the disposition of courtyards and streets, help create optimum shade in the summer and allow adequate sun penetration in the winter. (105 SOUTH FACING OUTDOORS **).

33. The hierarchy of positive private and public outdoor spaces provides order and direction within complexity, a sense of place and a sequence of movement which enhances the three-dimensional man-made setting.(106 POSITIVE OUTDOOR SPACE **).

34. Sixty per cent of the area of the old village is covered by buildings and streets. The latter takes up 16% and the former—primarily large clusters of connected individual buildings—44%. The connections within these clusters are achieved through the use of party walls and, occasionally, "sabat"s (room crossing street or cul-de-sac) (108 CONNECTED BUILDINGS *).

35. Main entrances to buildings are bold and clear in relation to their importance. These are the only facade elements in Arabic-Islamic architecture which are allowed to be given prominence through decoration. Their clarity is achieved by their location and a combination of elements such as steps, stone frames, color and studded design. (110 MAIN ENTRANCE **).

36. Transition from the street to the courtyard is handled by the use of "dribas" or "skifas" and occasionally a walled garden, or a row of tall trees visible from the street. (112 ENTRANCE TRANSITION **).

37. There are many locations within the village where the structuring of the open spaces can be easily perceived. A prime example of this is the village square. (114 HIERARCHY OF OPEN SPACE *).

38. Vaulted ceilings as used in Sidi Bou Sa'id seem to add to a building's sense of shelter. (117 SHELTERING ROOF **).

39. There are many usable roof spaces such as private roof gardens in Sidi Bou Sa'id. The two most prominent public 'roof gardens' are the "sahn" of the Mosque Complex and the open cafe adjacent to Impasse Thameur. (118 ROOF GARDEN *).

40. Visual goals for pedestrians are created by the variety of 3-dimensional shapes in the village. (120 PATHS AND GOALS *).

41. There is a wide variety of path shapes within the boundaries of the old village, created by the determinants of the building process, the camel/donkey and the hilly terrain. It is interesting to note that most streets have maximum lengths without a bend of 25 m : the limiting distance for recognizing a human face. Many of the irregularities of the streetscape are used for planting and seating. The use of wide gentle steps for level changes enhances the uses and visual appeal of the streets. (121 PATH SHAPE *) .

42. The use of the courtyard building as the primary growth module, the built-in entrance lobbies ("skifas") and the inward looking major rooms did not require that the buildings be set back from the street. In addition Islamic law recognized wall to wall dimensions for street widths. (122 BUILDING FRONTS *).

43. In normal use, the main square has a density of about 8–12 m²/person, denser than Alexander's recommendation of 14 m²/person the minimum required for a square to be sensed as being lively. (123 PEDESTRIAN DENSITY *).

44. Two cafes and various shops form activity pockets around the village square.(124 ACTIVITY POCKETS **).

45. The large flight of steps from the square to the Cafe des Nattes offers magnificent views of the village and the sea-people use it extensively for sitting on, and occasionally the cafe owner provides a role matt for the purpose. (125 STAIR SEATS *).

46. Although the minaret is the major focal point at the village scale, it is not located in the exact center of the built form. We also find that at the scale of the village square, the trees are located off center. (126 SOMETHING ROUGHLY IN THE MIDDLE).

Of the remaining 46 patterns identified by Alexander and embodied in Sidi Bou Sa'id, we continue elaborating some and indicating others by name and number only:

47. INTIMACY GRADIENT (127 **).

48. INDOOR SUNLIGHT (128 *).

49. Every traditional Arabic-Islamic house has one or more entrance rooms or lobbies "Skifa", which are totally incorporated within the perimeter of the house plan. It is usually used by the owner as a guest reception room for male visitors. Affluent owners tend to decorate the walls of the skifa with elaborately designed tile-work. (130 ENTRANCE ROOM **).

50. ZEN VIEW (134 *).

51. BED CLUSTER (143 *).

52. ROOMS TO RENT (153).

53. HOME WORKSHOP (157).

54. OPEN STAIRS (158 *).

55. BUILDING EDGE (160 **).

56. SUNNY PLACE (161 **) or Shaded place in Summer.

57. A street window type specifically developed by the Arab-Islamic culture is the "Maucharabieh". A bay window on the upper floor covered with a wooden lattice to allow the occupants to see

out without being seen. It is usually located on a busy street side, and often has built-in seating. (164 STREET WINDOWS *).

58. TERRACED SLOPE (169 *) .

59. TREE PLACES (171 **) .

60. The enclosing wall is an integral component of the Islamic garden. It defines the boundary of the man-made 'paradise'. It also provides privacy, security and sound protection. This concept is reinforced by the requirements of compact planning, so that in many instances the garden would be surrounded by a building on at least one or two sides. Sidi Bou Sa'id has a variety of small and large walled gardens.(173 GARDEN WALL *).

61. In large gardens trellises are used to provide shade for walkways. They are usually covered with grapevines, and are located adjacent to walls or as distinct walkways creating visual divisions within the garden space. (174 TRELLISED WALK **) .

62. VEGETABLE GARDEN (177 *) .

63. Alcoves are integral features of the two room types predominant in Sidi Bou Sa'id and the Tunis region. See chapter 7 for a definition and sketch plans of these rooms (179 ALCOVES **).

64. WINDOW PLACE (180 **).

65. MARRIAGE BED (187).

66. Bedrooms are not isolated entities but rather incorporated in multi-function rooms as alcoves. These alcoves are occasionally developed into a fixed bed with a wooden frame and curtains creating an 'entrance' effect. In affluent homes, these frames could be elaborately decorated. (188 BED ALCOVE **).

67. With the exception of primary rooms on the ground floor which have relatively equal heights, other spaces tend to have varying heights in response to anticipated use and/or technical constraints.(190 CEILING HEIGHT VARIETY **).

68. THE SHAPE OF INDOOR SPACE (191 **).

69. WINDOWS OVERLOOKING LIFE (192 *).

70. In addition to their insulating feature, thick walls used in the Tunis region (1 cubit or approximately 50 cm) prevent open doors and windows from obstructing usable space, and often contain recessed storage and shelving. (197 THICK WALLS **).

71. BUILT-IN SEATS (202 *) .

CONSTRUCTION DETAILS

72. Careful study of aerial photos of traditional Arabic-Islamic settlements reveals the equilibrium which has been achieved between formalistic and complex socio-cultural design requirements. This was possible because of the generative nature of the building process used. (205 STRUCTURE FOLLOWS SOCIAL SPACES **).

73. EFFICIENT STRUCTURE (206 *).

74. Traditional buildings in the Tunis region strike a good balance in the use of "bulk" and "secondary" materials. The primary bulk material, stone, is long lasting, easy to trim and maintain, a good thermal insulator and easy to recycle. Wood, a more easily depleted resource

than stone, is used sparingly as a secondary material for windows, doors and, occasionally, ceilings. The uniformity of the building materials tends to enhance the dignity and character of the built environment.(207 GOOD MATERIALS **).

75. ROOF LAYOUT (209 *).
76. FLOOR AND CEILING LAYOUT (210).
77. FLOOR–CEILING VAULTS (219 **).
78. ROOF VAULTS (220 *).
79. NATURAL DOORS AND WINDOWS (221 **).
80. LOW SILL (222).
81. DEEP REVEALS (223).
82. The large double entrance doors are only opened on special occasions or when moving furniture. Otherwise a small door inset into one of the larger leaves is used. Its height of 1.52 m(5 feet) requires that an adult bend down before entering a dwelling—symbolizing respect to his host. This inset low door traditionally common in most Islamic countries, also responds to privacy and security requirements.(224 LOW DOORWAY).
83. COLUMN CONNECTION (227 **).
84. STAIR VAULT (228 *).
85. RADIANT HEAT (230 *).
86. ROOF CAPS (232).
87. FLOOR SURFACE (233 **).
88. SOFT INSIDE WALLS (235 *).
89. FILTERED LIGHT (238 *).
90. RAISED FLOWERS (245 *).
91. CLIMBING PLANTS (246).
92. It is valuable to understand the importance of the location and characteristics of ornament in Islamic architecture (see chapter 4). Whether on the door and window surrounds, on the courtyard walls or, if the owner can afford it, on the walls and ceilings of interior rooms, ornament coalesces the different spaces and surfaces of the building and, at its best, is a reminder of the infinite variety and beauty of God's creations. (249 ORNAMENT **).

The existence of the preceding patterns in Sidi Bou Sa'id provides ample evidence of the high quality of its physical environment. However we should be aware that a successful physical environment cannot only be judged by the number of desirable patterns it embodies but rather how these patterns interact in a complex and poetic way. Such complexity implies that the total spatial environment can only be perceived and appreciated by a pedestrian who can sense the changes in level, direction, light, heat, texture, sound, scent and the degree of enclosure.[5] Le Corbusier

[5] Amos Rapoport. "Designing for Complexity", *Architectural Association Quarterly,* Vol. 3 No.1 (winter 1971), pp. 29–33.

recognized the importance of these attributes and mentioned several examples from Islamic architecture in his writings.[6]

But beyond the value of these patterns, possibly the most profound lesson which the village can offer us is the importance of the underlying building process and its component mechanisms: a simple set of building guidelines whose intentions are clear acting as criteria for performance and a versatile customary building practice that generates good "patterns" as demonstrated in this study's conclusions. Our architectural delivery system must be shifted from the conception of buildings as fixed static end products conceived and implemented within a limited time frame, to embrace the more timeless building principles and processes of responsive change and growth. Maybe then contemporary Western society would be capable of creating forceful and delightful environments such as Sidi Bou Sa'id.

---

[6]Le Corbusier frequently praised Islamic architecture and urban design, particularly after trips to Algeria and Turkey. The following translated passage appeared on page 24 of his *Oeuvre Complete de 1929-1934*, published by Les Editions Girsberger, Zurich, in 1935. It was related to his explanation of the Villa Savoye, which was built in 1929-31 in Poissy, near Paris:

"Arab architecture gives us precise information. It is appreciated by someone on foot; for it is while walking that one can see the development of its architectural patterns. This principle is at odds with Baroque architecture which is conceived on paper around a fixed theoretical point. I much prefer the way that Arab architecture conveys information."

SIDI BOU SA'ID AS A SUMMER RESORT IN THE 19TH CENTURY

Notable families who came to Sidi Bou Sa'id for their summer holidays left Tunis with an imposing retinue of servants carrying bedding and abundant provisions. One of the most delightful provisions was always a large copper plate with cakes made from couscous and thickly covered with dates, pistachios and almonds.

Already used to riding through the streets of Tunis, people of note rode by horse or mule to Sidi Bou Sa'id. Later they used a kind of closed carriage imported from Malta. Other chariots, these of Spanish origin, were reserved for the harem.

So it was that at dawn on the day that a wealthy Tunis family left for Sidi Bou Sa'id the gates of the city would issue forth horsemen, painted and armed caleches and open or covered four wheel chariots. This procession of domestics, provisions, children and adults followed the bank of the lake of el-Bahira until it reached the midpoint of its journey at about noon. Since the sun was already high in the sky the procession rested here before going on to Sidi Bou Sa'id which was reached by mid-afternoon.

It was quite a sight to see the richly harnessed donkeys and vehicles with their important passengers and colorful servants winding their ways up the hill to the summer palaces. The few permanent inhabitants of the town—fishermen, gardeners and shepherds—came running to welcome the visitors. The people from "far off" Tunis provided enough news and gossip to keep everybody entertained for weeks. Also, all around the town, shops were reopened and stocked with fruit and vegetables.

In the hottest part of the summer a new exodus was organized as the families would go down to the beach by foot or donkey and stay there for a day or several weeks. At the "chott" Sidi Bou Sa'id they built small wooden pile houses some distance out into the cool surf. Each house was a miniature version of the traditional palaces in Tunis except that the corridor was substituted by the footbridge leading from the beach to a covered central patio. The patio was surrounded by toilets, bedrooms and a living room with seats facing the sea. Although elegantly appointed these houses were brilliantly painted in greens, reds and blues in marked contrast to the beige terraces, pink rocks and whitewashed houses above.

Aside from their everyday duties the men spent a great deal of time amusing themselves. The various distractions to be found in salons were good conversation, music and singing. Dar Lasram was the place to go each morning to hear "nouba" and "malouf" (oriental and Andalusian music) played on violin, lute, drum and tambourine. Elsewhere card and other games were played until the small hours of the morning. One could see these men arriving at the cafes in the late afternoon followed by a servant with a carpet and a cushion. As soon as the cushion was placed in its usual position the cafe owner hurried over with a vase of sweet-smelling jasmine. In the cafe the patron could drink coffee or tea and smoke a water pipe while listening to storytellers or musicians.

Conversely the women would occupy themselves with the surveillance of the servants and the education of the children. They also met frequently; during such meetings talk about marriage was the most inexhaustible subject: the weddings of female relatives at which they had been guests, the wealth of the dowry, the enumeration and description of the clothes embroidered with gold and silver and the jewels worn by the young bride.

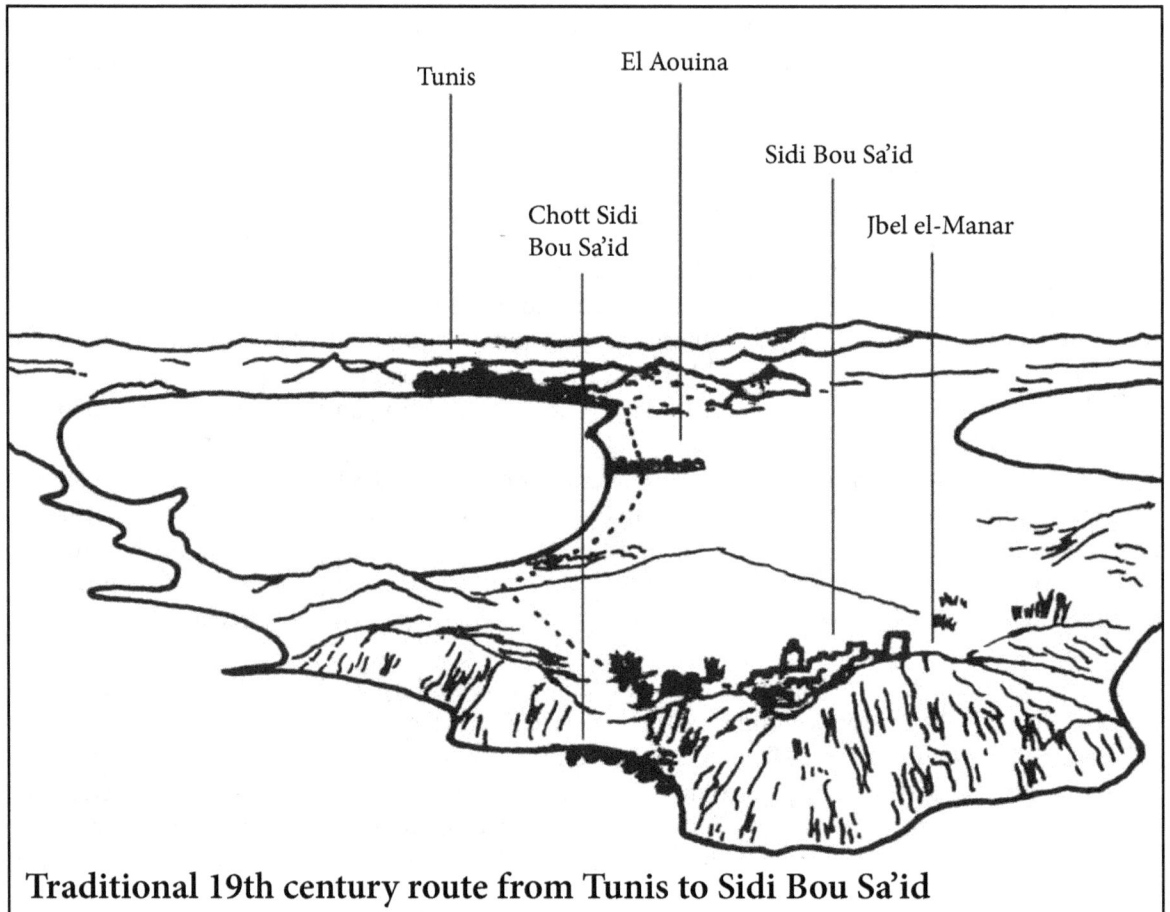

Traditional 19th century route from Tunis to Sidi Bou Sa'id

A less strict confinement was allowed for the women while in Sidi Bou Sa'id than would have been possible in Tunis. As long as she was accompanied by a servant it was always proper for a Tunisian woman to appear at the mosques, the marabouts and the cemetery. For all of the women of either great or modest wealth the biggest attraction was the "rbabiya" musicians who performed each Friday at the mosque-zawiya of Sidi Bou Sa'id. Numbering five or six they dressed identically in colored tunics over tight bouffant pants. They played violin, drum and a large drum with a copper cymbal. After the audience paid a small contribution the music would start—the religious chants of the rbabiya intermingling with the rhythmic plaintiveness of the drums and violins.

Typical Plan of Summer Pavillion at Chott Sidi Bou Sa'id

1. Foot bridge
2. Meeting room for men
3. Covered corridor
4. Bedroom
5. Kitchen
6. Living room
7. Built-in seating
8. Balcony over sea

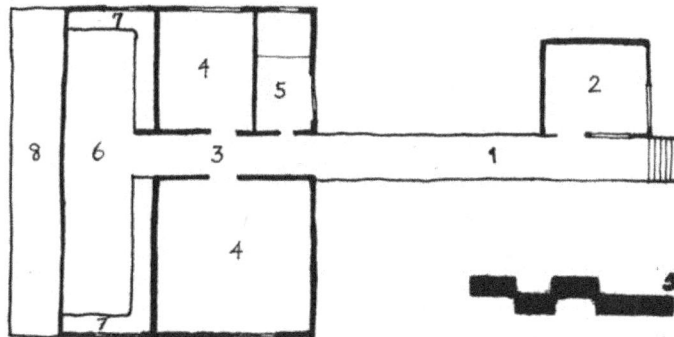

After J. Revault's *Palais et Residences d'été de la region de Tunis*, 1974.

DECREE OF 1915: THE PROTECTION OF ARABIC BUILDINGS IN SIDI BOU SA'ID

THE PROTECTION OF ARABIC BUILDINGS IN SIDI BOU SA'ID
Decree of August 6, 1915 (25 Ramadan 1333)

Praise be to God!

WE, MOHAMMED EN NACER PACHA-BEY, POSSESSOR OF THE KINGDOM OF TUNIS,

Seeing the decree of 14 January 1914 on the organization of the Communes;

Seeing the decree of 30 July 1909, approving the regulations of the public roads of the community of Sidi Bou Sa'id;

Considering that the Arabic construction of the town of Sidi Bou Sa'id constitutes a precious collection of artistic wealth which is worthy of conservation;

On the agreement of our Prime Minister: HAVE MADE THE FOLLOWING DECREE;

Article 1—It is forbidden for proprietors, managers, tenants, and holders of such titles, of houses or properties included in the perimeter indicated by a pink border on the map adjoining the present decree, to modify the exterior aspect of the facades of the buildings, of the vaults and roofs established along or above the streets, or visible from these streets, without specific authorization given by the President of the Commune, after approval by the Secretary General of the Tunisian government and on notice of agreement by the Service of Antiquities and Arts.

It is, in particular, forbidden:
1. To give to facades any ornament, cornice, banister, etc.
2. To paint facades with anything except whitewash;
3. To modify the style of doors, windows, balconies as well as iron grills and wooden trellises with which the windows and balconies are provided;
4. To transform the terraces which form the roofs;
5. To modify the layout and existing alignment of streets, squares, blind alleys.

Article 2—All new construction bordering the streets must present a facade in a style analogous to that of the old buildings existing in the immediate neighbourhood. Its height must not exceed that of the lesser elevated of the two immediately neighboring buildings.

Article 3—The total or partial reconstruction of existing facades, whose poor state, duly ascertained, may present a danger to public circulation, will be undertaken in a manner such that no modification is made to the original configuration.
Restoration work and maintenance of the vaults and arches above street level is to be executed with materials and in a style identical to that of the original work. No modification either in plan or in elevation may be introduced.

Article 4—Requests for authorization will be addressed to the President of the Commune with plans giving details of the facades or other work to be done, sections and elevations of sides to be approved in the form and in the conditions anticipating the regulations of the Department of Public Roads of the Commune of Sidi Bou Sa'id.
Where the project does not involve any modification of the exterior of the buildings, the President of the Commune will be able to deliver authorization conforming to the regulations in effect for normal reparation of houses.
In other cases, the Municipality will decide, if the work requested may be authorized after previous consent by the Secretary General of the Tunisian Government and on notice of agreement by the Service of Antiquities and Arts.

Article 5—All construction, reconstruction, restoration of any type of building without the authorization of the Municipality, or contrary to the approved plans, will result in the application of a fine of from 16 to 500 francs, while the immediate demolition of any unauthorized work remains mandatory.
In the case where such construction has been occupied, its demolition may be delayed by the concerned party for a period not exceeding 20 days from the time of notification; which will have come from the office by the attention of the municipal administration. The order for demolition will always be preceded by the proof of the illicit state of the buildings by an expert chosen by the President of the French Civil Tribunal or by the Tribunal of the Ouzara, according to the case; the resulting expenses of the official demolition will be recovered in the same way as matters of municipal tax.

Article 6—In the case where the lawbreaker takes no account of the notice to suspend the construction work undertaken without authorization and in violation of the directives of the present decree, he will be liable to penalty of imprisonment of from 10 days to 1 month, without removal of the fine set out in Article 5.

Article 7—Article 463 of the French penal code and Article 53 of the Tunisian penal code will be applicable to the lawbreaker.

Article 8—The affixing of any posters is prohibited in the street which leads through the souk of Sidi Bou Sa'id; in other streets it will not be tolerated that posters measure more than 50 cm on each side.

Places reserved for posting of acts of public authority will be designated by decree of the President of the Commune.

Article 9—All infractions of the provision of the first paragraph of Article 8 above will be punishable by a fine of from 25 to 200 francs.

Article 10—Our Prime Minister is charged with the implementation of the present decree.

See for promulgation and putting into execution:

Tunis, the 6th August 1915

The "Ministre Plénipotentiare", Resident General in the French Republic of Tunis,

ALAPETITE[1]

---

[1] Source: *Journal Officiel Tunisien,* 28 Aout 1915, No. 69–33ᵉ année. This decree was superseded by the decree of 17 September 1953 (8 Muharram 1373) entitled 'Protection of Sites'.

EXTENSION HOUSING FOR SIDI BOU SA'ID: A DESIGN PROPOSAL

This project was undertaken by Mr. George Guimond during his final term in the school following his return from Sidi Bou Sa'id. The challenge was to design housing within the village which would be in harmony with the existing traditional fabric and yet suitable for the requirements of contemporary Western style living.

The site chosen is adjunct to the old village located on its northwest extremity with a magnificent distant view. It is within an area designated by the Municipality of Sidi Bou Sa'id as a zone of special status for housing extension. The site is capable of accommodating 20–30 units, and the distribution of unit types are based on the ratio of 30% 2-bedroom, 50% 3-bedroom and 20% 4-bedroom.

The primary objectives for the design was to:

- Maintain the high standard of privacy within the units and social interaction in public spaces.
- Maintain cohesion with the existing fabric of the village, and the enhancement of its visual character.
- Maintain the views from the higher portion of the site

The proposed design indicates 25 units, seven of which are fully detailed, and comprise 4: 2-bedroom, 2: 3-bedroom and 1: 4-bedroom units. Four other units are recommended for filling an area adjunct to the site.

Although the design achieves the objectives set out, it fails to:

- Utilize the full potentialities of the courtyard house as a planning module. It would have been possible to achieve more units if larger housing group clusters were planned and serviced by one major through access with cul-de-sacs branching from it.
- To develop an appropriate building process with supporting guidelines which would achieve the objectives set out incrementally. The project as proposed can only be successfully implemented, when viewed as a complete entity designed and implemented by one contractor or authority on a "turnkey" basis.

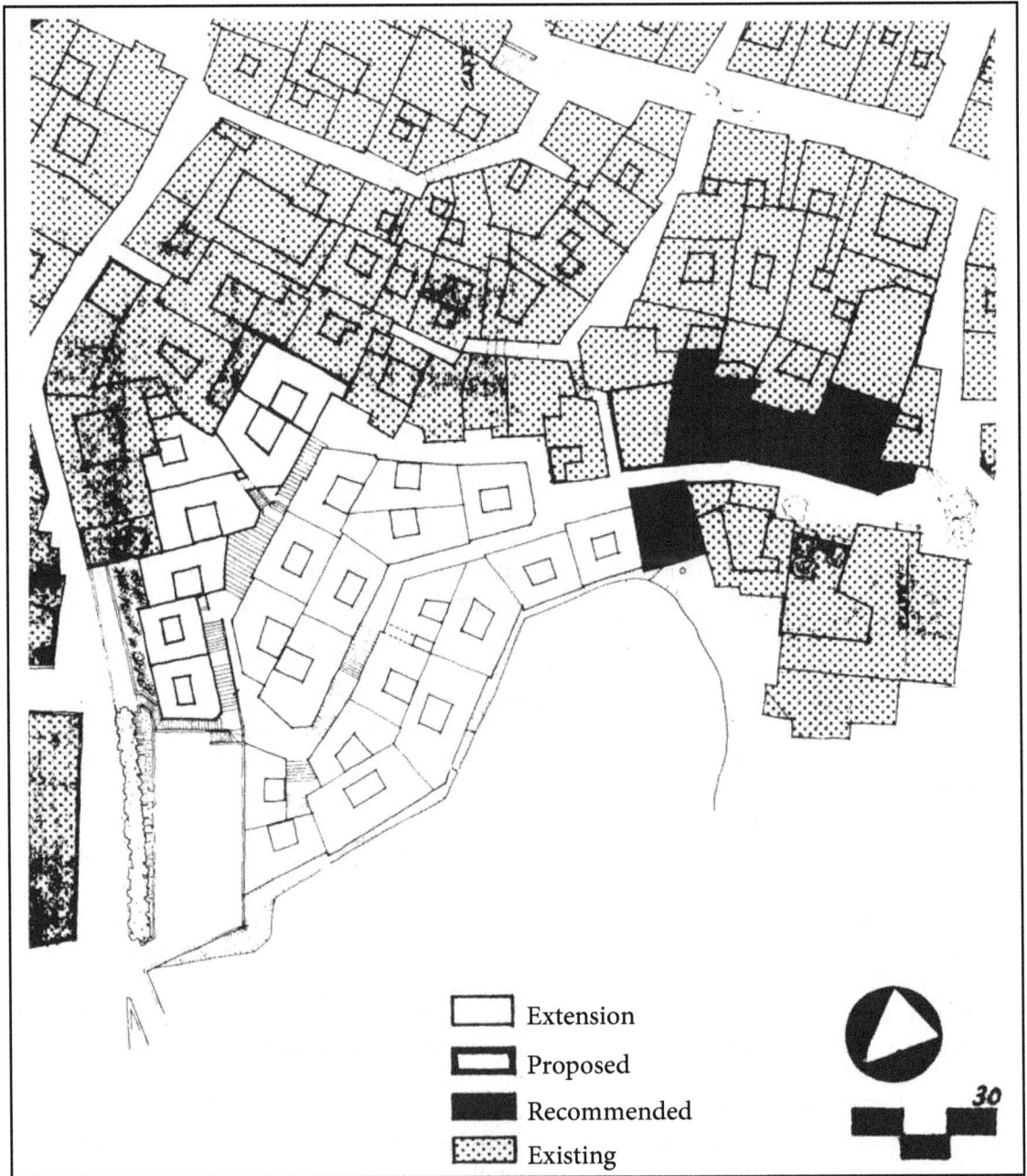

☐	Extension
☐	Proposed
■	Recommended
⬚	Existing

Site Plan

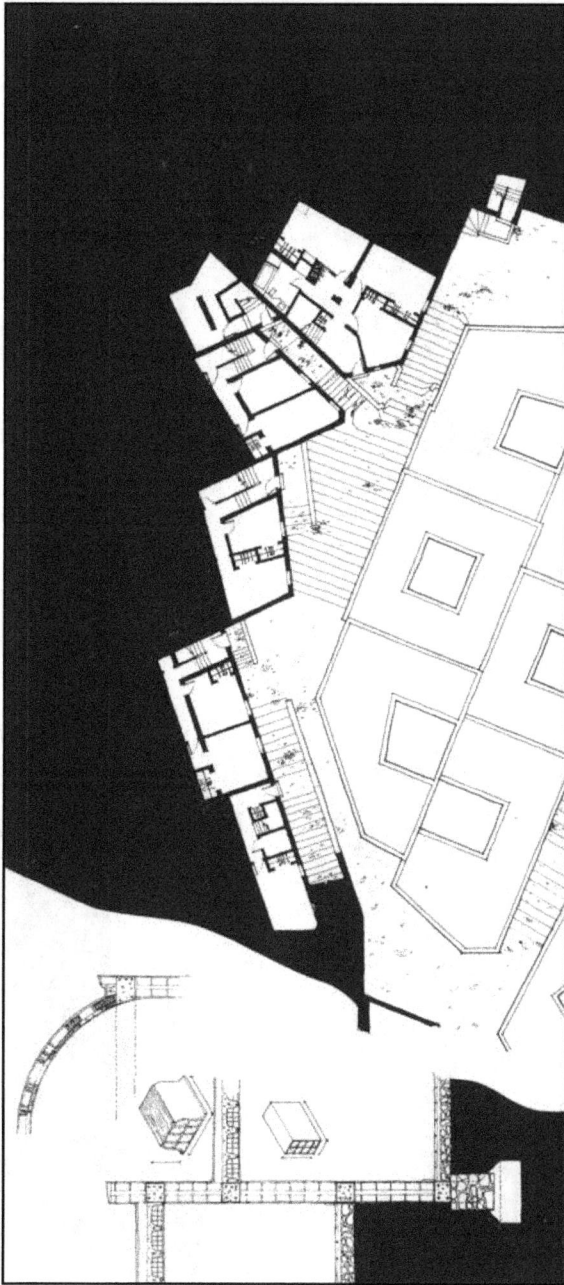

Entrance Level Plan

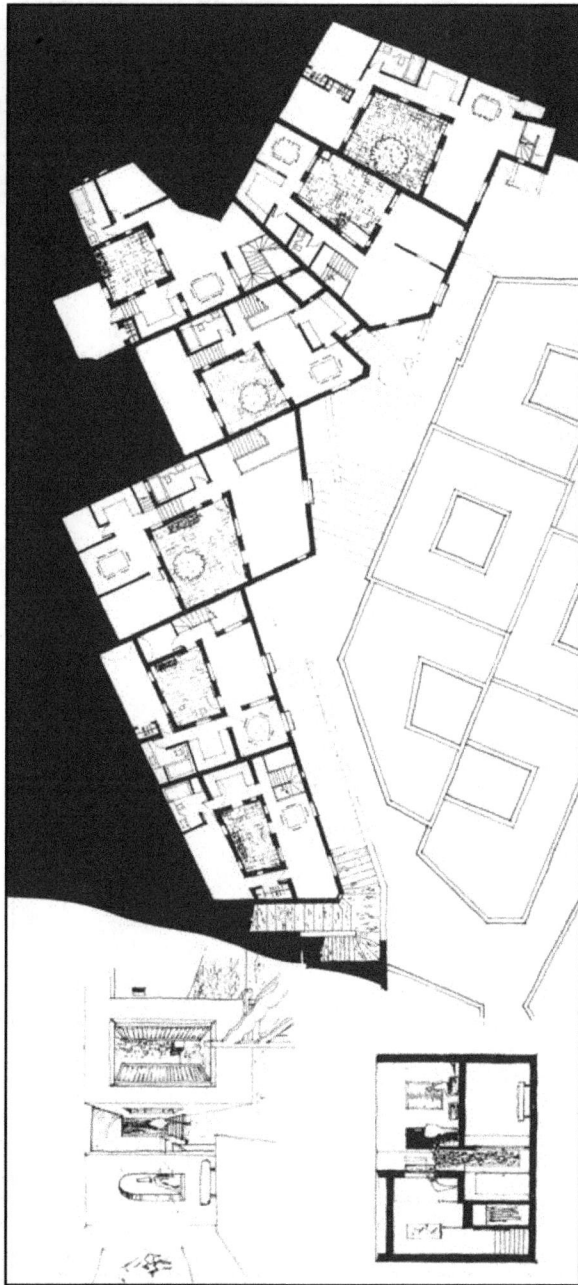

Upper Level Plan

Roof Plan

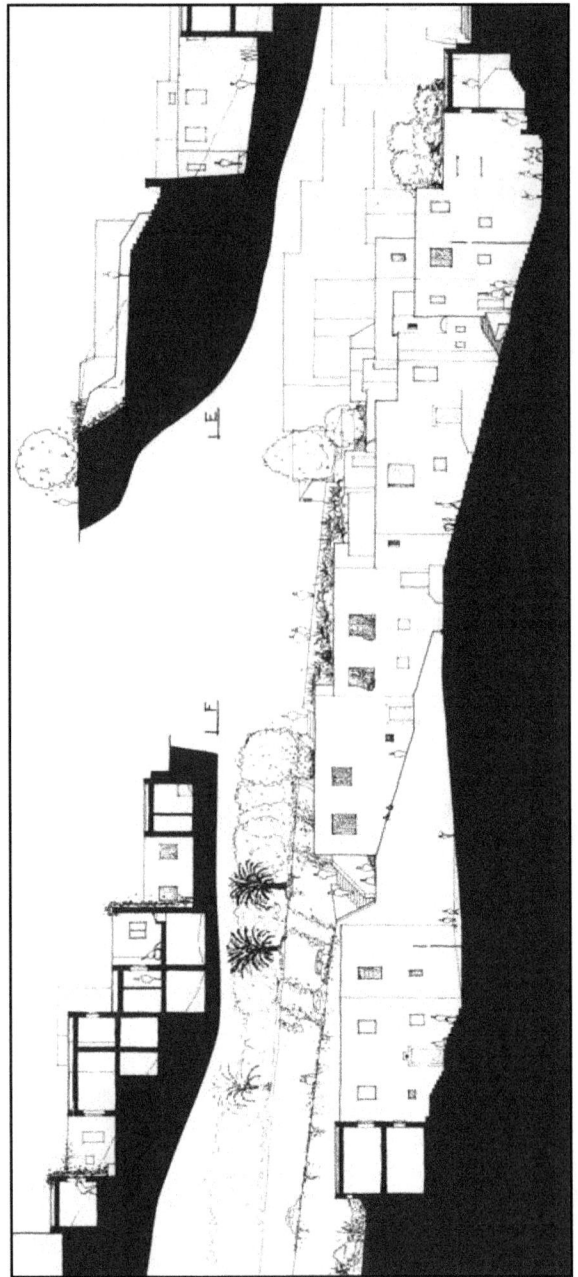

Sections/Elevation

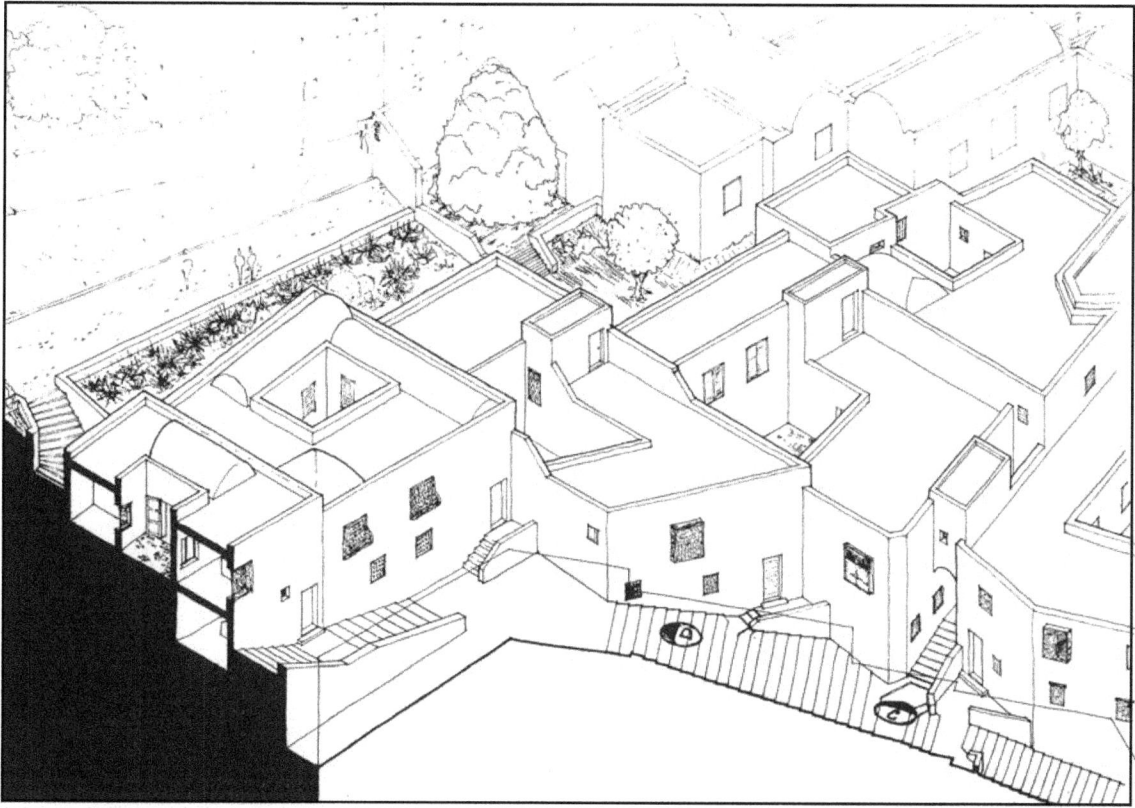

View from Southwest

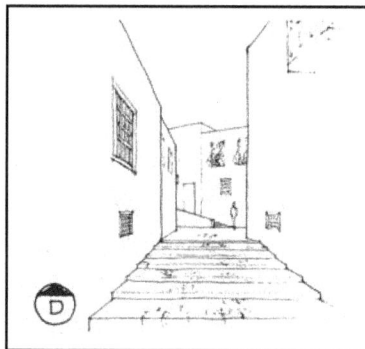

STUDENTS' LIFESTYLE IN SIDI BOU SA'ID

OUR HOME AND STUDIO

For a period of nine weeks our group of ten Canadian architectural students, and four spouses lived in Sidi Bou Sa'id, Tunisia for the purpose of studying the architecture of this beautiful village under the direction of Professor Besim Hakim. We invite you to accompany us to Hotel Bou Fares, our home and studio for that period of time.

Approaching Cafe des Nattes on Rue Docteur H. Thameur we find a terraced pedestrian street going off to the left just before reaching the cafe. Turning up this street, Rue Sidi Bou Fares, we walk up a series of steps and then continue up the grade until we reach No. 15, on the left side of the street. It marks a very inconspicuous doorway, with no other sign to indicate that we have reached Hotel Bou Fares; Welcome!

Prior to ten years ago the hotel served as a home for several families, although in its original state, it was the private home of the Bou Fares family, which gave their name to the present hotel.

In the center of the hotel is a large, beautiful courtyard, off of which open many blue colored doors. Two large trees, one olive and one fig are centered in either end of the courtyard and many beautiful and varied potted plants, grapevines, hibiscus and jasmine bushes are located elsewhere around the courtyard. It is well shielded from the sounds of the street: the children playing, the women on their way to the market, the call of the man who walks with his donkey through the streets bringing fresh vegetables for sale, etc.

In the courtyard near Maria's room during the first five weeks of our stay here one would often find several people gathered soaking up the warm rays of the sun while working, reading or simply relaxing. Moving closer to the trees we would find the group there at lunchtime trying to escape the hot rays of the sun. Also, as the weather cooled off and the sun became more precious, the noon meal was quite often served in this area as the sun's rays would be found here then.

During our stay we were always conscious of weather conditions as it would usually determine our location at any one time, be it inside or out, in a room, area of the courtyard, or hotel roof, where we might be found on warm days after the sun's rays had left the courtyard.

Our 'Studio' was highly mobile, made of make shift tables and other ingenious working tops. The work location varied, during the first half of our stay the students worked primarily in the courtyard, whereas most of the work was done in the rooms during the latter half of our stay, as the climate became relatively cold.

The students created a library and Jim Wright became the person responsible and acting as a librarian. All material was catalogued and located in his room, and any person borrowing had to sign it out. Black and white photographic processing was also carried out in one of the smaller rooms.

In effect Hotel Bou Fares was converted to a mini school of architecture during the day and a students' residence during the night. Following is a description of our food, some of our activities, and pleasures. We did enjoy our stay and delight in sharing it with you!

FOOD

Tunisian cuisine is truly an adventure worth experiencing. It can involve a lamb or dorado (local fish), couscous, a mechoui (barbecue), fish dishes, a tajine or briks a l'oeuf (eggs in pastry).

Each meal is served generally as a three course meal—salad or soup, a meat or fish dish and a desert which is often 'fruits of the season'. The ingredients for each course are bought fresh from the local market on a daily basis. From observation, the daily marketing is partly due to a lack of large refrigeration facilities in people's homes and also due to local custom. Certainly the local community market area is an ideal place to meet friends and catch up on the local gossip of the day.

Fish is bought fresh from the market or from the fisherman himself. In Sidi Bou Sa'id, the market offers calamases (squid), octopus, poisson rouge, mackerel and locally canned sardines and tuna. Vegetables and fruit are bought fresh throughout the year. Tomatoes, red and green peppers, chick peas, olives, carrots, squash, cauliflower, onions, zucchinis,, potatoes, turnips, parsley and beets are the main vegetables. Fruits appearing seasonally are oranges, tangerines, peaches, pomegranates, figs, dates, melons, grapes and apples.

Breakfast is not typically Tunisian or of much nutritional importance, consisting only of bread, jam, coffee, hot milk or tea.

Our description of food would not be complete or totally meaningful, without you, the reader, actually tasting a sample, so we are including recipes for two Tunisian dishes which our group particularly enjoyed during our stay in Sidi Bou Sa'id.

1. COUSCOUS WITH MEAT

2–3 lbs. stew meat, lamb or chicken
1 lg. onion
4 tbsp. tomato paste
½ tbsp. red pepper
1 c. olive oil
1 c. soaked chickpeas
6 c. couscous
Black pepper, salt

Choice of vegetables: pumpkin, turnip, parsnip, carrots, cabbage, celery, whole green and/or red peppers, potatoes. Soak chickpeas overnight. Cut meat into serving pieces and put them in the bottom of a "couscoussier".* Season with salt, pepper (red and black). Mince the onion and add. Pour in olive oil and brown the meat. Add 2 pints water, tomato paste and chickpeas. Cool 15–20 minutes. Add the vegetables: 3–4 whole potatoes (peeled), 3–4 medium carrots (cut in half lengthwise), 2 small turnips (quartered) and any other vegetables as desired. Add 1½ quarts of water and bring to a boil. Dampen the couscous with a little cold water and pour gently into the steamer. Be careful not to let it cake together. Place steamer over pot. Cool 30–40 minutes from the time the steam starts to rise. Take the steamer off the bottom pot and empty the couscous into a large shallow bowl. Sprinkle with fresh water and break up the lumps with a spoon so that each grain of couscous is separated from the next.

Put the couscous back into the steamer and replace it on the bottom pot, the contents of which have been cooking all this while. Cover, let steam awhile longer (no more than ½ hour) empty couscous into serving dish, skim off any fat from top of the bouillon. Add a little salted butter. Optional here to add 2 good pinches of cinnamon. Pour some of the liquid onto the couscous to moisten and mix lightly. Smooth the couscous out in dish. Salt the bouillon to taste. Arrange the vegetables and meat on top of the couscous. Let stand a few minutes. Serve. Remainder of bouillon can be poured over individual dishes.

* (a 3 piece steamer consisting of a large bottom pot, a colander-like steaming unit, and a lid.)

2. TUNA TAJINE

1 c. white beans
1 lg. tin tuna
Salt, black pepper
1 medium onion
1 tbsp. tomato paste
½ tsp. red pepper
Bread crumbs
½ c. cheese
Butter
6–8 eggs

Soak the beans overnight. Brown for 5–6 minutes in oil, an onion (minced). Add tomato paste, red pepper and the beans. Cover with water and bring to a boil. Reduce heat. Add tuna and let simmer, covered, for an hour. Put some of the sauce into pan at back of stove. Let the rest cool. Add to cooled sauce, crumbs made from a slice of bread, grated cheese, black pepper and salted butter. Salt to taste and mix 6–8 raw eggs into mixture. Pour into square pan and put in 350°oven. Tajine is cooked when no liquid remains on blade of knife. Cut in slices and serve hot. Pour remaining liquid over individual dishes.

STUDENTS' WORKDAY

The students' workday began at 9:30 a.m. and continued to 7 p.m. with one hour for lunch. Most mornings were devoted to discussions by the group with Professor Hakim, or if previous arrangements had been made some students would go out to visit a construction site or a house as part of their study schedule. Sometimes, classes were held in the courtyard (see hotel layout and photos) under the pear tree. However, on damp, cold or rainy days classes were held in one of the larger student's rooms.

The size of the group and the time allotted to studying the village gave students the opportunity of investigating it at various levels. For instance, the project was divided into various sections which collectively provided sufficient material for a comprehensive understanding of the town and its people. Each study section was undertaken by a small group of two or three students, and in this way the work was made easier and more efficient to compile.

Students undertook their analysis through various sources. For instance, they did site surveys, translated material from French, had lectures from various consultants working in Tunis, and made personal contacts with residents such as artists, architects, and businessmen. However, on-site surveys were the most important means of study.

During the earlier part of our stay most afternoons were devoted to the measurement of houses, streets, cafes, souks, mosque etc. These measurements were later used for analysis and to aid in the drawing of floor plans, elevations, sections, and details. Because of the shortage of working equipment this schedule was never rigidly adhered to.

Photographs were also taken of areas of study and photography periods were included in the working day schedule; an aspect which the students especially enjoyed. Some of the keener photographers in our group would go out before sunrise or just before sunset, when the village of Sidi Bou Sa'id is at its most beautiful.

Between five and six o'clock the souk and cafes come alive. This is the time daily tourist influx is at its peak and when many of the villagers, Tunisian or foreign take their afternoon stroll for a cup of tea or coffee. Students studying these areas found this time of day particularly exciting and were also able to compare the way the streets and shops function at various times of the day.

Students did not really object to working at all times of the day because their work was closely tied in with the village and its way of life. By working among the Tunisians, studying various aspects of the village, the group made many friends and were able to visit many buildings which were studied as part of their project. The initial breaking down of the cultural barrier was difficult especially because few people from our group were able to communicate effectively in French much less Arabic. But, as our faces became more familiar the heavy wooden doors which sealed off the entrance of many homes were opened to us.

As the deadline date for the final critique on the project approached, the tempo of working changed considerably. Students worked non-stop, in an effort to complete their drawings and correlate all the material accumulated. Very often you could have heard knocks on someone's door of a student trying to locate a .000 pen, a T-square, or a measuring tape for last minute measurements. The hotel hummed with activity at all times of the day and night.

LEISURE HOURS

The students took very few leisure days as such, although whenever they needed to break from their work routine they would take an hour or two to enjoy what the small village of Sidi Bou Sa'id had to offer.

One favorite means of recreation during the first four weeks of our stay was to go for a swim and sunbathing. The beach was about a fifteen minute walk, down 278 steps, through a tree-covered walk to the base of the promontory. Needless to say, the walk back to the hotel was not half as much fun. The beach was beautifully sandy and wide, the water temperature seldom fell below 60° F, to late November, however the group were so spoiled by the warm weather that there was very little swimming after the middle of November.

Probably the excuse for a break that was used the most often was to go and have tea. Within a few minutes walking distance of Hotel Bou Fares were several cafes which offered a beautiful view of the Bay of Carthage. The cafes are favorite places for the people to meet and play cards, dominoes or just get into discussions. They provided wonderful places to obtain an idea of the local way of life.

One activity that at first was enjoyable but eventually became a chore was going to the market for the day's supply of food. Two students accompanied by Hadi, our Tunisian helper, would set off shortly after breakfast to the market and general store at the foot of the hill where they made quite an efficient team. Hadi would choose the food, accepting or rejecting either prices or quality as the three decided; one student would check quantities and prices while the other student kept a record of the food bought and its cost. There were very few errors made. On the way back up the hill the bread would be bought and the olive oil bottle filled to complete the day's shopping

Another favorite pastime was shopping in the small open shops on the main street of Sidi Bou Sa'id. With their hand-embroidered native clothing of many brilliant colors, their rugs, blankets, pottery and leather goods, they made an inviting scene.

At times students would spend a day visiting Tunis, La Marsa or the ruins at Carthage, and at night playing cards, doing some macrame or working on their respective projects. Very seldom was boredom found at Hotel Bou Fares in Sidi Bou Sa'id.

Students' Lifestyle
in Sidi Bou Sa'id

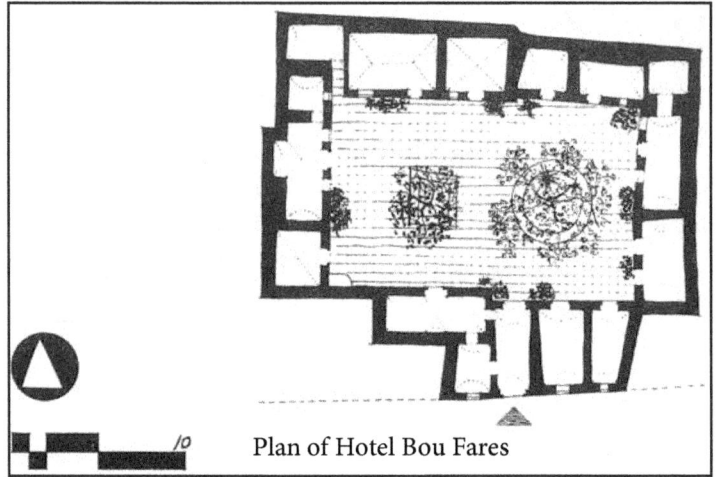

Plan of Hotel Bou Fares

ACKNOWLEDGMENTS

A study trip such as the one to Sidi Bou Sa'id took a great deal of pre-planning and organization, in fact the process was started on October 25, 1974, almost a year before the actual trip took place, when I gave an audiovisual presentation to students to determine how many would be interested in the idea.

Many people provided assistance and encouragement during the process of planning the trip and later when we were in Tunisia. I would like to take this opportunity on behalf of all participating students to thank the following individuals and organizations without whose assistance it would have been impossible to successfully accomplish the trip:

During the formative stages of planning the project, I am indebted to Dr. Peter Manning, Director of our School, for his enthusiasm, Mr. Ferid Mouldi, Director of the Tunisian National Tourist Board in Montreal, for the loan of slides and brochures about Tunisia, Mr. Abdelhamid Fekih, Director of ITAAUT (Institut Technologique d'Art d'Architecture et d'Urbanisme de Tunis), for his support and encouragement, and SOTUTOR (Societe Tunisienne de Promotion du Tourisme Jeune), which organized the group's accommodation in the Hotel Bou Fares in Sidi Bou Sa'id and the two week tour of Tunisia which began upon the arrival of the students in Tunis on September 28, 1975.

Many individuals and private citizens provided information, assistance and goodwill during our scheduled nine week stay in Sidi Bou Sa'id (October 12–December 12, 1975) I would like to thank all of them. The following provided information for which the group is very grateful: Jerome Woodford, Massimo Amodei, Luigi Barocci, Eric Hoechel, Jacques Marmey, Pere Louis, Antoine D'Ancona, the Bibliotheque Nationale, the British Embassy Library and the Office de la Topographie et de la Cartographie in Tunis.

During our nine week stay I arranged a program of eight speakers who came to the Hotel Bou Fares and talked to the students on an informal basis. The topics discussed were architecture and urban planning in North Africa, Islamic civilization and culture, symbolism in Islamic art and problems of rapid urbanization in developing countries. I extend our appreciative thanks to the following guest speakers: Michael Brammah, Pat Crook, Bernard Delaval, Abdulrazak Hilali, Dr. Mohammad Fadhel Jamali, Abbas Jamali, Aly Ben Salem and Jerome Woodford.

We also received assistance from Jane Rouleau and the following kind people who allowed some of our group to study the houses in which they were residing in Sidi Bou Sa'id: Paul and Martine Cahen, Mr. and Mrs. Ben Zarrouk, Gill and Catherine and Alain Chandlier and Noël Stremdoerfer. Our thanks also to Farouk Ben Miled and Wassim Ben Mahmoud for their invitations to visit them and to Baron D'Erlanger Jr. who was kind enough to take the whole group on a tour of his father's magnificent palace. Mr. Phillip M. Mackinnon, Vice-Consul in the Canadian Embassy at Tunis gave us his kind assistance and support when needed and a gracious farewell party at his home in Tunis.

Special thanks must be extended to Fatina Hijab and Elizabeth Wilson for their patience and skill in typing the original report.

Finally, my thanks on behalf of the group would not be complete without a special salute to Saleh Fezzani, the cook in the Hotel Bou Fares, and Hedi, his assistant, who made our lifestyle so delightfully palatable during those nine memorable weeks in Sidi Bou Sa'id.

BIBLIOGRAPHY

Arnold, Thomas W. *Painting in Islam.* Oxford University Press, 1928. Reprinted by Dover Publications, Inc. New York, 1965.

Ashihara, Yoshinobu. *Exterior Design in Architecture.* Van Nostrand Reinhold Co., New York, 1970.

Borg, Andre. "L'Habitat A Tozeur" *Cahiers des Arts et Techniques D'Afrique du Nord,* No. 5, 1959 pp. 91–107.

Brown, Carl L. (ed). *From Madina to Metropolis, Heritage and Change in the Near Eastern City.* The Darwin Press, Princeton, N.J., 1973.

Burckhardt, Titus. "Perennial Vaules in Islamic Art", *Studies in Comparative Religion,* Vol 1, No. 3, Summer 1967, pp 132–141.

Cantelli, M. *Essai de Typologie del'Habitat.* Association Sauvegarde de la Medina, Tunis, 1968/69.

Cragg, Kenneth. *The Call of the Minaret.* Oxford University Press, New York, 1964.

Cullen, Gordon. *The Concise Townscape.* The Architectural Press, London, 1961 and 1971.

Delaval, Bernard. "Urban Communities of the Algerian Sahara" *EKISTICS,* No. 227, October, 1974.

DeSelm, David and Ricci, Anthony. "SFAX, A Tunisian Medina", *Architectural Review,* December, 1970.

Direction Amenagement du Territoire, Ministre Economie National, Republique Tunisienne. *Plan D'Amenagement: Commune De Sidi Bou-Said* and six accompanying maps, Tunis, January, 1973.

Direction du Tourisme, Republique Tunisienne. *Tunis et sa Region*. Enquête d'Urbanisme. Societe Centrale pour l'Equipment du Territoire, Tunis, 1962.

Dunham, Daniel. "The Courtyard House as a Temperature Regulator" *The New Scientist* 8, September, 1960, pp. 663–666.

Ennabli, Abdelmajid and Slim, Hedi. *Carthage, A Visit to the Ruins*. Ceres Productions, Tunis 1974.

Fathy, Hassan. *Architecture for the Poor*. The University of Chicago Press, Chicago 1973.

———. *The Arab House In the Urban Setting: Past,Present and Future*. University of Essex, Carreras Arab Lecture,3 November, 1970. Longman Group Ltd., London, 1972.

Fodor, E. and Curtis, W. (eds). *Tunisia 1973*. David McKay Co., New York, 1973.

Goldfinger, Myron. *Villages in the Sun*. Praeger Publishers, New York, 1969.

Hodgson, Marshall G. S. "lslam and Image", *History of Religions,* Vol. 3, No. 2, Winter 1964, pp 220–260.

Jamali, Mohammed Fadhel. *Letters on Islam*. Oxford University Press, London, 1965.

Journal Officiel Tunisien: 28 Aout 1915, No. 69. Relatif a la protection des constructions arabes de Sidi Bou Said De'cret du 6 Aout 1915 (p 361).

Koenigsberger, O. H. et al: *Manual of Tropical Housing and Building—Part one: Climatic Design*. Longman Group Ltd., London 1974.

Mansour, Ezdine. "La 'Kharja' de Sidi Bou Said—Anachronisme ou acte signifiant?", *Dialogue*, No. 51, 25 August, 1975, pp 35–38.

Nasr, Seyyed Hossein. *Ideals and Realities of Islam*. George Allen and Unwin Ltd., London, 1966.

———. "Foreword" in *The Sense of Unity: The Sufi Tradition in Persian Architecture*, by N. Ardalan and L. Bakhtiar. University of Chicago Press, 1973.

Pellegrin, Arthur. "Sidi-Bou-Said: Le Site et son Histoire" *Bulletin Economique et Social de la Tunisie,* December 1955, No. 107, pp 123–146.

Project Tunis—Carthage. *Mise en valeur de Patrimoine monumental de la region de Carthage en vue du developpement economique.* Republique Tunisienne—UNESCO-PNUD, INNA-ASM, Tunis, 1971.

Rapoport, Amos. *House Form and Culture*. Prentice-Hall Inc. N.J. 1969.

Revault, Jacques. "Residences d'ete a Sidi Bou Said" *Cahiers des Arts et Techniques D'Afrique du Nord,* No. 6, 1960–61, pp 153–187.

———. *Arts Traditionnels en Tunisie.* Publications de l'office National de l'artisanat de Tunisie, 1967.

———. *Palais et Demeures de Tunis (XVI et XVII siecles).* Editions du Centre National de la Recherche Scientifique, Paris, 1967.

———. *Palais et Demeures de Tunis (XVII et XIX siecles).* Editions du Centre National de la Recherche Scientifique, Paris, 1971.

———. *Palais et Residences d'ete de la Region de Tunis (XVI et XIX Siecles).* Editions du Centre National de la Recherche Scientifique, Paris, 1974.

Rice, David T. *Islamic Art.* Frederick A. Praeger, New York, 1965.

Rudofsky, Bernard. *Architecture without Architects.* Musuem of Modern Art, New York, 1965.

Smith, James A., Jr. (ed): *Manuel d'Architecture et de Construction en Tunisie.* American Peace Corps. Tunis, August 1968.

Sylvester, A. *Tunisia.* The Bodley Head, London, 1969.

Spreiregen, Paul D.: *Urban Design: The Architecture of Towns and Cities.* McGraw-Hill Book Co., New York, 1965.

Von Grunebaum, G. E. "The Structure of the Muslim Town" in *Islam: Essays in the Nature and Growth of a Cultural Tradition.* Routledge and Kegan Paul Ltd., London, 1955, pp 141–158.

Zbiss, S. M. *Sidi Bou-Said.* Societe Tunisienne de Diffusion, Tunis, 1971.

INDEX

Bold text for drawings and photos. Arabic words in italic.

www.ingramcontent.com/pod-product-compliance
Lightning Source LLC
Chambersburg PA
CBHW062042090426
42740CB00016B/2991